Oxford Socio-Legal Studies

Rules and Regulators

OXFORD SOCIO-LEGAL STUDIES

Oxford Socio-Legal Studies is a series of books exploring the role of law in society for both an academic and a wider readership. The series publishes theoretical and empirically-informed work, from the United Kingdom and elsewhere, by social scientists and lawyers which advances understanding of the social reality of law and legal processes.

RULES AND REGULATORS

JULIA BLACK

CLARENDON PRESS · OXFORD
1997

Oxford University Press, Great Clarendon Street, Oxford OX2 6DP
Oxford New York
Athens Auckland Bangkok Bogota Bombay
Buenos Aires Calcutta Cape Town Dar es Salaam
Delhi Florence Hong Kong Istanbul Karachi
Kuala Lumpur Madras Madrid Melbourne
Mexico City Nairobi Paris Singapore
Taipei Tokyo Toronto
and associated companies in
Berlin Ibadan

Oxford is a trade mark of Oxford University Press

Published in the United States by
Oxford University Press Inc., New York

British Library Cataloguing in Publication Data
Data available

Library of Congress Cataloging in Publication Data

ISBN 0–19–826294 9

1 3 5 7 9 10 8 6 4 2

Typeset by Graphicraft Typesetters Ltd., Hong Kong
Printed in Great Britain by
Biddles Ltd., Guildford and King's Lynn

General Editor's Introduction

The relationship between rules and discretion has recently begun to attract considerable attention within socio-legal studies. Julia Black's detailed exploration of the nature of rules in the context of regulation, posing theoretical analysis with empirical investigation, is a welcome addition to this emerging literature. The book is valuable also in presenting us with an extended analysis of the regulation of financial services.

Dr Black pursues a number of purposes in her study. Her primary aim is to understand more fully the nature of rule-making in the regulatory process. She does this, in particular, by building on a jurisprudential and linguistic analysis of rules so as to provide a basis for proposing how rules could be used for regulatory purposes. This analysis is then connected with an enquiry into rule-use in the regulation of financial services. The author has a number of important ideas for those who study rule making, arguing that it is essential to understand policy making and decision making, quite apart from developing an appreciation of the potential, but also the limits of rules. She presents a subtle and complex picture of how various forces interact to affect both the content of a rule and the use to which it is put.

Julia Black's book fits naturally into the series of *Oxford Socio-Legal Studies*, in which a number of works that focus on regulatory behaviour and techniques or on legal rules and discretion have already appeared.

Keith Hawkins

Acknowledgements

I have been fortunate to receive considerable assistance in the course of researching and writing this book. In the early stages of my research, I benefited from time spent at Slaughter and May and at the Law Commission, particularly from discussions with Jack Beatson. Many regulators, regulated, academics, and others have been generous with their time, providing information and explanations, including Professor Jim Gower, Sir Kenneth Berrill, and Sir David Walker, all of whom I thank. For financial assistance during my doctoral studies I am indebted to the British Academy for their award of a major state studentship, to the research and scholarship funds of Lincoln College, Oxford, and to my parents.

I am grateful to those who have heard, read, or discussed with me various parts of this book in its previous incarnations, and whose comments, criticisms, and questions have led to further analysis, exposition, explanation, and deletion, including Rob Baldwin, Peter Cane, Paul Craig, Paul Davies, Denis Galligan, Doreen McBarnet, Chris McCrudden, and Dan Prentice. I particularly thank Chris McCrudden and Dan Prentice, who supervised my doctoral thesis, the research for which forms the basis for the analysis in this book, Rob Baldwin for his pertinent comments, and Denis Galligan, for his encouragement and support for the book's publication.

I also thank Mandy Tinnams for her work in transforming the manuscript into OUP format, and Richard Hart for his assistance.

Finally, I owe my greatest debt to Tim, for his tireless readings of innumerable drafts, for his comments, criticisms, insights, and suggestions, and for his encouragement, support, and friendship, without which this work may never have begun, and certainly its completion would have been a far harder task.

Contents

Abbreviations

ABI	Association of British Insurers
AHC	Accepting Houses Committee
AFBD	Association of Futures Brokers and Dealers
AIBD	Association of International Bond Dealers
ASLO	Association of Scottish Life Offices
BEQB	*Bank of England Quarterly Bulletin*
BJIBFL	*Butterworths Journal of International Business and Finance Law*
BMBA	British Merchant Bankers Association
BSA	Building Societies Association
CA	Companies Act 1989
CCBRs	Core Conduct of Business Rules
CP	Consultative Paper
CR	Core Rule
CSI	Council for the Securities Industry
DGFT	Director General of Fair Trading
DoT	Department of Trade
DP	Discussion Paper
DTI	Department of Trade and Industry
Fimbra	Financial Intermediaries, Managers and Brokers Regulatory Association
FOX	London Futures and Options Exchange
FSA	Financial Services Act 1986
FT	*Financial Times*
FTA	Fair Trading Act 1973
IBRA	Insurance Brokers Registration Act 1977
IBRC	Insurance Brokers Registration Council
ICS	Investors' Compensation Scheme
IDC	Indirect Customer

IFA	Independent Financial Adviser
IMRO	Investment Managers Regulatory Organisation
IOSCO	International Organisation of Securities Commissions
ISD	Investment Services Directive
ISRO	International Securities Regulatory Organisation
JBL	*Journal of Business Law*
JLS	*Journal of Legal Studies*
Lautro	Life Association and Unit Trust Regulatory Organisation
LD(CB)Rs	Licensed Dealers' (Conduct of Business) Rules
LOA	Life Offices Association
MCA	Maximum Commissions Agreement
MCP	Market Counterparty
MIBOC	Marketing of Investments Board Organising Committee
MLR	*Modern Law Review*
NASDIM	National Association of Securities Dealers and Investment Managers
OFT	Office of Fair Trading
OJLS	*Oxford Journal of Legal Studies*
PF(I)A	Prevention of Fraud (Investments) Act 1958
PIA	Personal Investment Authority
RCH	Recognized Clearing House
RIE	Recognized Investment Exchange
RIY	Reduction in Yield
ROLAC	Register of Life Assurance Commissions
RPB	Recognized Professional Body
RPC	Restrictive Practices Court
RTPA	Restrictive Trade Practices Act 1956
SEAQ	Stock Exchange Automatic Quotation system
SEQ	*Stock Exchange Quarterly*
SFA	Securities and Futures Authority

SIB	Securities and Investments Board
SRA	Self-Regulatory Association
SRO	Self-Regulating Organisation
TCSC	Treasury and Civil Service Select Committee
TSA	The Securities Association
UCITS	Undertakings for Collective Investment in Transferable Securities
UTA	Unit Trust Association

Introduction

Why do rule makers make the rules that they do? What difference does it make if a rule provides that 'sufficient' information should be given, rather than stipulating in detail exactly what information should be provided? Why produce guidance rather than a legally enforceable rule? Why provide that breach of a rule is not actionable in court, but only subject to disciplinary action by a regulator? How rules are used in regulation and how they should be used are issues of increasing concern, and the question of the formation of rules and their role in expressing and implementing regulatory policy has begun to attract the attention of those interested in the techniques of regulation. This represents a development on the traditional debate about rules within administrative law, namely the merits and demerits of rules, discretion, and adjudication as mechanisms for the implementation of public policy.[1] It also complements the more extensive work which has been done on discretion and enforcement, which essentially looks at the responses to rules of different actors: officials within organizations charged with the implementation and enforcement of policies[2] or those actors outside the organization whose behaviour the rules are meant to regulate.[3]

[1] D. L. Shapiro, 'The Choice of Rulemaking or Adjudication in the Development of Agency Policy' (1965) 78 *Harv. LR* 921; L. L. Fuller, 'The Forms and Limits of Adjudication' (1978) 92 *Harv. LR* 353; J. L. Jowell, 'The Legal Control of Administrative Discretion' (1973) *Public Law* 179; id., *Law and Bureaucracy* (New York, 1975); K. C. Davis, *Discretionary Justice* (Illinois, 1978); J. L. Mashaw, *Bureaucratic Justice* (Yale, 1983).

[2] K. Hawkins, *Environment and Enforcement* (Oxford, 1984); id., (ed.), *The Uses of Discretion* (Oxford, 1992); id. and J. M. Thomas, *Enforcing Regulation* (Boston, 1984); id., and R. Baldwin, 'Discretionary Justice: Davis Reconsidered' (1984) *Public Law* 570; D. J. Galligan, *Discretionary Powers* (Oxford, 1986); id., 'The Nature and Function of Policies within Discretionary Power' (1976) *Public Law* 332; G. R. Richardson with A. I. Ogus and P. Burrows, *Policing Pollution* (Oxford, 1983); B. M. Hutter, *The Reasonable Arm of the Law?* (Oxford, 1988).

[3] D. McBarnet, 'Law, Policy and Legal Avoidance' (1988) *JLS* 113; id. and C. Whelan, 'The Elusive Spirit of the Law: Formalism and the Struggle for Legal Control' (1991) 54 *MLR* 409; *eid.*, 'Beyond Control: Law, Management and Corporate Governance' in J. MacCaherty, S. Picciotto, and C. Scott, (eds.), *Corporate Control and Accountability* (Oxford, 1993).

The concerns of each of those who have looked at the role of rules in regulation have varied: attention has focused on their incidence,[4] the process of their formation,[5] their relationship with enforcement,[6] and their legitimacy.[7] The focus of this study differs again, and its aim is threefold. It is first to build on a jurisprudential and linguistic analysis of rules to develop an understanding of the nature of rules and as a result provide proposals for how rules could be used in the regulatory process; second, to integrate that analysis with examples of the use of rules in a particular regulatory system, that of financial services; and finally to understand in greater depth the nature of the regulatory rule making process.

Chapter 1 explores different theories of rules and of interpretation. It extrapolates from these to offer an analysis of rules and to develop suggestions for ways in which rules can be used in regulation, ways which take into account their nature and ameliorate their limitations. It proposes three different but related techniques: the use of different types of rules, the use and development of interpretive communities, and the adoption of a conversational model of regulation.

The analysis and proposals of chapter 1 form the framework for the consideration of the formation and use of rules in a particular regulatory system, that of financial services, and more particularly, regulation of the conduct of investment business. Chapters 2 to 5 examine the development of the financial services regulatory system from its inception, exploring the use made of rules. Chapter 2 looks at the reasons for the introduction of the regulation, and in particular the significance in that debate of the question, who

[4] G. Ganz, *Quasi-Legislation: Recent Developments in Delegated Legislation* (London, 1987); R. Baldwin and J. Houghton, 'Circular Arguments: The Status and Legitimacy of Administrative Rules' (1986) *Public Law* 239.

[5] M. Asimov, 'Delegated Legislation: United States and United Kingdom' (1983) *OJLS* 253; id., 'Non-Legislative Rulemaking and Regulatory Reform' (1985) *Duke LJ* 381; J. Beatson, 'Legislative Control of Administrative Rule-making: Lessons from the British Experience?' (1979) 12 *CILJ* 199; C. McCrudden, 'Codes in a Cold Climate: Administrative Rulemaking by the Commission for Racial Equality' (1988) 51 *MLR* 409; R. Baldwin, 'Health and Safety at Work: Consensus and Self-Regulation' in R. Baldwin and C. McCrudden, *Regulation and Public Law* (London, 1987); M. Cavadino, 'Commissions and Codes: A Case Study in Law and Public Administration' (1993) *Public Law* 333.

[6] R. Baldwin, 'Why Rules Don't Work' (1991) *MLR* 321; id., *Rules and Government* (Oxford, 1995).

[7] Baldwin and McCrudden, *Regulation and Public Law*, Ch. 3; Baldwin, *Rules and Government*; J. L. Mashaw, *Due Process in the Administrative State* (Yale, 1985).

should be the rule makers, what type of body should have responsibility for forming and implementing the regulation. Chapter 3 examines the changing role of rules within the regulatory system, and the impact which the institutional structure, and the rhetoric of 'self-regulation' which surrounds it, have had on the use of rules. In particular, the chapter illustrates the manner in which, and extent to which, the question of rule use can become a policy issue in its own right.

Chapters 4 and 5 focus on two particular areas of conduct of business regulation, the marketing of retail investment products and the regulation of the commission arrangements between fund managers, brokers, and market makers known as 'soft commissions'. The chapters examine the impact which the nature of the market, the characteristics of the product or arrangement being regulated, and the skill and experience of the investor, have on the development and use of rules, the role played by interest groups, other regulatory bodies and the perceptions of the regulators themselves in the rule making process, and the interaction of rule use with other techniques of regulation, highlighting the limits of rules.

Chapter 6 draws together examples of how rules have been used in the regulatory system, integrating the theoretical analysis of chapter 1 with the empirical findings of the other chapters. The chapter also seeks to explore in greater depth the nature of the rule making decision. It is suggested that understanding rule making requires an understanding of policy making, of decision making, and of the nature of rules, their limitation and potential. Drawing on the analysis of rule making by financial services regulators, it suggests that rule making may be a conscious and tactical exercise, but that the question of the extent to which the decision is a strategic one is separate from the question of the extent to which that decision is affected by a range of different factors and influences. Those factors may shape the strategy adopted, but they do not mean that strategy is not possible (although it may not always be present). The chapter illustrates how the institutional structure, the expectations which surround it, the interests and perceptions of those involved in the process, regulated, regulators, and government, the market context, and the dynamics of the regulatory system itself, interact to shape the form each other takes and the influence which each may have, and to affect not only the content of the rule but the use which is made of it.

Finally, it is suggested that certain aspects of the analysis of the formation and use of rules by financial services regulators may be generalizable to other contexts, namely the significance of the design of the regulatory system, of the market context in which the regulation operates and which it is attempting to regulate, and of the stage the regulatory system is in its evolution. The study thus aims to integrate a theoretical understanding of the nature of rules and their interpretation with an empirical analysis of the use of rules and their formation. In this way, it hopes to explain how in fact rules are used, and to suggest ways in which they could be used.

1 Using Rules

'In any large group general rules, standards and principles must be the main instrument of social control, and not particular directions given to each individual separately. If it were not possible to communicate general standards of conduct, which multitudes of individuals could understand, without further direction, as requiring from them certain conduct when occasion arose, nothing that we now recognize as law could exist.'[1] As Hart observed, rules are an inevitable feature of law and thus, we may add, of legal regulation; their limitations, however, are well documented and observed. Rules are inherently vague or indeterminate, and inherently over- or under-inclusive. As tools of decision making, they are imperfect; in Schauer's words 'rules function as impediments to optimally sensitive decision making. Rules doom decision making to mediocrity by mandating the inaccessibility of excellence.'[2] Their failure to control discretion is well recognized, by academics at least;[3] and the limitations of rules as a regulatory technique have been pointed out in the literature on enforcement and compliance.[4] Finally, rules are associated with 'command and control' regulation: a system of statutory rules backed by sanctions, the limitations of which have been documented and explored in a range of empirical and theoretical studies.[5]

How to make rules work has thus become an increasingly important focus of attention for those interested in regulation. A number of suggestions have been made which draw on empirical studies on the enforcement of rules: that rule makers should adopt

[1] H. L. A. Hart, *The Concept of Law* (Oxford, 1961), 121.

[2] F. Schauer, 'Formalism' (1988) 97 *Yale LJ* 509 at 539.

[3] K. Hawkins (ed.), *The Uses of Discretion* (Oxford, 1992), D. J. Galligan, *Discretionary Powers* (Oxford, 1986), R. Baldwin and K. Hawkins, 'Discretionary Justice: Davis Reconsidered' (1984) *Public Law* 570.

[4] R. Baldwin, 'Why Rules Don't Work' (1990) 53 *MLR* 321, id., *Rules and Government* (Oxford, 1995), D. McBarnet and C. Whelan, 'The Elusive Spirit of the Law: Formalism and the Struggle for Legal Control' (1991) 54 *MLR* 848, K. Hawkins, *Environment and Enforcement* (Oxford, 1984).

[5] For a recent assessment of different techniques of regulation see A. Ogus, *Regulation: Legal Form and Economic Theory* (Oxford, 1994).

a 'compliance-orientated' approach in rule making,[6] for example, or that responsibility for the formation of rules should be devolved to individual firms.[7] This chapter considers the empirically based observations of the limitations of rules in the light of the theoretical analysis of rules in jurisprudential and linguistic writing. The approach is thus to 'go back to basics': to understand the nature of the instrument which is being used, the properties of rules and their inherent limitations, and to see whether we can gain insights from this analysis which would enable us to make better use of rules as a regulatory technique. Three ways in which the limitations of rules could be ameliorated are suggested, none without its costs and/or trade-offs. The first is through a better appreciation and use of different types of rules. The second and third relate to the context in which rules operate: the nature of the regulatory community, and the style of regulation adopted.

The Nature of Rules

The three main problems associated with the use of rules in any context, and on which all who write about rules agree, are their tendency to over- or under-inclusiveness, their indeterminacy, and their interpretation.[8] These problems stem from two roots: the nature of rules and the nature of language. Prescriptive rules are anticipatory, generalized abstractions, and when endowed with legal status are distinctive, authoritative forms of communication. They are also linguistic structures: how we understand, interpret, and apply rules depends in part on how we understand and interpret language. In considering the nature and limitations of rules, a legal analysis of the roles which rules are asked to play in a regulatory system needs thus to be coupled to an examination of these linguistic properties.

[6] Baldwin, *Rules and Government*, Ch. 6, 'Why Rules Don't Work'.

[7] I. Ayers and J. Braithwaite, *Responsive Regulation* (OUP, Oxford, 1992), Ch. 4, 'Enforced Self-Regulation'.

[8] The jurisprudential literature on rules is extensive. For legal analyses of rules see in particular F. Schauer, *Playing by the Rules: A Philosophical Examination of Rule-Based Decision-Making in Law and Life* (Oxford, 1991), W. Twining and D. Miers, *How to do Things with Rules* (London, 3rd ed., 1991), H. Hart and A. Sacks, *The Legal Process* (Tentative ed., 1958); D. Kennedy, 'Form and Substance in Private Law Adjudication' (1976) 89 *Harvard LR* 1685; N. MacCormick, *Legal Reasoning and Legal Theory* (Oxford, 1978).

Inclusiveness

Rules are generalizations: they group together particular instances or attributes of an object or occurrence and abstract or generalize from them to build up a category or definition which then forms the operative basis of the rule. Say, for example, that following a lunch in a restaurant in which my black labrador dog, Rufus, has been particularly disruptive the proprietor wants to make a rule to ensure such disruption does not happen again. She will consider which aspects of the event should form the operative basis of the rule, what the rule should 'bite' on. In doing that, she would need to assess which of the various aspects of Rufus (Rufus, black, dog, mine, in restaurant) were relevant to the fact of the disruption. She could consider banning all black things or all things called Rufus, but, as far as we know, not all black things or indeed Rufuses are necessarily disruptive, and the fact that Rufus was black or his name was Rufus were not causes of the disruption. Rather she should focus on the fact that Rufus was a dog, and so form a rule, 'no dogs allowed'.

The rule in this example is straightforward, but the process of rule formation is not. In making the generalization, the rule maker is choosing from a range of individual properties which an event or object possesses; in making that choice she searches for the aspect of the particular which is causally relevant to the aim of the rule: the goal which is sought to be achieved or the harm which is sought to be avoided.[9] It is thus the overall aim or purpose of the rule which determines which among a range of generalizations should be chosen as the operative fact or facts for the ensuing rule. However in forming the generalization, which is the operative basis of the rule, only some features of the particular event or object are focused on and are then projected onto future events, beyond the particulars which served as the paradigm or archetype for the formation of the generalization. The generalizations in rules are thus simplifications of complex events, objects or courses of behaviour. Aspects of those events will thus be left out, or 'suppressed' by the generalization. Further, the generalization, being necessarily selective, will also include some properties which will in some circumstances be irrelevant.

[9] One of the fullest conceptual analyses of rule formation is Schauer, *Playing by the Rules*, 17–38, which is drawn on in this section.

Purpose thus interacts with the generalization. The inclusiveness of a rule (or more accurately, its generalization) is a function of the rule's purpose or justification. It is the imperfect match between the rule and its purpose which is represented in the description of rules as over- or under-inclusive. This mismatch can occur for three reasons. First, as noted, the generalization which is the operative basis of the rule inevitably suppresses properties that may subsequently be relevant or includes properties that may in some cases be irrelevant. Secondly, the causal relationship between the event and the harm/goal is likely to be only an approximate one: the generalization bears simply a probable relationship to the harm sought to be avoided or goal sought to be achieved. Thirdly, even if a perfect causal match between the generalization and the aim of the rule could be achieved, future events may develop in such a way that it ceases to be so. As Schauer states:

> [i]n part because human beings are fallible, in part because they have imperfect knowledge of a changing future, and in part because the world itself is variable, rules premised on the empirical relationship between generalisation and justification remain vulnerable to future discoveries or events that would falsify what had previously been thought to be universal or exclusive truth. Thus even rules that seem now to be neither under- or over-inclusive with respect to their background justifications retain the prospect of becoming so.[10]

It follows from this that over or under-inclusiveness, although inherent, is likely to be exacerbated in certain circumstances, viz., where the context in which the rule operates is one which is subject to frequent change, where the course of change is unforeseeable, where the range of situations in which the rule will apply is great, and where there is an uncertain causal relationship between the events, objects or behaviour focused on and the harm to be avoided or goal to be achieved. Further, the analysis thus far has assumed that the rule is formed in reaction to an observed or experienced event.[11] Where the rule is formed in anticipation of events or behaviour, then the likelihood of over- or under-inclusiveness is enhanced as the causal relationship between those events and the harms or goals is likely to be ill understood. This may be the case where the rules are formed in anticipation of changes which are about to occur in the environment in which the rules operate

[10] Schauer, *Playing by the Rules*, 35.

[11] This indeed is Schauer's assumption.

or where the rules are themselves constitutive of a new arrangement, for example a market restructuring, the functioning or operation of which they are then attempting to regulate.

Inclusiveness can be taken as a sign of the 'success' or 'failure' of a rule. Legal rules, and particularly regulatory rules, perform social management and instrumental functions.[12] Rules are embodiments of policy decisions, and their success is measured in terms of the extent to which they ensure that the substance of policy is achieved. The fundamental demand for congruence between the rule and its purpose derives from this instrumental view. Under-inclusion can represent 'missed targets'; over-inclusion, excessive intrusion. The problems of over-inclusive rules in practice, particularly when used in association with an enforcement strategy which emphasizes prosecution for breach of the rule, have been well documented by Bardach and Kagan.[13] Where over inclusiveness at 'rule-level' is not mitigated by flexible application at the 'site-level',[14] they argue, this leads to both economic inefficiencies and in particular to damaging social implications, as regulatees suffer the experience of being subjected to unreasonable regulatory requirements. This in turn affects their attitude to the regulation, undermining commitment to it, destroying co-operation, generating perceptions of injustice, and stimulating political and legal resistance.[15]

The implications of over- and under-inclusive rules have also been analysed from an economic perspective by Ehrlich and Posner, who argue that rules which are over- or under-inclusive are inefficient: over-inclusive rules can discourage socially desirable behaviour, under-inclusive rules encourage socially undesirable behaviour.[16]

[12] In Summers's analysis of the techniques of law, administrative-regulatory techniques were one of five ways in which law could perform its social management function, the others being grievance-remedial, penal, public benefit conferral or distributional and facilitative of private arrangements: R. S. Summers, 'The Technique Element in Law' (1971) 59 *California LR* 733, and R. S. Summers and C. Howard, *Law, its Nature, Function and Limits* (1972).

[13] E. Bardach and R. Kagan, *Going By the Book: The Problem of Regulatory Unreasonableness* (Philadelphia, 1982).

[14] For an analysis of the difference between 'rule-level' and 'site-level' inclusiveness see ibid., 7. Baldwin also uses the distinction: *Rules and Government*, 177.

[15] Bardach and Kagan discuss the nature and consequences of 'unreasonableness' in *Going by the Book*, Chs. 4 and 5.

[16] I. Ehrlich and R. Posner, 'An Economic Analysis of Legal Rulemaking' (1974) 3 *J Legal Studies* 257; see also J. S. Johnston, 'Uncertainty, Chaos, and the Torts Process: An Economic Analysis of Legal Form' (1991) 76 *Cornell LR* 341.

Their solution to the problem of inclusiveness is increased precision of the rule. By increasing precision, they argue, the rule maker can ensure that socially undesirable behaviour is discouraged, and socially desirable behaviour encouraged, so bringing society nearer to its desired allocation of resources. Whether this is in fact the only or most effective approach to the problem of inclusion, however, is considered below.

Indeterminacy

Rules are also inherently indeterminate. Their indeterminacy arises in part from the nature of language, in part from their anticipatory nature, and in part because they rely on others for their application. Their indeterminacy matters because rules, particularly legal rules, are entrenched, authoritative statements which are meant to guide behaviour, be applied on an indefinite number of occasions, and which have sanctions attached for their breach.[17] It is thus important to know whether this particular occasion is one of those in which the rule should be applied. The most familiar exponent of the indeterminacy of legal rules is Hart, who described rules as having a 'core' of meaning and a 'penumbra of uncertainty' or 'fringe of vagueness'.[18] The indeterminacy arises not because the meaning of the word is unclear in itself,[19] but because in applying the rule the question would always arise as to whether the general term used in the rule applied to this particular fact situation. 'Particular fact situations do not await us already marked off from

[17] There is a wider critique of both the nature and implications of the indeterminacy of legal rules advanced by critical legal theorists which goes to the question of the legitimacy of law, and particularly of adjudication. It is not the purpose of this analysis to enter into this debate (and see further n. 33 below). For expressions of the indeterminacy thesis and the link with legitimacy see, e.g., J. Singer, 'The Player and the Cards: Nihilism and Legal Theory' (1984) 94 *Yale LJ* 1; A. Altman, 'Legal Realism, Critical Legal Studies, and Dworkin' (1986) 15 *Phi. & Pub. Aff.* 205; D. Kennedy, 'Legal Formality' (1973) 2 *J Leg. Stud.* 351 and 'Form and Substance' (1976) 89 *Harvard LR* 1685. For a consideration (and refutation) of this part of the indeterminacy thesis see K. Kress, 'Legal Indeterminacy' (1989) 88 *Calif. LR* 283; J. L. Coleman and B. Leiter, 'Determinacy, Objectivity and Authority' in A. Marmor (ed.), *Law and Interpretation* (Oxford, 1995).

[18] Hart, *The Concept of Law*, 124–6. In his five part series of articles on law and language Glanville Williams also spoke of the 'core' and 'penumbra' of rules: G. Williams, 'Language and the Law' (1945) 61 *LQR* 71, 179, 293, 384; and (1946) 62 *LQR* 387.

[19] This analysis of indeterminacy thus differs from the radical indeterminacy thesis in jurisprudence and literary theory which focuses on the questions of meaning and interpretation; on this see the discussion of interpretation below.

each other, and labelled as instances of the general rule, the application of which is in question; nor can the rule itself step forward to claim its own instances.'[20] There will be cases in which the general expression will be clearly applicable; in others it will not. There may be fact situations which possess only some features of the plain case, but others which they lack.

This indeterminacy in application Hart described as the 'open texture' of rules. The concept of open texture was drawn from a theory of language developed by Waismann,[21] although Hart recast it in his theory of rules,[22] and it has been used by others, notably Schauer, to show why rules can be inherently indeterminate.[23] In Hart's analysis, as in Schauer's, open texture stems from the inability of rule makers to anticipate all future events and possibilities: 'the necessity for such choice is thrust upon us because we are men, not gods'.[24] So even if consensus could gradually be built up as to the 'core meaning' of a particular term, the vagaries of future events would mean that there would still be instances 'thrown up by nature or human invention' which would possess only some of the features of the paradigm case or cases but not others.[25] Waismann's example illustrates the point: although we may think that we had a precise definition covering all cases when we established that if something has properties, *a, b, c,* and *d,* it is an *x,* and if something does not have those properties, it is not *x,* when we encounter something which is only two-thirds *b,* this unanticipated contingency creates a vagueness where none had hitherto existed. Rules thus have an inherent vagueness which stems not from language but from the prospective generalizations which characterize rules—even if determinant, the limits of human foresight mean that the least vague term may turn out to be vague when applied to a situation unforeseen when the term was defined.[26]

[20] Hart, *The Concept of Law,* 123.

[21] F. Waismann, 'Verifiability' in A. G. N. Flew (ed.), *Logic and Language: First Series* (Oxford, 1951), 117–44.

[22] For a discussion of the relationship of Hart's use of the concept to Waismann's theory see B. Bix, *Law, Language and Legal Determinacy* (Oxford, 1993), 7–35.

[23] Schauer, *Playing by the Rules,* 35–7.

[24] Hart, *The Concept of Law,* 125; and see Schauer, *Playing by the Rules,* 35.

[25] Hart, *The Concept of Law,* 123; Schauer, *Playing by the Rules,* 36. Both Hart and to an extent Schauer find the 'core' meaning of a term to derive from consensus as to its interpretation: see further below.

[26] Linguistic theory further suggests that the 'core meaning' which Hart ascribed to rules may not be as determinate as he suggested. In Wittgenstein's analysis, language contains 'family resemblance' concepts, in which the category borders

Interpretation

Rule making thus involves simplifications, suppressions, and assessments of probable causation; it is at best an imperfect business; moreover a rule is hostage to future developments which render the application of the rule uncertain. The rule may be over- or under-inclusive in relation to its overall purpose, and a rule can never be sufficiently explicit or precise to cover every potential eventuality, as the analysis of indeterminacy indicates. Rules thus need a sympathetic audience if they are to be interpreted and applied in a way which will further the purpose for which they were formed; rule maker and rule applier are to this extent in a reciprocal relationship.[27] Such a sympathetic interpretation is essentially what those who advocate a purposive approach to interpretation demand. Problems of inclusiveness and determinacy or certainty can be addressed by interpreting the rule in accordance with its underlying aim. By contrast, the purpose of the rule could be defeated if the rule is interpreted literally, if things suppressed by the generalization remain suppressed.

Rules also need an informed audience, one which understands the context of assumptions and practices in which the rule is based, which gave rise to it, and which it is trying to address. As practices change, the application of rules needs to change with them. As we have seen, rules can never be sufficiently explicit to cover every circumstance. Nor can they ever express all the tacit understandings on which the rule is based as to those practices or to the state of the world. A rule 'no dogs allowed' relies on the shared understanding of what a 'dog' is; it does not need to then go on to define 'dog' into its semantic components. To the extent that the rule does have to define the terms which it contains, it becomes increasingly precise, with consequent implications for inclusiveness and formalism, complexity and certainty, discussed below.

could change depending on the context in which it was used: see G. P. Baker and P. M. S. Hacker, *Wittgenstein: Understanding and Meaning* (Oxford, 1980), 320–43. Sainsbury further argues that some terms are intrinsically vague: there are no boundaries between when the term applies and when it does not: R. M. Sainsbury, 'Is There a Higher Order Vagueness?' (1991) 41 *Philosophical Qly.* 167.

[27] The reciprocal nature of the relationship between rule maker and rule enforcer is emphasized by Fuller, the two roles being occupied in his analysis by the legislative draftsman and the judge: Fuller, *The Morality of Law* (New Haven, rev. ed., 1969), 91; see also Twining and Miers, *How to do Things with Rules*, 193–4.

A rule, then, is only as good as its interpretation. To follow Hart again, rules cannot apply themselves, they rely on others for their application.[28] To be applied, rules have to be interpreted. The significance of the interpretive strategy adopted for the operation and effectiveness of rules is illustrated by McBarnet and Whelan's study of accounting regulation. They examined the effect of the conscious adoption by the regulated of a formalist interpretation of the rules, one which focuses on the 'literal meaning' of the rule. They dubbed the strategy 'creative compliance': the deliberate and tactical use of an alternative interpretive strategy, one of literalism or formalism, to circumvent the purpose of the rule; compliance with the 'letter' rather than the 'spirit'.[29] So, although a purposive interpretation could ameliorate some of the limitations of rules, such an interpretation may not in practice be that which the rule receives. The problems of interpretation are not confined to creative compliance; they also cover the honest perplexity of those subject to the rule of its application in a particular circumstance, which in turn can affect the certainty of the rule's operation. Given then the centrality of interpretation for the operation of rules, how can the rule maker know how the rule will be interpreted and applied? What is the relationship between rules and their interpretation? The theoretical literature exploring the relationship between rules and interpretation is considerable and spans legal, literary, and linguistic theory. It is worth exploring it, albeit briefly, as it is suggested that the insights from this literature are relevant for an analysis of rules and could provide a basis for addressing one of the central problems with rules: their interpretation and application (even by well-intentioned addressees concerned to 'do the best' by the rule).

The interpretive debate is as to both theories of adjudication and theories of language, and the concerns of the former can underly debates on the latter. Theories of adjudication do not concern us here, but theories of language and interpretation do.

[28] Hart, *The Concept of Law*, 123.

[29] McBarnet and Whelan, '*The Elusive Spirit of the Law*', *eid.* 'Beyond Control: Law, Management and Corporate Governance' in J. McCaherty, S. Picciotto, and C. Scott (eds.), *Corporate Control and Accountability* (Oxford, 1993), McBarnet, 'It's Not What You Do, But the Way that You Do It: Tax Evasion, Tax Avoidance and the Boundaries of Deviance', in D. Downes (ed.), *Unravelling Criminal Justice* (London, 1991).

In the notorious Hart-Fuller debate, Fuller advanced a purposive or instrumentalist approach to interpretation. In applying a rule the purpose of the rule should be the guide, Fuller argued, not just the language of the rule. If applying the rule strictly according to its terms would lead to a result inconsistent with the purpose of the rule, then it should not be so applied.[30] In Llewellyn's words, '[w]here the reason stops, there stops the rule'.[31] The countering formalist argument, most recently advanced by Schauer, is that words are capable of having a meaning which is independent of the particular purpose of that particular rule.[32] Application of rules to those situations which are covered by the literal meaning of the rule may or may not be normatively desirable, it is argued, but it is analytically possible.

The contemporary jurisprudential debate draws directly on linguistic and literary theory concerning the meaning and interpretation of language and texts: interpretation thus becomes associated with questions of determinacy and indeterminacy (although in a different sense to that described above). The debate is essentially whether language has an intrinsic, objective meaning: whether 'meaning resides "in" language somewhat the way furniture resides in rooms' (objectivism);[33] whether all language and its interpretation is simply subjective, dependent on the reader alone (nihilism);[34]

[30] L. F. Fuller, 'Positivism and Fidelity to Law—A Reply to Professor Hart' (1958) 71 *Harvard LR* 630, id. *The Morality of Law.*

[31] The instrumentalist or purposive approach is advocated by Llewellyn's 'Grand Juristic Style', K. Llewellyn, *Common Law Tradition* (Boston, 1960).

[32] Hart, 'Positivism and the Separation of Law and Morals' (1958) 71 *Harvard LR* 593, id., 'Definition and Theory in Jurisprudence', in *Essays in Jurisprudence and Philosophy* (Oxford, 1983) 21; Schauer, 'Formalism', id., *Playing by the Rules*, 54–62.

[33] G. Graff, '"Keep off the Grass," "Drop Dead," and Other Indeterminacies: A Response to Stanford Levinson' (1982) 60 *Texas LR* 405 at 405. The degree to which the position of objectivity is held varies considerably from those who argue that words have a 'natural' meaning: M. Moore, 'A Natural Law Theory of Interpretation' (1985) 58 *S Calif. LR* 277, id., 'The Interpretive Turn in Modern Theory: A Turn for the Worse?' (1989) 41 *Stanford LR* 871; D. Brink, 'Legal Theory, Legal Interpretation, and Judicial Review' (1988) 17 *Phi. & Pub. Aff.* 105 and 'Semantics and Legal Interpretation (Further Thoughts)' (1989) 2 *Canadian Journal of Law and Jurisprudence* 181–91, to those who try in less extreme ways to assert the possibility of objective meaning, see e.g., O. M. Fiss, 'Objectivity and Interpretation' (1982) 34 *Stanford LR* 739. For a discussion of objectivity see A. Marmor, 'Three Concepts of Objectivity', in A. Marmor (ed.), *Law and Interpretation.*

[34] For critical legal theorists who expound the thesis of radical indeterminacy, see e.g., references cited at nn. 17 and 36. This view is also held by those who, with a certain amount of dismay, see it as the logical consequence of the rejection of the objectivity thesis, see e.g., S. Levinson, 'Law as Literature' (1982) 60 *Texas LR* 373.

or whether the distinction objective/subjective is inappropriate: meaning is constituted by interpretation, which is in turn a function of varying combinations of shared understandings, knowledge of language, conventions, and context (conventionalism).[35]

It is not necessary for these purposes to enter into this debate: we are not concerned with meaning *per se*, and whether there is an objectively 'correct' or 'real' meaning, for example. Rather what we are concerned with is how that rule *will* be interpreted and applied by those it is regulating; not how it should be. In this vein, the most suggestive line of work is that of the conventionalist school, which is concerned with how the meaning of rules is constructed and hence how rules are interpreted and applied.

The writing in this area is extensive; however within it the writings of Wittgenstein have been some of the most influential.[36] Wittgenstein was concerned with unreflective rule following, in mathematics or language, and not with legal rules. His theory has nevertheless spawned a considerable debate on legal rule following and application. He argued that automatic, unreflective rule following arose from shared judgements in the meaning and application of that rule.[37]

> If language is to be a means of communication there must be agreement not only in definitions but also (queer as this may sound) in judgements.[38]

Judgements include all the connections we make in our actions between language and the world: between a rule and its application,

[35] The 'middle way' is found by a range of writers through various routes. One of the most trenchant rejectors of the objective/subjective dichotomy, however, is Stanley Fish: S. Fish, *Is There a Text in This Class?* (Cambridge, Mass., 1980) and *Doing What Comes Naturally* (Oxford, 1989).

[36] Wittgenstein has been borrowed by many participants in the debate to bolster their arguments, including Fuller, and the critical legal theorists, notably S. Kripke, *Wittgenstein on Rules and Private Language* (Cambridge, Mass., 1982), C. Yablon, 'Law and Metaphysics' (1987) 96 *Yale LJ* 613 (book review), id., 'The Indeterminacy of the Law: Critical Legal Studies and the Problem of Legal Explanation' (1985) 6 *Cardozo LR* 917, M. Tushnet, *Red, White and Blue* (Harvard, 1988). For criticism of the use of Wittgenstein to support the radical indeterminacy thesis of the CLS writers, see e.g., C. Wright, Critical Notice (1989) 98 *Mind* 289, and Bix, *Law, Language and Legal Determinacy*, 36–45, who also argues that Hart's analysis of rules was Wittgensteinian in its approach at 52, and further id., 'Questions in Legal Interpretation', in A. Marmor (ed.), *Law and Interpretation.*

[37] G. P. Baker and P. M. S. Hacker, *Wittgenstein: Rules, Grammar and Necessity* (Oxford, 1985), 249; and *eid., Understanding and Meaning* (Oxford, 1980), *eid., Scepticism, Rules and Language* (Oxford, 1984).

[38] L. Wittgenstein, *Philosophical Investigations* (G. E. M. Anscombe, trans., New York, 1968, 3rd ed.) s. 242; Bix, *Law, Language and Legal Determinacy*, 42.

for example, or between how we have used a term in the past and whether we apply it to a particular new instance.[39] Agreement in judgements arises in turn from shared understandings arising from shared 'forms of life'. The concept of forms of life is cultural; different educations, interests, concerns, human relations or relations to nature constitute distinct forms of life.[40] It includes social contexts, cultures, practices, and training and forms the framework in which our use of language occurs (or our language-game is played, to adopt Wittgenstein's terminology). There are no shared rules without shared patterns of normative actions, and so shared judgements about justifications, criticisms, explanations, descriptions. The interpretation and application of a rule will thus be clear where there is agreement as to the meaning of the rule; agreement in turn comes from shared forms of life.

This argument has given rise to considerable controversy as to its meaning and implications. Most readers of Wittgenstein agree, however, that what this does not mean is that a consensus has to be obtained before the meaning of a rule is understood or the correctness of its application can be assessed. Wittgenstein draws a subtle but crucial distinction between the agreement which comes from forms of life which constitutes the background to the rule, and the internal relation between a rule and acts that accord with it. The background agreement enables us to follow rules in the same way, but it does not determine the correctness of a particular act in relation to a rule. 'We do not determine whether a flower is red by first asking everyone around what they think the flower's colour is.'[41]

[39] For discussions see Baker and Hacker, *Wittgenstein: Rules, Grammar and Necessity*, 229–51, *eid.*, *Wittgenstein: Understanding and Meaning*; J. McDowell, 'Non-Cognitivism and Rule-Following' in S. Holtzman and C. Leich (eds.), *Wittgenstein: To Follow a Rule* (London, 1981); Bix, *Law, Language and Legal Determinacy*, 36–62; C. McGinn, *Wittgenstein on Meaning* (Oxford, 1984).

[40] As Baker and Hacker explain in *Wittgenstein: Rules, Grammar and Necessity*, 242: 'different cultures form different conceptual structures, adopt different forms and norms of representation, limited only by the vague boundaries of the concept of a form of representation or a language. Of course, in advance of a particular question and a specific context it would be quite pointless to draw hard and fast distinctions between what counts as the same and what counts as different forms of life. Such distinctions depend upon the purpose and context of different kinds of investigation.'

[41] L. Wittgenstein, *Zettel* (G. E. M. Anscombe trans., G. E. M. Anscombe and G. H. von Wright (eds.), California, 1970) quoted in Baker and Hacker, *Wittgenstein: Rules, Grammar and Necessity*, 172.

What relevance has this for the formation and use of rules? As noted above, Wittgenstein was concerned with unreflective and automatic rule following. Interpretation and application of legal rules poses different issues, in part because in law the scope for differing yet 'correct' interpretations is far less than in other uses of language, the margin of acceptability of interpretation is significantly lower, and in part because law has its own rules of interpretation and application.[42] What can be drawn from his analysis for the purposes of understanding the nature of legal rules and their interpretation, however, are three things.

First, that saying a word or rule has a 'literal' or 'plain' meaning means simply that meaning which participants from a community would unreflectively assign to it.[43] A word may have a different 'literal' meaning in different languages, dialects, communities or contexts. It may be that in a community certain terms have very specific meaning; that meaning may not be shared by others outside. So 'jellies' may mean a particular drug to one community, or a type of dessert to another. Words may have particular technical meanings which may be alien to other language users: legal terms provide obvious examples ('consideration' in forming a contract does not mean a display of kindness), others could be terms commonly used in a particular industrial or commercial sector. However, it may nevertheless be the case that some words or phrases

[42] As Graff states, 'the practical concerns of the law occasion the imposition of a number of *artificial* restrictions on interpretive procedure, restrictions that do not apply outside the legal context. These restrictions arise from practical, ethical considerations rather than epistemological ones': '"Drop Dead," "Keep Off the Grass," and Other Indeterminacies', 411. Some, e.g., Posner, deny that literary theory has any relevance for law: R. A. Posner, 'Law and Literature: A Relation Reargued' (1986) 72 *Virginia LR* 1351; for a rebuttal see S. Fish, 'Don't Know Much About the Middle Ages: Posner on Law and Literature' (1988) 97 *Yale LJ* 777. More particularly, for warnings against the wholesale application of Wittgenstein to law (although support for its usefulness) see Bix, *Law, Language and Legal Determinacy*, 51–3.

[43] Indeed, this was the description of plain cases which Hart adopted: 'The plain case [*sic*], where the general terms seem to need no interpretation and where the recognition of instances seems unproblematic or "automatic", are only the familiar ones, constantly recurring in similar contexts, where there is general agreement in judgements as to the applicability of the classifying terms.' Hart, *The Concept of Law*, 123. It is also that adopted by Glanville Williams, who argued that 'words have no proper meanings', save in two senses: commonly accepted meanings, which may not be current among the community as a whole but confined to a particular section of it, and special meanings assigned by a particular person: 'Language and the Law', 384.

commonly have clearer meanings than others. In particular, evaluative terms will normally have a greater range of potentially acceptable interpretations than descriptive terms, particularly quantifiable ones ('reasonable speed' as opposed to '30 miles per hour'). Nevertheless, it may be that words which appear to be open to a wide range of interpretations, 'reasonable' or 'fair' for example, may in fact have very specific meanings in a particular community: what is considered to be a reasonable speed may be interpreted quite specifically (as 20 miles per hour, for example) in a particular community.

Secondly, because meaning and hence the application of a rule is not an objective fact but is contingent on the interpretive community reading the rule, there is no objectively clear rule or plain case. The clarity of a rule is not an objective assessment; rather as Fish notes it is a function of agreement within an interpretive community: 'agreement is not a function of clear and perspicuous rules; it is a function of the fact that interpretive assumptions and procedures are so widely shared in a community that the rule applies to all in the same (interpreted) shape'.[44] This analysis bears directly on the question of certainty of the rule: certainty in relation to a rule means that all who are to apply the rule: regulated, enforcement official, adjudicator, will adopt the same interpretation of the rule. What the conventionalist theory indicates is that certainty is not solely a function of the rule itself, it is a function of the community interpreting the rule. This, it is suggested, has significant implications for forming and using rules, which will be addressed below.

Finally, the idea of community constructed interpretations offers a theoretical basis for understanding many of the empirical observations as to the responses to rules of those subject to them in bureaucracies and regulatory systems. Studies of bureaucratic behaviour indicate that rules which contain wide, evaluative terms may be interpreted in a quite particular way by officials who are applying them.[45] As we have seen, the regulated may adopt a deliberate interpretive strategy, one of literalism, to defeat the purpose of the rule. The analysis indicates that creative compliance is not simply a failure to adopt a purposive approach, however, although it is that;

[44] Fish, *Doing What Comes Naturally*, 122.

[45] D. J. Gifford, 'Discretionary Decisionmaking in the Regulatory Agencies: A Conceptual Framework', (1983) 57 *South Calif. LR* 101; id., 'Decisions, Decisional Referents, and Administrative Justice' (1972) 37 *Law and Contemp. Problems* 3; Baldwin

it is a refusal to 'read in' to the rule things which are suppressed by the generalizations or abstractions which the rule uses, and most significantly a refusal to recognize the tacit understandings on which the rule is based and on which it relies. These understandings may be as to the purpose of the rule, they may also be as to the state of the world or other unformulated rules of conduct. A rule maker can never make sufficiently explicit the tacit assumptions on which the successful application of the rule depends; she will always be prey to those who adopt a 'literal' interpretation of a rule.

Using Rules

The above analysis indicates the extent to which, even before the problems of decision making, policy implementation, and enforcement are faced, regulation through rules has limitations which stem from the inherent nature of rules themselves. It may be possible to address at least some of the problems of regulating with rules through focusing on these inherent limitations to see to what extent they can be ameliorated. The next section suggests three strategies which could be pursued separately or in combination to this end: the use of different types of rules, the development and use of interpretive communities in regulation, and the adoption of a 'conversational model' of regulation. Some of the institutional implications of each are also indicated. These are not suggested as panaceas for all the rule-related ills that beset regulation; in particular they do not address the problem of what the rule should provide and the regulatory technique that should be adopted: franchising, licensing, disclosure, price, 'command and control'.[46] However, they are preferred as some of the potential ways in which more effective use could be made of rules in regulation by addressing the issues of flexibility and certainty in regulation, of adaptability and inclusiveness, of 'honest perplexity' as to the rule's meaning and application, and of creative compliance. They also help to explain some of the assumptions which are made about rules and regulatory structures in wider political and academic debates, and some of

and Hawkins, 'Discretionary Justice'; K. Hawkins, 'The Use of Legal Discretion: Perspectives from Law and Social Science', in K. Hawkins (ed.), *The Uses of Discretion* (Oxford, 1992); id., 'Discretion in Making Legal Decisions' (1986) 43 *Washington and Lee LR* 1161.

[46] For a discussion of a range of regulatory techniques see Ogus, *Regulation.*

the strategies which we will see in the subsequent chapters rule makers have used in the field of financial services in an attempt to improve the effectiveness of rules.

Rule Type

The first way in which the limitations of rules can be addressed lies in the rule itself: what type of rule is written. The possible implications of adopting rules of different types are alluded to in many discussions of rules, indeed the rules/standards/discretion debate makes extensive assumptions as to the effects of different types of rule. Discussions of rules, in both jurisprudential and administrative / bureaucratic contexts, tend to identify two broad types of norm, rules and standards.[47] Rules are usually seen as relatively precise formulations: 'a legal precept attaching a definite legal consequence to a definite detailed state of fact'.[48] Standards are seen as less precise, requiring some judgement in their application. A number of assumptions are involved in these distinctions, from which a range of consequences are seen to flow. Rules are associated with 'formalism' or 'legalism' and rigidity on the one hand, but certainty and uniformity on the other. In the administrative literature they are associated with the formal model of bureaucratic rationality, decision according to the literal letter of the rule, and with a low level of discretion. Standards are seen as allowing or prompting a more 'purposive' approach, so affording flexibility in their application and conferring greater discretion, but also entailing uncertainty and dangers of discrimination and partiality. They are associated with substantive rationality: decisions made on an individualized basis in accordance with the overall goal or purpose of the rule. 'Rules' and 'standards' are thus seen as monoliths representing competing models of rationality. The resolution of the competing demands of these rationalities, of certainty and flexibility, uniformity and individualization, is in turn seen to be a matter of combining rules and standards to achieve the 'right balance' of discretion at any one time.[49]

[47] For a discussion of the rule/standard and rule/principle dichotomies see R. Dworkin, *Taking Rights Seriously* (London, 1977), 22; Kennedy, 'Legal Formality' and id., 'Form and Substance'; Schauer, 'Formalism'; L. Alexander and K. Kress, 'Against Legal Principles', in A. Marmor (ed.), *Law and Interpretation.*

[48] R. Pound, *Jurisprudence* (New York, 1959) vol. 1, 124; for a similar definition see J. L. Jowell, *Law and Bureaucracy* (New York, 1975), 135.

[49] See, e.g., the discussion in Galligan, *Discretionary Powers*, Ch. 4.

The implications as to the use of types of rules are thus alluded to, but the distinction between rules and standards which dominates discussion of rules in the context of bureaucratic decision making provides an inadequate characterization of prescriptive rules for the purpose of considering the uses of rules within a regulatory system. Those concerned with the uses of rules have suggested a more complex analysis. Diver identified three dimensions to rules, transparency, congruence, and accessibility or simplicity.[50] Transparency refers to the ease with which the rule can be understood ('[a] transparent rule, like a transparent window, allows each observer to see the same thing—to reach the same conclusion about legal consequences when confronted with the same evidence').[51] Congruence refers to the inclusiveness of the rule, and simplicity or accessibility to the number of steps required by the rule and the quantity and accessibility of the evidentiary inputs that it demands. In his study of the use of delegated legislation, Baldwin builds on Diver to identify five dimensions: legal form or status (the mode of promulgation of the rule: statutory instrument, code); legal force or effect, associated prescription or sanction; specificity or precision (Diver's dimension of simplicity); accessibility and intelligibility (which refers to physical availability, and ease of comprehension); and scope or inclusiveness (Diver's dimension of congruence).[52]

Combining a legal with a linguistic analysis of rules, we can build on and rationalize these dimensional analyses by identifying four dimensions to rules: the substance and scope of a rule; its character; its legal status and the sanction attaching to it; and its linguistic structure. The first two dimensions, the substance of the rule and its character relate to the two dimensions of rules in the standard linguistic analysis of rules. Any rule can be formulated into two parts to take the canonical form: 'if *x*, then *y*'.[53] 'If *x*' is the factual

[50] C. S. Diver, 'The Optimal Precision of Regulatory Rules' (1983) *Yale LJ* 65, at 67–8; id., 'Regulatory Precision', in K. Hawkins and J. Thomas, *Making Regulatory Policy* (Pittsburgh, 1989).

[51] Diver, 'Regulatory Precision', 200–1.

[52] Baldwin, 'Why Rules Don't Work', 321–2; id., *Rules and Government*, 8–11.

[53] This analysis draws on G. Gottleib, *The Logic of Choice* (London, 1968), especially Ch. 3, who argues that for a statement to be a rule, it must be capable of being broken down in this manner. Other users of this analysis are R. Twining and D. Miers, *How to Do Things With Rules*, 141–4; N. MacCormick, *Legal Reasoning and Legal Theory*, 43, 45; Schauer, *Playing by the Rules*, 23–4; and in political science, C. Hood, *Administrative Analysis: An Introduction to Rules, Enforcement and Organisation* (London, 1986), Ch. 2.

predicate of the rule, the generalization discussed above.[54] 'Then *y*' is the consequence, what happens when the instances embraced in the generalization occur: it may be that a person is then permitted or required to act or refrain from acting.[55] The substance of the rule is thus its operational facts or factual predicate, what makes it 'bite'; its scope or inclusiveness is a function of the relationship of the operational facts to the rule's purpose, as explained above. The consequence of the rule may be described as its character; in law the consequence characterizes the rule as mandatory, directory, discretionary or permissive.[56]

The third dimension of status and sanction reflects the context of the present analysis of rules, viz. the use of rules in a regulatory system. The rules may be of direct or indirect legal effect (breach may give rise to sanction, or be of evidentiary nature only, for example), may be contained in legislation, statutory instrument, statutory or voluntary code, or in contractual form in licences, franchises or association membership agreements. They may have criminal or civil sanctions attaching to them, or give rise to disciplinary action by the regulatory body only in the form of expulsion from an association, a fine or publication of the fact of breach, for example.

The fourth dimension is the linguistic structure of the rule, and has three aspects: precision or vagueness, simplicity or complexity, and clarity or opacity.[57] The *precision or vagueness* of the rule draws most strongly on linguistic analysis and refers to the degree to which the operative facts of the rule are specified. There are a number of ways in which a rule could be vague.[58] There could be lack of specification as to the manner in which an action is to be performed ('inform', 'publish'), or as to time or place ('promptly', 'within the

[54] In Gottlieb's terms, the *protasis*: Gottlieb, *The Logic of Choice.*

[55] In Gottlieb's analysis, the *apodosis*: ibid.

[56] For a linguistic analysis of legal rules which analyses the use of different modals of 'may', 'shall', and 'must' as carrying the meanings of permission, ordering, and prohibition see D. Kurzon, *It is Hereby Performed: Explanations of Legal Speech Acts* (Philadelphia, 1986), Y. Maley, 'The Language of the Law', in J. Gibbons (ed.), *Language and the Law* (London, 1994), 20.

[57] Although expressed in terms of opposites, these descriptions are really of points at either end of spectrum rather than of rigid 'either/or' categories: precision or vagueness, e.g., is a matter of degree.

[58] Different analyses identify a range of different forms of vagueness: see, e.g., R. M. Kempson, *Semantic Theory* (Cambridge, 1977) (on which this section draws); F. Bowers, *Linguistic Aspects of Legislative Expression* (University of British Columbia, Canada, 1989), Ch. 3; Williams, 'The Language of Law', 179–95.

vicinity'). The rule could be referentially vague or indeterminate in the sense described above: although the meaning of the word is commonly understood, it may be difficult in certain cases to decide whether it applies to certain objects or arrangements ('vehicle'). The rule is thus vague in its particular application in a particular instance. Further, the meaning of the word itself could be vague in that it is evaluative ('reasonable', 'fair', 'suitable'). Or finally, it could be vague in that it uses generic terms (superordinates) which refer to a whole class of objects or events rather than specific terms which refer to particular components of that class (hyponyms): ('fruit' as opposed to 'citrus fruit', or more specifically, 'lemon'; 'financial instruments' as opposed to 'securities', or more specifically, 'shares'; 'information' as opposed to 'written information on costs and expenses').

The *simplicity or complexity* of a rule's structure is that aspect which is closest to Diver's dimension of simplicity and refers to the number of factual situations or assessments involved in a determination of the rule's applicability. For example, a simple rule would be one which provided, 'no licences may be granted to firms with less than twenty-five employees', or (more vaguely) 'licences will only be granted to those who are fit and proper'. A complex rule would be one which stated, 'licences may be granted to firms which comply with the following conditions . . .' and which set out a list of criteria which have to be met or assessments made. A rule may thus be simple but precise, or complex but vague, and vice versa. Simplicity refers to the number of operative facts, precision to the specification of those facts.

Finally, the *clarity or opacity* of a rule refers to the extent to which the rule is understood by those applying the rule, be they following or enforcing the rule. The aspect of clarity has been stressed by a range of different writers on rules,[59] but it is worth reuniting this aspect with its theoretical roots, partly to 'come clean' as it were about assumptions which underlie this analysis of rules, and partly in anticipation of the next section of this chapter. The identification of the aspect of clarity or opacity of a rule in fact expresses a particular theory of language: that of the conventionalists outlined

[59] e.g., Fuller's description of the 'clarity' of a rule in *The Morality of Law*, 63–5, Kennedy's 'formal realizability' of rules in 'Form and Substance', 1687–8, and Diver's 'transparency': 'Regulatory Precision', 200–1.

above. Clarity, it is being suggested, is a subjective assessment; it is a function of the interpretation which the rule receives in a particular community. Certain words may indeed have commonly received meanings ('fire'), others may be technical terms, receiving a common interpretation in one community, but not more widely ('bill of exchange', 'derivative'). Rules which contain evaluative statements ('fair', 'reasonable', 'due care') are probably going to be less clear than rules which refer to objects (vehicle) or to measurable quantities, be it of time, speed, length (30 days, 50 miles per hour, 10 miles). It may nevertheless be the case that a particular evaluative term has a particular meaning in a particular community, in which case that rule will be clear to members of that community, although opaque to those outside it. 'Due despatch' may commonly mean the next working day in some areas of business, for example. Or 'fit and proper' may be interpreted by licensing officials in accordance with a particular criteria.[60]

Choice of Rule Type

The dimensions of rules essentially represent decision points in the formation of rules; indeed choice of rule type may be a significant aspect of regulatory policy, as chapter 3 indicates. The dimensional analysis of rules suggested here enables us to appreciate the full nature of that choice. In this respect the rules / standards distinction underplays the decisions involved in rule making and fails to appreciate the range of uses of rules. It tends to focus on only one dimension of rules, their linguistic structure, and within that is confined to the precision or simplicity of a rule; further it assumes that there is a necessary relationship between different dimensions: a 'rule' is always precise and certain; a standard vague and unclear. There is no necessary analytical relationship between any of the dimensions, however. A rule can be of legislative status but be opaque. A rule can be simple but vague, opaque yet precise.

[60] Hawkins's study of decision making by officials in accordance with legislative or internal bureaucratic rules emphasizes the role norms, values, conventions, and practices can play in structuring or routinizing decisions under apparently broad discretionary rules: K. Hawkins, 'Using Legal Discretion' and 'On Legal Decision Making'; and see also Gifford, 'Discretionary Decision Making in the Regulatory Agencies'; A Conceptual Framework and 'Decisions, Decisional Referents, and Administrative Justice'; L. M. Friedman, 'Legal Rules and the Process of Social Change' (1967) 19 *Stanford LR* 786; Galligan, *Discretionary Powers*, 109–63. Decision making in the formation of rules is considered in Ch. 6.

The more precise a rule, though, the more likely it is that it will be under-inclusive, but as inclusiveness is a function of the purpose of the rule rather than its structure then again there is no necessary linear relationship between precision and inclusiveness.[61]

There is, moreover, no necessary and direct relationship between precision and certainty. 'Certainty' may indeed be a function of a number of dimensions.[62] It could be provided through specification as to manner, time or place, or through the clarity of a rule; it could however be destroyed by complexity.[63] Greater precision may therefore affect the certainty of the rule if it leads to complexity. Similarly, 'flexibility' may also be a function of a number of dimensions. It could be conferred by the vagueness of a rule, or its legal status and the sanction (or lack thereof) attaching to it. In this (latter) way, a precise rule could be rendered flexible if it was embodied in a voluntary code or guidance, breach of which did not of itself give rise to a sanction.

Rule makers can thus form different types of rules: rules with different scope, character, status, sanction, and structure. It must be noted, however, that the extent to which this is possible depends in a statutory system on the provisions of the primary legislation; frequently the rule maker may not have a full range of rule making powers and may be restricted to forming rules the sanction and status attaching to which have been predetermined by the legislature.[64] If the rules are to be embodied in legislation and be subject to criminal sanction, therefore, the ability of the rule maker to use, for example, the status and sanction of the rule to compensate for

[61] This counters Ehrlich and Posner's analysis; further, as the dimensional analysis indicates, their analysis of rules is only partial and moreover their prescription of precision brings its own problems: Ehrlich and Posner, 'An Economic Analysis of Legal Rulemaking', discussed above, text accompanying n. 16. Their analysis is also criticized by Baldwin who argues in addition that they take insufficient account of different compliance seeking strategies on the part of the enforcer: *Rules and Government*, 178.

[62] It is ultimately a function of the community interpreting the rule: see below.

[63] The impact of complexity in producing uncertainty in practice has been noted in a range of studies: S. Breyer, *Regulation and its Reform* (Harvard, 1982), 78–9 (discussing the effect of the fourteen separate criteria for issuing licences by the US Federal Communications Commission), S. Long, 'Social Control and the Civil Law: The Case of Income Tax Enforcement', in H. L. Ross (ed.), *Law and Deviance* (California, 1981), S. Surrey, 'Complexity and the Internal Revenue Code: The Problem of Management of Tax Detail' (1964) *Law and Contemp. Problems* 673.

[64] For a full study of delegated legislation see Baldwin, *Rules and Government*; G. Ganz, *Quasi-Legislation: Recent Developments in Delegated Legislation* (London, 1987).

over-inclusiveness or otherwise reduce formalism is reduced. Clearly, for rule makers to be able to use the full potential of rules, they need to be able to form rules of a wide range of types.

How could rule type be used? What are the possible implications of using different types of rules? Take first the dimension of status and sanction. The status and sanction of a rule can be used to ameliorate the over- or under-inclusiveness of a rule: if the rule is simply of the status of guidance, with no sanction for its breach, then problems of over-inclusiveness are addressed: the rule does not impose a sanction or pose a reason for action in those situations which do not further its purpose. Alternatively, a precise rule can be given flexibility if it is purely recommendatory, or its breach leads only to a discretionary sanction.

Using rules of different structures can also serve the function of distributing discretion or decisional jurisdiction within a regulatory system. Rules which are less precise, containing more evaluative terms or greater use of general descriptive or 'class' terms, leave more room for the person applying the rule to assess whether and how the rule should apply in any particular instance. As the analysis of vagueness and indeterminacy indicates, the inherent indeterminacy of rules means that this requirement to exercise judgement in the application of a rule can never be eliminated; its degree can however be altered. A rule which stipulates a maximum speed of 30 miles per hour confers less discretion than one which requires drivers to drive at a reasonable speed.

Rules with a vague structure can be combined with a permissive character to increase the level of discretion conferred. Primary legislation confers considerable amounts of discretion to ministers or regulatory bodies through the use of vague and permissive rules: 'the Secretary of State may make rules regulating the conduct of investment business', or 'may by rules establish a scheme for compensating investors' are two examples from the Financial Services Act 1986.[65] Alternatively, if the rule maker wants to try to control the interpretation and application of the rule she then may adopt a more precise rule (although this strategy may not always be effective, see below), and/or one which is mandatory or prohibitive in character.

The structure of the rule can also affect the interpretive strategy

[65] Ss. 48 and 54 respectively.

which is adopted in relation to it. That rule structure will affect interpretation is indeed the operative assumption in the rules / standards / discretion debate where precise rules are associated with a formalist strategy of interpretation, vague rules a purposive one. Creative compliance is also facilitated by, and partly dependent on, particular rule structures, notably specific and precise rules which do not contain evaluative terms.[66] Changing the structure of the rule and using vaguer terms which are more evaluative, could thus trigger a different interpretive strategy. So rather than having a sign 'no vehicles in the park', the sign could state 'nothing which inhibits the peaceful enjoyment of the park shall be allowed'. Changing the rule's structure is indeed one strategy which regulators in accountancy and financial services have deliberately adopted in an attempt to prevent formalistic interpretations.[67] The difference between the two types of rule is that the former, 'no vehicles in the park', could be read in two ways: as either a statement of the end in view (no vehicles to enter the park) or as an instrument to achieve an end which is not stated in the rule (peaceful enjoyment). The latter, by contrast, explicitly states that end. Thus at one level, a 'purposive' rule implicitly tries to address the problem of probabilistic cause in the formation of the substance or operative facts of the rule by identifying in the rule not the cause of the harm to be avoided or goal achieved, but rather that harm or goal itself ('peaceful enjoyment' rather than 'vehicle'). The revised rule may still bar the injured veteran's cavalcade, but will at least allow in wheelchairs and the statue of a truck. At another level, the essential difference between a rule which is vague and one which is precise, for strategies of interpretation at least, is that the former may use evaluative terms which not only may have a greater range of interpretation, but which require consideration of the aim of the rule in its application. Rules may thus address the problem of formalistic interpretation by using terms which do not have a commonly accepted or literal meaning, but which rather are evaluative, requiring the exercise of judgement on the part of those applying the rule.

[66] For a further analysis of other factors on which creative compliance relies, see Baldwin, *Rules and Government,* 186 n. 3 and 189, and below Ch. 6.

[67] See further Ch. 3, and in accountancy, McBarnet and Whelan, 'The Elusive Spirit of the Law' and 'Its Not What You Do but the Way That You Do It'.

Tensions and Trade-Offs

There are inevitably tensions and trade-offs involved in the choice of rule type, however. The most obvious tension, although by no means the only one, is that between flexibility and certainty. Further, the implications of using rules of different types are not so straightforward as the above discussion may suggest. Empirical work on bureaucratic decision making under rules indicates that the automatic association of interpretive strategy, or indeed of relative amounts of discretion, with rule type may be misplaced.[68] Precise rules may not control bureaucratic discretion, they may simply displace it.[69] Alternatively, rules which appear to confer wide discretion and to require judgement in their application (and so the purposiveness which is attributed to them) have been shown in practice to quickly be interpreted in a very particular, and perhaps inflexible, way through the development of practices in case-load handling, for example, or the influence of institutional norms and values.

Using rules to control the behaviour of regulatees rather than bureaucratic officials can pose slightly different problems. As noted above, precise rules, far from improving congruence or controlling behaviour, may also enable 'creatively compliant' behaviour on the part of the regulated: compliance with the literal meaning of the rule which subverts its purpose. The potential of those subject to the rules to behave in such an opportunistic fashion was encapsulated by Holmes's Bad Man; McBarnet and Whelan's research into the implementation of accountancy rules illustrates the extent to which this behaviour is facilitated by, and indeed dependent on, precise and complex rules.[70]

Further, some types of rules may be more suited to some enforcement systems and strategies than others. Economic analysis of systems of private enforcement suggests that as such systems are likely to result in enforcement and sanctioning of all breaches of rules then to minimise the inefficiency resulting from over-enforcement, rules would have to be more precise and err on the side of under-inclusion.[71] The over- or under-inclusion of rules is

[68] Hawkins (ed.), *The Uses of Discretion*, Galligan, *Discretionary Powers*, and references cited at n. 60 above.

[69] Baldwin and Hawkins, 'Discretionary Justice'.

[70] Although see above n. 66.

[71] R. Landes and R. A. Posner, 'The Private Enforcement of Law' (1975) *JLS* 1.

not in these circumstances mitigated by the enforcement process. Drawing on his study of health and safety regulation Baldwin suggests that 'bright line' rules are more suited to a deterrent strategy of enforcement as they facilitate prosecution; however where a compliance strategy of enforcement is adopted, involving negotiation, advice, education, and compromise with the regulatee, then less precise rules can aid the enforcement process.[72]

So there are trade-offs to be made between, for example, wanting to reduce the regulatee's discretion but also to facilitate an enforcement strategy of compliance rather than sanctioning or deterrence; or wanting to pre-empt creative compliance yet also ensure the prosecutability of rules; or wanting to avoid over-inclusiveness but also avoid complexity and the loopholes that result from precision. However, rule type can nonetheless be used to limit some of the inherent limitations of rules and achieve a degree of compromise in the trade-offs involved. The dimensional analysis indicates that tension between certainty and flexibility, for example, need not be the foundering reef of regulation which is often supposed.[73] Both flexibility and certainty are a function of a number of dimensions, in particular rule structure, status, and character. Rules of different types could be used within a rule system to provide both adaptability and assurance. For example, the rule system could combine vague, simple rules which have sanctions attached for their breach, with precise, complex rules which have no sanction attached to them but which provide guidance for compliance with the vague and simple rule. Indeed, it is through such a combination of rule types, that the financial services rule makers have attempted to resolve the tension between flexibility and certainty.[74]

The problems of control, literalism, and ensuring full and appropriate use of the discretion granted by the rule are in contrast essentially problems relating to interpretation. They may in part be addressed by the use of vaguer, purposive rules, as discussed above. The problem then is ensuring that the discretion is utilized, and

[72] Baldwin, 'Why Rules Don't Work' and *Rules and Government*, 143–57. For the identification and discussion of the distinction between 'compliance' and 'sanctioning' or 'deterrent' strategies of enforcement see K. Hawkins, *Environment and Enforcement* (Oxford, 1984).

[73] Rule type could further be used in combination with interpretive communities and with a conversational model of regulation discussed below to address the tension of flexibility and certainty.

[74] See Ch. 3 below.

in the way that the regulator wants it to be. In addressing this, rule type has to be used in conjunction with additional techniques of rule use, in particular, the use of interpretive communities.

Interpretive Communities

The second way in which some of the problems relating to rules may be addressed lies not in the rule itself but in the context in which it is formed, followed, and enforced. As was noted above, the contingency of the application of the rule on the interpretation it receives suggests a particular vulnerability of rules. Because of the need to rely on others to apply and interpret the rule the rule maker needs to know how the rule will be interpreted: will it be interpreted by persons acting in good faith and with an intent to 'do the best by the rule', or in the vein of Holmes's Bad Man: literally, opportunistically, seeking and exploiting loopholes or 'gaps' in the rule. In a bureaucratic context, will the rule be interpreted as conferring discretion to enable the rule to be applied in a manner which could reduce problems of inclusiveness and improve congruence, or will this discretion be in practice restricted, and the rule simply be interpreted in accordance with particular criteria, norms or a particular culture of the bureaucracy applying it?[75]

The rule maker also has to know whether the terms that he or she uses will be clear to those interpreting the rule, and so whether the rule will give the certainty that is so demanded. This has to be known with some precision essentially because, as noted above, meaning for rules is critical; rules are not like literary texts where the more meaning and interpretation that can be found the better; for rules, only one interpretation will be accepted as 'correct'. For the rule to 'work' in the sense of being applied in a way that would further the overall aims of the regulatory system, then the person applying has to share the rule maker's interpretation of the rule; they have to belong to the same interpretive community. If they do not, then the rule will fail in this sense at least.

Finally the rule maker has to know the extent to which the

[75] As Lempert observes, 'where rules accord a range of discretion to a decision maker, the decision maker may be both less and more constrained than he appears': R. Lempert, 'Discretion in a Behavioural Perspective', in Hawkins (ed.), *Uses of Discretion*, 227.

rule's addressees can be relied upon to 'read in' the tacit assumptions on which the rule is based. For as Fish explains, '[a] rule can never be made explicit in the sense of demarcating the field of reference independently of interpretation, but a rule can always be received as explicit by someone who hears it within an interpretive preunderstanding of what the field of reference could possibly be'.[76] This has a direct bearing on the question of the degree of precision which is necessary in a rule. The greater the shared understanding of the rule and the practices it is addressing, the more the rule maker can rely on tacit understandings as to the aim of the rule and context in which it operates, the less the need for explicitness, and the greater the degree to which simple, vague rules can be used.

How can such shared and informed understandings of rules be assured? The key may lie in the development and use of interpretive communities. The notion of interpretive communities suggested here draws on that of Fish, who describes them as:

> not so much a group of individuals who shared a point of view, but a point of view or way of organizing experience that shared individuals in the sense that its assumed distinctions, categories of understanding, and stipulations of relevance and irrelevance were the content of the consciousness of community members who were therefore no longer individuals but, insofar as they were embedded in the community's enterprise, community property. It followed that such community-constituted interpreters would, in their turn, constitute, more or less in agreement, the same text, although the sameness would not be attributable to the self-identity of the text, but to the communal nature of the interpretive act.[77]

It is not proposed to take Fish's notion completely, but rather to suggest that his idea of interpretive communities may contain seeds for the development of a notion of regulatory interpretive communities; of those involved in the regulatory system, rule makers, regulatees, enforcers, adjudicators, sharing interpretive strategies. Such interpretive communities are in essence constituted by institutional practices which may exist in the form of shared cultures, norms, goals, definitions, and can be created through,

[76] Fish, *Doing What Comes Naturally*, 125.

[77] Fish, *Doing What Comes Naturally*, 141. See further *Is There a Text in This Class?* (Harvard, 1980), 'Fish v. Fiss' (1984) 36 *Stanford LR* 1325, 'Don't Know Much About the Middle Ages' and *Doing What Comes Naturally*, 141–60.

for example, training and education. A regulatory strategy which uses interpretive communities could provide the germ of solutions for the problems of uncertainty and 'honest perplexity' and the problem of explicitness.[78] Interpretive communities could also address the practice of creative compliance and perhaps serve to create what may be termed *instinctive* compliance, in two ways. First, through the development of a tacit knowledge and understanding which can inform the application of the rules; secondly, by overcoming the opportunistic approach to rules which is the basis of creative compliance. It is one thing having the tacit understandings necessary for the 'correct' application of the rule, it is another thing using them.

Indeed, creative compliance and certainty raise two distinct but related problems. In the demand for certainty what is being sought is the assurance that my interpretation of the rule will accord with others', in particular that of the person or institution that ultimately has the responsibility for determining the application of the rule. Certainty has been traditionally associated with greater specification and precision, with all the implications that has for inclusiveness, flexibility, and so on. The implicit assumption is that only precision can guarantee sufficient commonality of interpretation. Greater precision is thus usually seen to be necessary where there is a large number of regulatees or enforcement officials.[79] Vaguer terms, either as to manner, time, place, level of description, or evaluative terms have a greater interpretive range and so traditionally are seen as more flexible but less certain. If, however, either the meaning of that term or the range of interpretations

[78] Intepretive communities are not a panacea for all rule-related ills, and as the discussion of the institutional implications indicates, may raise some of their own, particularly with respect to their accountability. Further, with respect to enforcement they may not alleviate the need for precise rules to aid a deterrent or sanctioning enforcement strategy. This strategy actively uses prosecution, and Baldwin notes is facilitated by precise rules. However, it is suggested that one of the reasons why precise rules are favoured in these cases is because such rules do not allow much room for argument as to interpretation, and so the regulatee cannot argue that the enforcement official's interpretation is the wrong one. The real issue, thus, is not rule precision, but whether the enforcement official's interpretation is accepted as authoritative by the regulatee. If, therefore, both the regulatee and the enforcer know that the latter's interpretation will in fact be that which is adopted, then the need for a precise or 'bright line' rule to effectively confer that authority (by reducing the range of possible interpretations so that there can be no argument that the regulatee has breached the rule) is sidestepped.

[79] See e.g., Diver, 'Regulatory Precision'.

that would be accepted as correct could be assured, then vague terms would be clear, and so could also confer certainty.

Interpretive communities are a way that mutuality of interpretation could be assured without further specification by rule. What is necessary then is that the rule maker, regulated, and enforcer share those norms, values, goals that give rise to a shared understanding as to the rule's meaning and application.[80] This is normally achieved in law through the use in the formulation and application of rules of those trained in legal practice who have an understanding of judicial rules of interpretation. The most obvious example is the conventions of parliamentary counsel in drafting statutes, which follow closely judicial rules of interpretation. However, outside the context of rules embodied in legislation, judicial involvement in the rule application process could in practice be a source of uncertainty if those judicial rules of interpretation are different from, or indeed alien to, those which the regulator and regulated would adopt. Indeed it is a frequent criticism of the relationship of the courts and regulators that courts 'do not understand' regulators or the practices they are regulating; the implicit charge is that courts impose an interpretation or allow an interpretive strategy that the regulator or regulated (at least in the absence of professional legal advice) would not share. Moreover, the criticism of 'legalism' is one frequently levelled at regulation which adopts a judicial approach to interpretation, and it is the ability to use 'non-legal language' which is preferred as one of the advantages of voluntary codes.[81]

Certainty, or mutuality of interpretation between regulator, regulated, and enforcer, could in these circumstances be achieved in a number of ways. The legislature could, for example, confer power on the regulator to formulate rules which had evidential status and which thus served as guides for the interpretation of vaguer legislative provisions, instructing the court, in effect, as to their interpretation. In a non-statutory regime, the regulator could operate entirely through rules which had no legal basis, statutory or contractual. The court's role in interpretation of those codes would then occur only in the context of judicial review, if that body is

[80] In the legal and regulatory context, it is the final adjudicator who will determine the particular interpretation of the rule and interpretive strategy to be adopted.

[81] See generally Ganz, *Quasi-Legislation*, Baldwin, *Rules and Government*, P. P. Craig, *Administrative Law* (London, 3rd ed., 1993), Ch. 7.

deemed to be subject to that jurisdiction.[82] Alternatively, the legislator could, for example, provide that breaches of regulatory rules were not actionable in civil suit, so eliminating the possibility of private enforcement (by individuals), and leaving the monopoly of enforcement to the regulator by making breaches subject to regulatory disciplinary action only, and not to action in the courts. In the latter instances, where the court's role in interpretation of the rules is limited, the system could be described as being 'closed off', and the number and range of different institutions involved in the rule formation and application process is significantly reduced.[83]

The use and development of interpretive communities through 'closing off' could address the problem of creative compliance. The opportunistic use of rules is a possibility only because the formalistic interpretation which the regulatee is applying is itself seen as a valid interpretive approach within the legal system. The legal system can explicitly change the interpretive approach that it adopts to prevent such behaviour;[84] however from a regulator's point of view the regulator cannot determine when a court will do this, and when it will not. Attempting to guide or instruct judicial intepretation may reduce some of the uncertainty but it is a relatively indirect strategy. 'Closing off' the regulatory system from external court control, enabling the regulator to have a monopoly over the interpretation and application of the rules, is more direct as it enables the regulator to set the interpretive strategy to be adopted. The regulator may thus be able to resist the pressures for formalism by adopting a range of rule types within the rule system: by formulating rules of vague structure but with regulatory sanction for their breach,[85] and rules of precise and even complex

[82] On the susceptibility of self regulatory bodies to judicial review, see J. M. Black, 'Constitutionalising Self Regulation' (1996) 59 *MLR* 24.

[83] The institutional implications are discussed further below. It is precisely the attempt to close off the regulatory system, to exclude those who do not share the practices, norms or culture of the regulated community which it is suggested was implicit in the formation of SIB's ten Principles in 1990. The outsiders in this instance were the courts: restricting their civil jurisdiction with respect to a breach of the rules enabled the use of vaguer, more evaluative rules. See further Ch. 3 below.

[84] e.g., in tax see *Furniss* v. *Dawson* [1984] AC 474 which explicitly stated that substance not form be looked at; similarly with respect to leases and licences, *Street* v. *Mountford* [1985] AC 809.

[85] 'Regulatory sanction' means a sanction imposed by the regulator, in contrast to one imposed by the court.

structure but which have no sanction attached to their breach. In relation to both the issue of certainty and creative compliance, then, interpretive communities, particularly if they are constituted by closing off, can enable a change in the types of rules used and their effectiveness.

Interpretive communities can also address the problem of explicitness, and may perhaps (to be admittedly optimistic) help to promote 'instinctive compliance' with the rules. As Fish notes, to be inside an interpretive community means to be already and always thinking and perceiving within the norms, standards, definitions, routines of that community and to share an understanding of the goals that both define and are defined by that context.[86] The greater the degree to which these are common amongst those writing, applying, and enforcing the rules, the less which has to be rendered explicit. This has implications both for the degree to which rules have to use precision in an attempt to control (which is reduced), and for the ability of rules to cope with a greater range of contingencies or changes which may arise (which is enhanced).[87]

What the development of an interpretive community would have to achieve to promote 'instinctive compliance' is the displacement of the interpretations, and norms, values, understandings, conventions which give rise to them, of regulatees and officials by those of the rule makers. This would be the ultimate stage in its development. At the very least, however, what is aimed at is the development of a reciprocity or mutuality of interpretation between regulated and rule maker. This is unlikely to occur spontaneously. It is not envisaged that interpretive communities will simply emerge in an organic process; they have to be actively developed. A crucial part of their development is ensuring that the interpretation ultimately accepted as 'correct' by the adjudicator is in accord with the regulator's. However, even if the system is 'closed off', and so the rule maker can rely on the adjudicator to confirm her interpretation of the rule, relying solely on adjudication is insufficient. The aim in developing interpretive communities is to develop

[86] Fish, *Doing What Comes Naturally*, 127, 303.

[87] This suggested relationship between prescription or explicitness and understanding could explain the often expressed attitude of financial services regulators that detailed rules are necessary where regulation is an untried and untested exercise. Conversely, successive chairman of SIB have stated that as soon as they feel happy that the regulated will in fact read into the rule a greater range of tacit understandings, and will adopt a common (and regulator-sanctioned) interpretation of rules, then vaguer, more evaluative rules could be used. See further below, Ch. 3.

mutuality of interpretation amongst all those involved in the regulatory process: rule maker, enforcer, regulated. This requires an educative as well as a command approach. Training and education of all involved in the process, including that given formally to enforcers and regulated, or by enforcers through the enforcement process, provide more subtle tools which could have greater continuous effect.

The use and development of interpretive communities has significant implications for the design of the institutional structure of the regulatory system. Indeed, it could be argued that it is the attempt to create, and/or to use existing, interpretive communities which lies behind the advocation of self-regulation as a system of regulation. Self-regulation is often seen to mitigate the problems of rules both by minimizing the inevitable limitations of rule makers' foresight and knowledge through the use of experts in the area (on the basis, presumably, that whilst all rule makers are fallible, some are more fallible than others) and through the particular context in which the rules operate. Self-regulation is seen to offer flexibility and sensitivity; to facilitate the use of vague, purposive rules rather than precise and complex ones, to avoid the problems of 'legalism' and literalism, and to offer regulation with a 'light touch' in contrast to the heavy and indiscriminate boot of command and control regulation.[88] All are attributes of interpretive communities. A self-regulatory system is essentially a system which is self-contained: it is the rule maker, regulated, and enforcer.[89] The process of rule making, rule interpretation, and rule application are contained within the system. Moreover, those within it may share a common training, background, norms, commitment or understanding. The rule maker can make rules in the confidence that the rules will receive a high degree of consensus as to their interpretation, and that the rule maker's interpretation will be confirmed in the application and enforcement process. That at least is the theoretical ideal. It is also the policy ideal for many.

[88] A. C. Page, 'Self Regulation and Codes of Practice' (1984) *JBL* 24, id., 'Self Regulation: The Constitutional Dimension' (1986) 49 *MLR* 141, C. Graham, 'Self Regulation', in H. Genn and G. Richardson, *Administrative Law and Government Action* (Oxford, 1995), A. Ogus, 'Re-thinking Self Regulation' (1995) 15 *OJLS* 97.

[89] There may be an institutional separation of regulator and regulated via an agency forming and administering the rules, but this is an organizational rather than conceptual issue.

However, conferring a monopoly of the formation and application of rules to a regulatory body, effectively 'closing off' the regulatory system from external interference, has significant implications for the accountability of such regulators. These could be addressed by ensuring that members and others affected by the regulation are involved in the formation of the rules,[90] and by a particular judicial approach to the interpretation of such rules. This would require the courts to give precedence to the regulator's interpretation of its rules, striking it down only if it was not within the range of interpretations that could be reasonably expected of the rule. Such an approach to the Takeover Panel's rules was suggested by Lord Donaldson in *Datafin*;[91] a similar approach has been suggested by Craig (although with respect to statutory bodies).[92]

Rules and Regulatory Style: A 'Conversational' Model of Regulation

Ensuring a mutuality of interpretation through the formation of an interpretive community addresses principally the problems of interpretive strategy and certainty. It is also suggested that some of the other limitations of rules, notably those of inclusiveness and difficulties in foresight, can be met through the adoption of a 'conversational model' of regulation. In order to explain this idea, we need to reflect again on the nature of rules and their inherent limitations.

Both over- and under-inclusiveness and 'open texture' pose a problem for rules because of the particular nature of rules as authoritative communications. Over-inclusive legal rules have the effect of punishing conduct which it was not intended should be prohibited by the rule; under-inclusive rules of failing to prohibit or encourage behaviour which would further the rule's purpose; each is an aspect of a rule's ineffectiveness. The linguistic analysis of the use of generalizations in conversations suggests two ways in which these effects of over- and under-inclusiveness can be mitigated. The first has already been mentioned above in the consideration of rule type:

[90] For detailed proposals of how this could be achieved, see P. Harter, 'Negotiationg Regulation' (1982) 17 *Georgetown LJ* 1.

[91] *R* v. *Panel on Takeovers and Mergers, ex p. Datafin* [1987] 1 All ER 564.

[92] Craig, *Administrative Law*, 375–8. For an application of a similar approach in the US see *Chevron USA* v. *NRDC* 467 US 837 (1984) 84. For a more general discussion of the relationship of the courts to self-regulatory bodies see J. Black, 'Constitutionalising Self-Regulation' (1996) 59 *MLR* 24.

limiting the sanction imposed for breach of the rule, or indeed removing any sanction (by making compliance with the rule voluntary or giving the rule the status of guidance only, for example). The second is a change in the regulatory style which is adopted, not simply the type of rule.[93] If a regulatory or enforcement strategy is adopted which makes either formal or informal use of waivers or modifications of the rules, a similar process of adjustment of the generalization can occur in regulation as occurs in conversation.

In conversation, the problems of generalizations and to an extent of open texture can be, and are, resolved by explanation and latitude in interpretation and understanding on the part of those participating.[94] For example, if whilst walking in the park my friend, looking at a toy truck, refers to 'that vehicle', I would understand to what she was referring and not necessarily correct her or question her description, although I may think it an odd use of the word. Or I may state that the weather is always miserable in February, but it is open to me to then immediately qualify that by saying there may be days in February in which the sun shines; or accept that in Australia the weather in February is in fact very pleasant. Conversation uses generalizations, and can tolerate them simply because it has the capacity for qualification, clarification, and embellishment. It is when this process of adjustment cannot or does not occur that the over- or under-inclusiveness of generalizations and the indeterminacy of rules poses a problem. It is precisely in legal rules that this adjustment is problematic. If in conversation I were to declare that all dogs should be banned from restaurants, it would be open to me to qualify this by saying, but of course I don't mean guide-dogs. Rules, particularly legal rules, however, are entrenched. The rule applies to all dogs; if a guide-dog enters, then there has been a breach of the rule.

Mitigating the problems of inclusiveness, then, and indeed open texture, could be addressed if the regulatory style could simulate that of a conversation between regulator and regulated. What would this 'conversational model' of regulation look like? Four characteristics come to mind, which are not mutually exclusive but not all

[93] Although again the two can be used in combination.

[94] For discussions of the differences in the use of language between conversations and rules see Schauer, *Playing by the Rules*, 38–42 and Bix, *Law, Language and Legal Determinacy*, 19, 184, on which this discussion of the conversational use of language draws.

of which may be present in any one system at any one time. First, the (formal) approach of rule adaptation through amendments to rules. The problem of inclusiveness is thus addressed through changes to the rule: the extension or reduction in its scope, for example, or through changes in specification, precision, through clarification, deletion or embellishment. This approach, however, may be neither feasible nor desirable in situations where the rule making process is expensive in terms of time and resources. Nor is it necessarily desirable where the rules apply to a large number of regulatees, simply because the dangers of unforeseen consequences of change are great, even where the process of changing rules is cheap; where however regulation is through a contractual or quasi-contractual mechanism, franchise or licence, for example, then rule changes could be an attractive option as they would affect only that operator.[95]

A second (formal) policy of rule adaptation through exceptions and waivers granted on an individualized basis by the regulator could have a similar 'conversational' effect, but the problems associated with amending rules are reduced. The rule continues to apply to other regulatees; it is simply adjusted with respect to individuals. This may mean that the regulation 'fits' individual circumstances more appropriately, but may be opposed on the grounds of lack of uniformity of treatment. The adjustment in the application of rules through the granting of waivers and exceptions may also be expensive to operate in terms of regulatory time.[96] Moreover, it would be more acceptable for reasons of consistency, certainty, and avoidance of retroactivity for the adjustment to take the form of exceptions from rules rather than via extensions of rules to fit events or things which are currently excluded from the rules. Over-inclusiveness can thus be addressed; the problem of under-inclusiveness may remain. This suggests that the strategy should be used in combination with vague, over-inclusive rules which are supplemented by more specific (although potentially under-inclusive) guidelines for regulatees and enforcers.

[95] This is not to say that it would be a 'harm-free' strategy: if frequent and continuous, rule changes could create uncertainty for the regulatee, making it difficult to develop long-term business strategies, e.g., and affecting its share price.

[96] See P. H. Schuck, 'When the Exception Becomes the Rule: Regulatory Equity and the Formulation of Agency Policy through an Exceptions Process' (1984) *Duke LJ* 163.

Thirdly, a system of individualized application of general rules could be developed. This could either be in a model akin to Ayers and Braithwaite's 'enforced self-regulation' in which individual firms formulate their own rules under the supervision of a regulatory body. Or it could be that the regulator negotiates with a firm how a vague rule should apply to it: for example what reserves a particular bank has to have to comply with the requirement that they be 'adequate'.[97] The point is that there exists a continual communication, a conversation, between regulator and regulated as to the application of the rule or rules. It is probable, however, that this style of regulation will only be effective in circumstances where the regulated are not only well-intentioned and well-informed but also well resourced; in other words, have good information about the intended operation of the regulation, are committed to it, and have the resources, both organizational and economic, to formulate their own rules.[98] Moreover, given the level of commitment of regulatory resources necessary to assess the different rules which firms formulate or to negotiate the individualized application of a rule, it may also be necessary that the regulatees be relatively few in number.

Finally, a (formal or informal) strategy of enforcement which is one of 'compliance' rather than 'deterrence' operated on the ground by enforcement officials could be adopted, and indeed enforcement studies suggest already is in certain circumstances. This has a similar effect as the operation of exceptions or waivers (the rule is not applied), but it occurs at a different level within the regulatory system, and may have greater problems of consistency and legitimacy associated with it.[99] A compliance strategy of

[97] Note that 'enforced self-regulation' differs from the others in that it is essentially a method of rule formation, rather than the application of existing rules. A hard distinction may not always be drawn between the two (the effect on the regulatee is the same under rule amendment, waiver, individual specification or this method of formation: the rule is adjusted to suit individual circumstances), but there are differences both in the degree to which the regulation is 'tailored' to suit the individual, and also in the design of the regulatory system, notably in the procedures for rule formation and in the role played by the regulator. This has implications for the issues of entry to and standing within the conversation: see below.

[98] For criticism of enforced self-regulation and a discussion of its limitations, see Baldwin, *Rules and Government*, 162–4.

[99] See Bardach and Kagan, *Going by the Book*, in particular Chs. 5–7, who also identify several reasons why enforcement officials may be reluctant to operate a

enforcement is one in which enforcement officials focus on improving compliance with the regulations by informing the regulatee of how to comply in the future rather than imposing sanctions for past infringements. A deterrence strategy of enforcement is one in which all breaches are sanctioned. As noted above, under a deterrence strategy, or indeed under a system of private enforcement (which has a similar effect), the problems of over- and under-inclusiveness of rules are not mitigated by the enforcement process: every occasion in which there has been a breach of the rule is sanctioned.[100] Under a compliance strategy, in contrast, some of the limitations of rules can be addressed by the waiver of the rule in that particular circumstance, or the negotiation of the application of the rule to new and unforeseen circumstances. It may be possible then to use over-inclusive rules knowing that their application can easily be waived.[101] Rules and enforcement may thus be in a reflexive relationship: rules may affect the enforcement strategy which can be used,[102] but the enforcement strategy may also influence the type of rules which may be adopted.[103]

Adoption of different forms or aspects of the conversational model of regulation may have the benefit of enabling the more precise 'targeting' of the rule; however the model does have its own limitations. It may be subject to institutional constraints. As noted, it may be easier to operate in a context of relatively few regulatees. If regulation is via licence or franchise of individual operators, or is of a monopolistic or oligopolistic industry or simply one in which

'compliance' model of enforcement. Such a strategy has nonetheless been observed as the principal strategy in regulation of pollution and health and safety in the UK, at least with regards those regulatees who are ill intentioned and ill informed: Hawkins, *Environment and Enforcement*; Baldwin, 'Why Rules Don't Work'; B. M. Hutter, *The Reasonable Arm of the Law* (Oxford, 1988). Holland's study of the operation of the Cadbury Code on corporate governance reveals a similar approach to enforcement being adopted, but not by a regulatory body rather by other market participants, in this case pension funds: J. Holland, 'Self Regulation: the Financial Aspects of Corporate Governance' (1996) *JBL* 127.

[100] Above, text accompanying n. 71. One of the problems of a private system of enforcement is that it does not allow for a conversation to occur.

[101] The problems of extending under-inclusive rules, noted with respect to the formal approach of modification or waiver, also apply here.

[102] Baldwin, 'Why Rules Don't Work' and *Rules and Government*.

[103] For a discussion of the reasons why in practice it may not, however, see Baldwin, *Rules and Government*, 164–74, Bardach and Kagan, *Going By the Book*, especially 153–213. It may also affect the role that rules consequently play in the regulatory process: see below, text accompanying n. 108.

there are relatively few operators then there may be greater potential for the regulator and regulated effectively to conduct a conversation as to the application of the rules at the more formal level of waivers, no action letters or rule changes. It may also be easier to use vague rules in these circumstances, with the particular application being negotiated with each individual regulatee and changed according to circumstances, for example; alternatively detailed rules can be used but changed or waived when application may not further the rule's purpose. These constraints could nonetheless be addressed to an extent, however. For example, a system of waivers and no action letters, or even of 'on-line' consultation and advice as to the application of rules in particular circumstances, could possibly still operate in a context of a large number of regulatees, if adequate record keeping of waivers or advice given ensured consistency in treatment of regulatees. A compliance-orientated enforcement strategy is similarly not necessarily constrained by numbers, although as with the use of waivers, for it to work effectively it may be reliant on considerable regulatory resources in terms of time and personnel (although these may still be less than those necessary for a deterrence strategy).[104]

The conversational model also raises more fundamental questions, however, notably of what is the relative standing of those conducting the conversation, and indeed, between who is it conducted. With respect to the relative positions of those involved in the conversation, it may not be that the regulator has in practice the stronger position. The model requires in particular significant resources of time, information, and expertise on the part of the regulator to assess the need, for example, for a waiver, the negotiation of the rule's application or the implications of the rules which the regulated has formulated, resources which may be lacking. The regulator may thus be at a considerable disadvantage in terms of assessing the need for adjustments to the rule or the appropriateness of those rules which the firm has formulated. Further, although the regulator may have the ultimate authority to decide whether to grant the waiver or to enforce the rule, thus suggesting that it is the regulator which has a stronger position in any negotiation, the regulator

[104] On compliance strategies see K. Hawkins and J. Thomas (eds.), *Enforcing Regulation* (Boston, Mass., 1984), and the discussion between F. Pearce and S. Tombs, 'Ideology, Hegemony and Empiricism' (1990) 20 *BJCrim.* 423, and K. Hawkins, 'Compliance Strategy, Prosecution Policy and Aunt Sally' (1990) 20 *BJCrim.* 444.

may in fact be seeking to avoid prosecution for reasons of time, money, and in the interests of maintaining long-term regulatory relationships;[105] if the regulated is aware of this, then the regulator's position of strength may be more apparent than real.

Problems of time, information, and expertise apply generally to any aspect of the formation and use of rules, and are not unique to the conversational model. Adopting a conversational model of regulation does however raise significant questions of accountability, simply because systems designed to increase participation and openness may more easily operate at the stage of rule formation rather than rule application and enforcement. Adopting a conversational model, especially one which involves a compliance strategy of enforcement, is a regulatory approach which it is difficult for other regulated firms or individuals and those outside the system to observe and monitor. The conversation, particularly when it occurs at the level of enforcement officers, is likely to be a dialogue between regulator and regulated, rather than a discussion embracing a wider constituency.

The questions of entry to and participation in that conversation which are thus raised may be addressed in different ways, depending on the type of conversational model adopted at any particular time or in any particular case. To the extent that it may be easier to design a system which involves a wider range of interests in the process of rule formation, then entry to and participation in that process may be designed into a conversation which proceeds by formal rule amendments or into the strategy of enforced self-regulation, which as noted is essentially a process of rule formation. It may also be incorporated into a system of waivers, at least to the extent of *post hoc* review of those granted. This may be easier when waivers are granted or application of the rule negotiated in a formal process, for example of request by the firm to the regulator. Where waivers or the negotiated application of the rule occurs informally and at a lower level in the regulatory system, notably at the level of enforcement officers, then the process is less visible, so less transparent and less monitorable, unless information flows within the organization facilitate the transmission of information of what

[105] See R. Cranston, *Regulating Business: Law and Consumer Agencies* (London, 1979); Hawkins, *Environment and Enforcement*; Richardson, Ogus, and Burrows, *Policing Pollution*; Hutter, *The Reasonable Arm of the Law*; Hawkins and Thomas (eds.), *Enforcing Regulation*.

happens at the enforcement stage further up the organization.[106] Further, ensuring that others can participate in the conversation when it occurs at the level of enforcement officers could make significant demands on the time of both regulator and regulated, render the process unwieldy, and perhaps affect the willingness of either the regulator or regulated to participate in the conversation at all.[107] Adoption of this type of conversational model thus may mean, however, that even if the rule formation process was one of negotiation between or otherwise involved the participation of a wide range of interests, those interests may be, and indeed enforcement studies indicate are, effectively excluded from the implementation of that rule in the enforcement process. Participation at one stage in the regulatory process, rule formation, is negated at another, the application of the rule to particular circumstances.

Finally, the model itself raises the issue that if the rule is observed more in the waiver than in the application, then the strategy of waivers may be in danger of undermining the rule itself. The rule becomes not a tool to achieve a certain aim, but the framework for subsequent negotiation between regulator and regulated.[108]

Conclusion

By extrapolating from a theoretical study of rules and their interpretation, a number of potential strategies of rule use may be developed to address the inherent limitations of rules. These may be the adoption of different rule types; structuring the context in which rules operate: the use and development of interpretive communities; or altering the way in which rules are applied: the adoption of a 'conversational model' of regulation. These strategies are not mutually exclusive, although each has its limitations and drawbacks.

[106] For suggestions that such information flows may frequently be blocked, see Baldwin, 'Why Rules Don't Work' and *Rules and Government*, Ch. 6.

[107] On the prerequisites for successful negotiation, see P. Harter, 'Negotiating Regulation' (1982) 71 *Georgetown LJ* 1.

[108] See J. L. Comaroff and S. R. Roberts, *Rules and Processes: The Cultural Logic of Dispute in an African Context* (Chicago, 1981); G. Teubner, 'Juridification: Concepts, Aspects, Limits, Solutions', in G. Teubner (ed.), *Juridification of the Social Sphere* (Berlin, 1987); M. Galanter, 'Legality and its Discontents: A Preliminary Assessment of Current Theories of Legalization and Delegalization' (1980) *Jahrburch fur Rechtssozolgie und Rechtstheorie* 11.

The analysis and suggestions proposed in this chapter are general in their application and are not confined to the role of rules in financial services regulation. The subsequent analysis suggests that two of these proposed uses of rules, rule type and the development of interpretive communities, have however been adopted by financial services rule makers. It also indicates that the reasons for using rules in particular ways can extend well beyond attempts to address the inherent limitations of rules. The regulators have used different types of rules to achieve a wide range of goals, and indeed the question of how rules should be used has on occasion been an issue of regulatory policy in its own right. The following chapters examine the formation and use of rules by financial services regulators, exploring the reasons why regulators make the rules that they do.

2 The Development of the Regulatory Structure

Before we can start to examine in depth the rule making process of financial services regulators and the ways in which they have used rules, it is necessary to step back and consider the institutional context in which they operate. This is necessary not only in order to set out their formal powers, but also, and more importantly, in order to understand the dynamics of the structure and the tensions and frictions which it contains and which have had a significant impact on the rule making process and the uses made of rules. These in turn can only be understood by examining the history and development of the structure, the growth of that structure out of existing institutional relationships, and the impact which the perceptions of both the legitimacy and effectiveness of different types of regulatory arrangements, self and statutory, have had on it. The history of the structure, itself characterized by a combination of accident, coincidence, and design, thus explains both the formal, structural elements of the regulatory system and its legal framework, and the less formalized expectations and tensions which pervade it. The chapter therefore explores the development of the structure, the blueprint for reform provided by Gower, and the ways in which events unrelated to his reports ensured that his proposals were adopted, and indeed became solutions to problems largely unforeseen at the time of their formulation. It examines the process leading up to the White Paper, and then the manner in which, and reasons why, the delicate balance struck in that White Paper was crucially altered over the course of the passage of the Bill. Finally, it develops a characterization of the structure which resulted, and explores briefly why that characterization matters in contemporary debates concerning the nature of the regulatory structure.

Designing the Regulatory Structure

Regulation of financial services has historically been characterized by a complex blend of statutory and non-statutory regulation.[1]

[1] For a conceptual analysis of the role of self-regulation prior to the Financial

Under the Prevention of Fraud (Investments) Act 1958, the immediate predecessor to the 1986 Act, the Department of Trade (DoT) was responsible for authorizing unit trusts and conferring either licences or exemptions on those who dealt in securities. Licences were granted on application, and could only be revoked if a person ceased to be 'fit and proper'. Licensed dealers were subject to the Licensed Dealer (Conduct of Business) Rules 1960. Members of associations recognized by the DoT, the Stock Exchange, and those regulated by the Bank of England were exempt, as were managers and trustees of unit trusts, anyone whose main business was not dealing or who dealt only with exempted or licensed dealers, or acted as principal, or acted for or on behalf of a licensed dealer or recognized association. Investment advisers and managers were not covered by the Act and were unregulated. The incidence of regulation was thus fragmented and moreover the administration of the system of licences and exemptions had led to the development of what Gower described as a 'fringe and an elite', where exemption was regarded as a status symbol.[2]

The activities of those, largely exempted, firms participating in the securities markets were loosely overseen by two bodies. The first was the Joint Review Body, described by the Wilson Committee as a 'major institutional change'[3] and by Gower as 'a small liaison committee of officials' of the DoT and the Bank.[4] It was charged with the general oversight of the supervision of the securities market and the identification of potential gaps in arrangements. It met about twice a year, did not publish minutes, and did not report to anyone. The second was the Council for the Securities Industry. The CSI had been set up by the Bank of England to co-ordinate self-regulation among all users and practitioners in the securities markets, essentially Exchange members and those exempted under the PF(I)A.[5] It had formed a Code of Conduct

Services Act 1986 see A. C. Page, 'Self Regulation: The Constitutional Dimension' (1986) 49 *MLR* 141; the Wilson Report also provides a good survey of the development, nature, and regulation of financial institutions prior to 1980: *Report of the Committee to Review the Functioning of Financial Institutions*, Cmnd. 7937 (HMSO, 1980), and an analysis of the nature, advantages, and disadvantages of self-regulation at 1099–110.

[2] L. C. B. Gower, *Review of Investor Protection, Discussion Document* (HMSO, London, 1982), para. 5.10. In 1981 over there were over 400 exempted dealers, mainly merchant banks, licensed deposit takers or insurance companies.

[3] Wilson Report, para. 1161.

[4] Gower, *Discussion Document*, para. 3.34.

[5] CSI, *Annual Report* 1979, para. 2.

for Dealers in Securities in 1980[6] but it had decided not to introduce a similar code for investment managers in 1979, having found 'no evidence of abuse'.[7] The CSI produced annual reports, but had no formal powers and no permanent staff.

The most important actor in the informal regulatory network was the Bank of England. Though it had no specific remit in the securities field, its role, as Gower commented, was more important and pervasive than merely the control it exercised over banking and deposit taking institutions under the 1979 Banking Act. 'As the instigator of the [Takeover] Panel, a member of the CSI and an overseer of markets it has a finger in every pie except insurance.'[8] As well as initiating the Panel and CSI, it instigated and supervised the creation of other self-regulatory groups, for example the Association of Licensed Dealers in Securities,[9] and the Association of Futures, Brokers and Dealers,[10] both of which ultimately became SROs under the FSA. The important think tank, the City Capital Markets Committee, was established by the Bank, and was regularly consulted by the DoT. The Bank's influence was as a policy actor and regulatory initiator, however; it did not directly regulate the securities industry.

In the area of insurance, the blend of governmental, self-, and no regulation was just as complex, but the experience of self-regulation was far less successful. The DoT monitored life companies under the Insurance Acts, but this did not cover the sale of life assurance. The Policyholders Protection Act 1975 set up a statutory compensation scheme financed by a levy on industry, but there was no product regulation, and no effective regulation of intermediaries. The Insurance Brokers Registration Act 1977 (IBRA) (only brought into force in 1981) required intermediaries

[6] Following the recommendation of the Directorate for Financial Institutions that member states implement a Code of Conduct relating to transactions in transferable securities for investors. See CSI, *Annual Report* 1979; the Code is contained in CSI, *Annual Report* 1980.

[7] Ibid., para. 36.7.

[8] Gower, *Discussion Document*, para. 3.33.

[9] ALDS was founded in 1979, and under the suasion of the Bank changed its name to NASDIM (National Association of Securities Dealers and Investment Managers) to broaden its membership in 1982. In 1983 NASDIM was recognized as an Association of Dealers in Securities under the Prevention of Fraud (Investments) Act 1958 and in the frantic period of SRO formation in the autumn of 1985 it merged with Lutiro (Life and Unit Trust Intermediaries Regulatory Organisation) to form Fimbra.

[10] Formed in 1984 as a consequence of scandals in the commodities markets.

selling life assurance to register and be subject to certain levels of training and competence. However, it only applied to those who called themselves 'brokers' and so could easily be avoided by the use of a different title, 'adviser', for example. There was an element of self-regulation with the major trade associations drawing up their own codes of conduct,[11] and the introduction of a 'cooling off period' in 1980, following Government pressure. However, industry wide attempts at self-regulation were not particularly successful. The experience of the IBRA, the complaints structure,[12] and most significantly the failure of the industry to agree on maximum commission levels for salesmen,[13] illustrated the fragmented and competitive nature of the life assurance industry. It was this fragmentation, principally over commission levels, which led Gower to conclude that 'self-regulation has failed because life offices have been unable to establish a professional body which embraces all of them or the intermediaries through whom their policies are marketed.'[14]

Gower concluded that the distinction between governmental and self-regulation had become blurred, with no apparent rationale for the choice of one method of regulation over another.[15] He was adamant that if the system was to be reformed both the substantive regulation and the institutional structure had to be altered for

[11] The British Insurance Association, Life Insurance Association, and Institute of Insurance Consultants.

[12] The Insurance Ombudsman Bureau was established in Mar. 1981 to provide a conciliation and settlement service for personal policyholders insured with members of the Bureau, though it had no power over intermediaries. Two-thirds of the UK insurance companies joined, but the rest set up a rival organization, the Personal Insurance Arbitration Service.

[13] In an attempt to control rising commission levels and to ensure that an intermediary's advice was not driven by the commission level attached to a product, in 1981 the two principal trade associations, the Life Offices Association and Association of Scottish Life Offices, introduced a commissions agreement to which all life companies had to comply which set maximum commission levels. However the agreement quickly broke down as members left the Associations in order to pay higher commissions, and it was formally abandoned in 1982. The Government refused to accede to life offices' demands for statutory controls, and a further agreement, the Register of Life Associations Commissions, was introduced in 1984 in the midst of an escalating commissions war. This was effectively replaced by the Maximum Commissions Agreement administered by Lautro until it was declared anti-competitive by the OFT acting under s. 114 in 1988: OFT, *The Life Assurance and Unit Trust Organisation*, Mar. 1988. On the latter, see further Ch. 4.

[14] L. C. B. Gower, *Review of Investor Protection, Report, Part I* (Cmnd. 9128) (London, 1984) para. 8.18.

[15] Gower, *Discussion Document*, para. 3.44.

the regulation to work.[16] He criticized the DoT's performance in administering regulation under the PF(I)A, in which licences and exemptions had been freely granted, but the authorization of unit trusts had been tightly controlled, with authorization taking months and being given on the basis of unknown and unpublished criteria. Based on the DoT's record as a regulator Gower argued that the likely result of departmental regulation would be:

> junior staff acting in accordance with rules derived from past precedents which would destroy flexibility, prevent desirable initiatives and constitute a code of esoteric law and lore largely unknown to those it affects.[17]

Gower was no more enamoured by the existing system of self-regulation, which he felt had not served the investor well thus far. If self-regulation was to be effective, he argued, it had to be more than 'the current propensity to trust people to behave themselves'.[18] Self-regulation had benefits and advantages which should be used, but it should be subject to surveillance otherwise it could degenerate into nothing more than a system of cartels with rules which were seldom reviewed and ineffectively enforced.[19]

In proposing a new structure, he argued that governmental and self-regulation should be seen not as antithetical but complementary.[20] The Government should decide major questions of public policy, but its role should be 'residual and supervisory'; it should not be involved in the day-to-day business of regulation. Self-regulation and statutory regulation should be welded into a coherent statutory framework 'in which each would perform what it does best working harmoniously together'.[21] The Act should lay down the basic requirements which those conducting investment business would have to observe, prohibit certain activities, and should empower a Department or self-standing Commission[22] to make rules which would cover the whole range of investment business and apply directly to firms regulated by it.[23] The day-to-day regulation should be administered by self-regulating associations (SRAs), who would not be recognized unless they satisfied certain conditions. These should be stated in the Act and not left to the

[16] Ibid., para. 8.01. [17] Ibid. [18] Ibid., para. 6.04.
[19] Gower, *Report, Part I*, para. 2.03.
[20] Gower, *Discussion Document*, para. 6.02. [21] Ibid., para. 6.04.
[22] This question he left open, Gower, *Report, Part I*, Ch. 3, and see below.
[23] Ibid., paras. 7.07–7.15.

discretion of the Secretary of State.[24] They should include the demonstration of a need for an SRA, that the agency had rules relating to the admission, suspension, expulsion, and discipline of members, investigation of complaints, procedures for monitoring and enforcement, requirements that members be 'fit and proper' in terms of their character, training and experience, and financial resources, and their constitution such that it would secure 'adequate independence of its governing body from the sectional interests of its members'.[25] The rules of the SRAs should provide protection at least equivalent to that provided by the rules of the Commission,[26] and either the Commission[27] or the Secretary of State should have power to amend or revoke these rules.[28]

His proposed structure mirrored in form that of the US Securities and Exchange Commission (SEC), and was in a sense an institutionalization of what could have partly evolved under the PF(I)A, but which due to the wide granting of exemptions, had not. The PF(I)A had permitted members of recognized associations to be exempt from the statutory rules if the association had rules which were equivalent to the LD(CB)Rs. He deliberately left open the question of whether the regulation should be supervised by the Department or a statutory commission, but clearly favoured the latter. His arguments in favour of a statutory commission were that regulation would then be formed and enforced by persons with knowledge of the industry, and so would provide more flexible regulation and operate in a more harmonious relationship with the City. Arguments against a commission were the dangers of capture, and the complexity of the institutional structure which would result, with a complicated set of relationships between the Department, Commission, and SRAs.[29]

Gower's proposals were far-reaching, and the reform of the regulatory structure was only one part of them. The initial reaction to the Discussion Document was hostile and Gower was sceptical about its prospects.[30] Indeed it was assumed by the City, the Stock

[24] Ibid., para. 6.15. [25] Ibid., para. 6.17. [26] Ibid., para. 6.29.

[27] Gower, *Discussion Document*, para. 8.04.

[28] Following criticism of his original proposal that the Commission should have the power to revoke or amend the SRAs' rules: L. C. B. Gower, *Review of Investor Protection, Report, Part II* (London, 1985) para. 6.36.

[29] Gower, *Report, Part I*, paras. 3.01–3.14.

[30] Gower, *Discussion Document*, para. 7.02.

Exchange, and the Bank that Gower's proposals either did not, or need not, apply to bodies which were currently exempted under the PF(I)A 1958. The decision to pursue reform of the regulatory structure stemmed principally from the unforeseen consequences of the agreement, brokered by the Bank, between the Government and the Stock Exchange in July 1983, whereby the Government agreed to instruct the OFT to drop the action against the Exchange's rules which it was currently taking to the Restrictive Trade Practices Court, if in return the Exchange would agree to reform its rules, under the supervision of the Bank of England.[31] It quickly became clear that the reform to the Exchange's rules would have far-reaching implications, leading to the abolition of single capacity and opening the way for foreign, well capitalized firms to enter the market. The current regulatory structure could not effectively regulate this new market, for reasons considered below; a new system was necessary. In the subsequent debate the question of instrument choice, what regulatory structure should be developed, assumed predominance.

The Need for Change

The need for change was seen to come principally from the change in the participants in the industry. The entry of foreign, particularly US firms, to the markets destroyed the homogeneity of participants on which the previous system of regulation had depended. The assumption was that self-regulation could work only where there was a common community of understanding; where shared norms, culture, practices enabled business to be conducted on the basis of trust, with the collective norm being reinforced by representatives of the group on their behalf if any one dissented. New entrants upset this situation: they would not share the group's norms, the mutual trust in business (manifested in the fear of litigation), and would not respect those currently accepted as the enforcers of these norms.

Changes in the structure of the markets also had consequences for the way that business would in future be conducted. The demise

[31] For a fuller discussion of the background of this agreement see M. Reid, *All Change in the City: The Revolution in Britain's Financial Services Sector* (London, 1988); M. Moran, *The Politics of the Financial Services Revolution: The UK, US and Japan* (London, 1991).

of single capacity, in which the roles of broker and dealer had been separated, and the growth of financial conglomerates offering 'one stop financial shopping' had the consequence that a firm would be facing significant conflicts of interest in the conduct of its business. It was this which caused the Bank to move from its initial position that those exempted under the PF(I)A should be excluded from the new regulatory framework and to argue for regulation. 'How in these circumstances can the full blooded *caveat emptor* case retain any credibility? The direct and indirect conflicts of interest inherent in the plurality of functions to which financial institutions aspire are so manifold that the investor cannot be left wholly to look after himself.'[32]

Conflicts of interest were seen to require regulation for two reasons. The first related to levels of confidence investors would have in the City. Regulation was necessary, it was argued by the Bank, Exchange, and Government, to prove that London was a safe place to do business.[33] If business abused positions of trust, this caused loss to individual clients and a loss of confidence in the market, which drove out trade. The second stemmed from the private law of agency and fiduciary duties.[34] Many of these conflicts were not new, and some had been dealt with in the Stock Exchange rules, for example churning.[35] The 'elegant solution'[36] of the functional division between brokers and jobbers had avoided many, although not all, of the conflicts. In the absence of this enforced separation of interests, firms would be able to act in the dual capacity of brokers and market makers, bringing an immediate conflict between their interests as principal and their duties as agent. A more worrying prospect was the combination of dual capacity with fund management, so called 'triple capacity'. If fiduciary and agency law were to apply strictly, business as it was proposed to be conducted would effectively be barred. Indeed, specific exemption from private law was sought by some of the major firms, but refused.

[32] R. Leigh Pemberton, 'Insurance in a Changing Field' (1984) *BEQB* 195.

[33] See e.g., R. Leigh Pemberton, 'Changing Boundaries in Financial Services' (1984) *BEQB* 40 and Stock Exchange, *Conflicts of Interest and their Regulation, Discussion Document,* 1984 *SEQ* 18.

[34] See generally, P. D. Finn, *Fiduciary Obligations* (Sydney, 1977).

[35] Permanent Notice C-101.

[36] E. George, 'Changes in the Structure of Financial Markets: A View from London' (1984) *BEQB* 75.

It was recognized by Gower and the Bank particularly that the application of fiduciary law to the new ways of conducting investment business was simply too unclear to provide firms with the certainty as to their duties and obligations which they needed in order to function efficiently. Common law could not provide this certainty, and definitely not in the time necessary before the restructuring of Big Bang took effect. 'Private law failure' was then a powerful, albeit subsidiary reason, for the need for regulation. Regulatory rules had to be formed.[37]

That new conduct of business regulation was necessary does not on its own explain why the FSA was introduced. Indeed, the CSI and Stock Exchange introduced their own codes for conflicts of interest in 1984, partly as a bid to indicate their credibility as regulators and ensure a place in the anticipated regulatory framework. These Codes were felt to be insufficient, however, not because of their substance, but because of the nature of the body issuing them. The failure was thus perceived to be an institutional one. With respect to the Exchange, the Bank made it quite clear that whatever its previous history as a regulator, simply for jurisdictional reasons the Exchange could not be the sole, or even principal, regulator for conflicts of interest.[38] Conflicts could arise between the member firm and its parent or sibling companies, and the Exchange would only have direct regulation over one part and conflicts could arise where there was no member involvement at all.[39] In the case of the CSI, it had no powers and little authority in the City and it was never proposed that it should continue in its present form. However, the CSI represented the umbrella self-regulatory body that those in favour of self-regulation wanted to preserve.[40] In other words, self-regulation as currently practised was insufficient to cope with the new regulatory challenges.

[37] The nature of the relationship between the rules and private law has been the subject of a Law Commission review: see Law Commission, *Fiduciary Duties and Regulatory Rules: A Consultative Paper*, CP No. 124 (London, 1992) and *Fiduciary Duties and Regulatory Rules*, LC No. 236 (London, 1995).

[38] R. Leigh Pemberton, 'The Future of the Securities Market' (1984) *BEQB* 189.

[39] Ibid.

[40] Both the City Capital Markets Committee and the Bank of England envisaged that the CSI would become a high-level investor protection council, supervising the body which would be supervising the self-regulating agencies: *FT*, 17 Feb. 1984 and 4 Apr. 1984. They wanted the Secretary of State to have to seek its approval before recognizing SRAs or subsequently intervening in its affairs: Barry Riley, 'Gower, After the City Upheaval', *FT*, 30 Apr. 1984.

Statutory or Self-Regulation?

Gower had provided a prototype structure, but the restructuring of business in the City prompted by the 1983 agreement meant that this structure, if it was to be adopted, had to meet changes in the industry which were more far-reaching than had ever been anticipated. The rationales for reforming the regulation, and the objectives attributed to it, changed significantly between the publication of the Discussion Document in 1982 and the passing of the Act in 1986. Initially, Gower was essentially concerned to implement a system of effective regulation which would 'protect reasonable people from being made fools of', and which would rationalize the situation which he faced in 1981. Concerns and priorities shifted radically after the 1983 Goodison/Parkinson agreement away from the predominantly investor protection concerns which had prompted Gower's review to a more market-orientated approach. The need for change in the securities markets, its degree and the speed at which it was set to occur had four consequences: the regulatory structure envisaged by Gower had to be adapted to meet a far larger structural change within the industry than was initially anticipated, the agenda for reform was not simply investor protection but the promotion of the City as an international centre of finance, the substantive regulation would have to provide for the conflicts of interest which were inevitably to intensify, and the new regulation had to be implemented with all possible speed. In an uncertain business climate, the form that the post Big Bang regulation would take needed to be established quickly if foreign firms were to enter the market.

The two tier structure of SROs and an umbrella body was broadly accepted; where the differences lay were in the nature, role, and status of that umbrella body. Should it be a statutory commission, as Gower had envisaged, or, as the Bank, CSI, and City Capital Markets Committee preferred, a self-regulatory 'son of CSI'?[41] The option that the regulation should be administered by a Department was never seriously contemplated, even by Gower, and was ruled off the agenda at an early stage. The case for a statutory commission, on the other hand, was advocated strongly by the financial press, and was bolstered in late 1983 and 1984 by a sharp

[41] Gower, *Report, Part II*, para. 1.09.

increase in the levels of fraud, and by the experience of Lloyds. Its supporters argued that it would be independent from the industry and so produce tough regulation, effective enforcement, and so provide high levels of investor protection and combat fraud. Constitutional arguments were introduced in support, in particular that only a statutory body could be granted the strong policing powers necessary to combat fraud. For the City, the Government, and the Bank, however, a statutory commission was held up to stand for everything that was bad about regulation. Staff would be civil servants, or on civil servants' pay scales, which would guarantee low quality staff with a lack of sensitivity and expertise in the financial services sector. Regulation would be by legislation, cumbersome and inflexible, and rules would be rigidly applied. The result would be ossification, and a flight of business from London.

In the City, certain parts of government, and certainly in the Bank, regulation by an independent statutory commission was thus seen as the worst possible scenario; there was a deep aversion to instituting an equivalent of the US Securities and Exchange Commission, and they remained committed to self-regulation. The Bank and the City were used to and invested considerable faith in a system of self-regulation; moreover, the Government's ideology did not support the creation of more statutory regulatory bodies. Most significantly, the Bank's prime concern was the desire to develop London as the key European financial centre, and efficiency, integrity, and financial innovation were watchwords of the Bank's policy. It argued that this could be achieved only through self-regulation. This would enable practitioners to retain control of the regulation, determine its intensity and application, and combine formal regulation with a flexibility and sensitivity that would foster confidence and not impede financial innovation. It would also ensure the commitment of those it regulated to high standards of conduct; all those advantages, in other words, which Gower attributed to a statutory commission.[42] However, given its experience of the Stock Exchange and the damage that rules of unsupervised regulatory bodies could inflict on London as a whole, the Bank was determined to maintain an overall supervisory role. Largely to this end, in early 1984 the Governor established the Governor's Advisory Group (GAG) to advise him 'as a matter of some urgency on the structure and

[42] See, e.g., R. Leigh Pemberton, 'The UK Approach to Financial Regulation' (1986) *BEQB* 48.

operation of *self regulatory* groupings that would most appropriately cover all types of securities activity (including investment management) together with commodity and financial futures, and which could in practice be formed in the near future'.[43] Subsequent to its report in August 1984[44] (which was never published), the Bank entered discussions with the DTI. The outcome was the White Paper, published in January 1985.[45]

The balance between statutory and self-regulation proposed by the White Paper was struck slightly differently from Gower's initial proposals. Crucially, the umbrella body would be neither a Department nor a statutory Commission, but two practitioner bodies whose powers would be delegated to them by the Secretary of State if they satisfied specified criteria, and who would be funded by the investment industry. Their rules and constitution had to provide adequate investor protection and comply with the principles set out in the Act, which echoed those which Gower had set down for the recognition of the self-regulating associations. Two bodies were proposed: the Securities and Investments Board (SIB) and the Marketing of Investments Board (MIB), later formed as the Marketing of Investments Board Organising Committee (MIBOC). These bodies would recognize SRAs, and ensure that they had the ability to regulate the admission and conduct of their members and that their rules provided a standard of investor protection equivalent to those of the Boards. The SRAs, as Gower had suggested, would be organized on a functional basis, but there was no provision as to their number.

In order for the system to work, the Paper stated, there had to be minimum of government or parliamentary interference: rule changes could not be the subject of their approval. Instead, the body would report annually to the Secretary of State, who would

[43] R. Leigh Pemberton, 'The Future of the Securities Markets', 193–4. The members of the group (described in *The Economist* (26 May 1984) as a 'roll call of the great and the good') were: Martin Jacomb, Chairman of VC Kleinwort Benson and Deputy Chairman of CSI; Sir Nicholas Goodison, Chairman of the Stock Exchange; John Barkshire, Chairman of Mercantile House; Brian Corby, Chief Executive of Prudential; David Hopkinson, Chairman of M&G Investment; Bill Mackworth Young, Chairman of Morgan Grenfell; Sir Jeremy Morse, Chairman of Lloyds Bank; David Scholey, Chairman of S. G. Warburg; Mark Weinberg, Chairman of Hambro LA; and Richard Westmacott, senior partner of Hoare Govett.

[44] And that of the parallel group for the life assurance industry which was appointed by the DTI, chaired by Marshall Fields.

[45] DTI, *Financial Services in the UK—A New Framework for Investor Protection*, Cmnd. 9432 (HMSO, 1985).

lay the report before Parliament and he could withdraw delegated authority from the body if it did not conform to the Act. The Secretary of State and the Bank of England would appoint the Board of SIB, the Secretary of State alone would appoint the Board of MIBOC, in consultation with the industry. In addition the Secretary of State would retain certain powers in relation to competition and international obligations: he would be able to revoke or amend rules where they were in conflict with international obligations, or where following a report of the OFT, he judged that they were significantly anti-competitive, beyond the degree required for the purpose of protecting investors or maintaining proper standards in the industry.

The proposals aimed to strike a careful balance between the different institutions involved, and the Paper was disarming in its presentation of their nature and relationship. Crucially, the Government itself retained no control over the day-to-day operation of the regulation or formation of the rules, save on international and competition issues. It was clear that SIB[46] would in fact have the position of a self standing commission, but its status as a private company, and more importantly the granting of powers to the Secretary of State rather than to SIB, disguised its nature.[47] The voluntary nature of the SROs was strongly emphasized. The Paper stated that the Board 'may' want to use them, SROs could come forward if they wanted to, and that there were no restrictions on their number or scope. In terms of the relative positions of the bodies and their accountability, SIB had control over the granting and revocation of authorization of the SROs, but no further powers. It could apply to court for injunction and restitution orders, and prohibit persons from engaging in investment business, but it had no general investigative powers, although the Government indicated a willingness to provide these.[48] The SROs governed their own membership, and SIB could not alter their rules.

In appearance, therefore, the SROs seemed to have retained the autonomy to regulate themselves to which the Stock Exchange was accustomed. The powers of SIB and the SROs ran in parallel, each regulating its own set of firms. SIB's involvement was restricted

[46] It was quickly realized that MIBOC would be merged with SIB once the rules had been formulated.

[47] The powers were only exercisable by SIB once the Secretary of State had issued the necessary delegation order.

[48] Cmnd. 9432, para. 5.10.

in essence to initial recognition and ultimate revocation. There were no specific requirements as to the governing structures of the SROs, and the Paper made no provision akin to that made for SIB and MIB's constitutions: to ensure that the governing councils had adequate independence from sectional interests. The equivalency requirement echoed the provision in the PF(I)A, but so few had been subject to its requirements its impact had not been felt. Finally, there were certain areas of vagueness in the Paper, principally concerning the relative rule making roles of the bodies, which were open to interpretation.

The balance proposed in the White Paper was described by Gower as 'an ingenious one—and presented in a way so ingenious as to amount almost to a confidence trick'.[49] The reasons for its presentation were political; concerns when striking this balance had not solely centred on the most effective way to regulate. The Government was aware of the City's unveiled hostility to a statutory body, and equally aware of the need for the City's co-operation if the system was to work at all. The Government depended on it for the quality staff which it sought, and the City were clear in their statements that such staff would not be forthcoming if the system were made statutory and if the SROs were not given real responsibility.[50] Yet there had been further scandals in the commodities markets and an increase of concern over the levels of fraud in the securities markets.[51] These, combined with the drive to increase private share ownership through privatization, meant the Government also had to reassure Parliament and the public that it was strengthening statutory responsibility for investor protection and was determined to prevent fraud.

The pressure for a strong statutory element in the regulation increased subsequent to the White Paper. Three events significantly affected the political climate in which the Bill was debated. The first was the resignation of the chief executive of Lloyds, whose

[49] L. C. B. Gower, '"Big Bang" and City Regulation' (1988) *MLR* 1, 11.

[50] Such warnings, prominent in the passage of the Act, continued to be made: see, e.g., IMRO's *Modification Note*, Dec. 1989, in relation to SIB's working paper, *A Forward Look*, Oct. 1989, which envisaged a more central policy role for SIB.

[51] Not abated by the purchase by the bank Singer and Friedlander of British Telecom privatization shares intended for institutional investors but in fact allocated to its executives and private clients (an internal inquiry concluded there had been no bad faith), and the allegations of multiple share applications investigated by the Director of Public Prosecutions.

inquiries into a previous misappropriation of members' funds had been curtailed by the chairman of Lloyds. This heightened concerns that self-regulation would simply be self-interested regulation, and would fail to be sufficiently objective and independent to provide high levels of investor protection. It fuelled calls for a statutory system, and for the inclusion of Lloyds in the new regulatory regime.[52] Largely to stem the latter demands, an inquiry into whether the 1982 Lloyds Act provided protection for members' interests comparable to that proposed under the Financial Services Bill, chaired by Sir Patrick Neill, was ordered in January 1986 following Tory and Opposition pressure.[53] The second was the failure of Johnson Matthey Bank, which called into question the conduct of the Bank of England's supervisory responsibilities.[54] The third was the increasing concern over fraud in the City, recognized in the Government's creation in 1984 of the Fraud Investigation Group and highlighted by the publication in January 1986 of the Roskill report on the conduct of fraud trials.[55] The collapse in the autumn of 1986 of a licensed dealer firm with the loss of millions of pounds of investors' money[56] heightened concerns that fraud

[52] In Nov. 1985 the chief executive of Lloyds, Ian Hay Davidson, had resigned when attempts were made by Lloyds to change his terms of reference, which were not defined in the 1982 Act. Davidson had been brought into Lloyds by the Bank in 1983 to reform the market after a series of scandals in which millions of pounds of underwriting members' funds had been misappropriated.

[53] See, e.g., in relation to SIB's powers and the composition of its Board, 1985/6 Standing Committee E c. 207 (Brian Sedgemore, Con.). The inadequacies of the 1982 Act were used in arguments by Tory backbenchers in favour of making SIB a statutory commission (e.g., 1985/6 Standing Committee E c. 757–8, Tim Smith). Bryan Gould (Lab.) argued that 'at Lloyds the regulators themselves became tarnished by the very practices they should have been outlawing. It is from this basis that the House should approach the whole question of regulating the City.' HC Debs. vol. 96 c. 979. The Opposition wanted Lloyds brought within the ambit of the Act.

[54] JMB was bought by the Bank for £1 in a rescue operation in Oct. 1984. Following an investigation by the Bank it found that JMB had made some suspicious loans for which it had made no specific provision in the accounts and which it could not cover; after failing to find private companies to support JMB, it was nationalized. The Bank's action had been prompted by JMB's position in the bullion markets and the fears of the loss of confidence that could result from its failure in that market and the linked silver and foreign exchange markets, which would affect London's position as a financial centre. See 'The Bank of England and Johnson Matthey Bankers Ltd', *Reports and Accounts of the Bank of England 1985.*

[55] *Report of the Committee on Fraud Trials, Chairman Lord Roskill* (London, 1980).

[56] The firm, McDonald Wheeler, collapsed in Oct. 1986. Although the Bill was by this stage in the Lords, it strengthened the case of SIB and those anxious to see a strengthening of the Bill, and was much cited in debates.

was a significant issue which needed to be addressed by tough regulation and strong policing powers. These, it was felt by many, could only be given to a statutory body. The issue of fraud and the need to secure prosecutions was climbing ever higher on the political agenda,[57] and prior to the introduction of the Bill the DTI indicated that it was considering strengthening the investigative powers of SIB in relation to fraud.[58]

These events gave rise to a lack of faith in self-regulation and many MPs on both sides of the House doubted whether the regulatory structure proposed in 1984–5 could really survive the structural upheavals of Big Bang. There was a high degree of cross-party support for a stronger statutory framework, and for SIB to be a fully statutory, independent commission. Half of the amendments which significantly strengthened the position of SIB were tabled by Tory back-bench MPs.

Changing Priorities: From Bill to Act

The Act is a highly technical piece of legislation, and the legislative process groaned under its strain.[59] The Bill was subject to a huge number of amendments, the majority of which were Government amendments tabled in the Lords as a result of last minute representations by firms who suddenly realized that they would be subject to the provisions of the Act. There were over 300 amendments on Report stage in the Commons, and over 750 amendments in the Lords, over 400 on Report stage there. The bill ended the process 50 per cent longer, with 3 new schedules and 46 new sections. The result, as Gower stated, 'is an Act of great complication and frequent obscurity'.[60]

The impact of the process on the design of the institutional structure was significant not because of any major revision, but because the delicate balance struck in the White Paper was subtly altered by key changes of detail. The climate in which the Bill was debated was one which was far more in favour of a stronger statutory element to the regulation than the Bank of England had been.

[57] In a letter to David Steel the Prime Minister pledged measures to strengthen and extend the regulation, *FT*, 4 Dec. 1985.

[58] *FT*, 22 Nov. 1984, 26 Nov. 1984.

[59] See, e.g., comments made at HL Debs. vol. 479 cc. 87–9 and 255–8, vol. 480 c. 684–6.

[60] Gower, 'Big Bang and City Regulation', 29.

By the end of the legislative process the institutional structure proposed in the White Paper and largely incorporated in the Bill had undergone a number of changes which had essentially added to the powers of the designated agency, which was now named as SIB. The balance created by the White Paper was altered in some fundamental respects, but without introducing the coherency to the regulatory structure that the full-scale adoption of Gower's proposals might have afforded. Indeed, examining the passage of the Bill prompts the suggestion that the legislative process can in many ways be described as 'mandated incrementalism'. The clause by clause scrutiny of the Bill which is the hallmark of the legislative process meant that the changes in the regulatory structure were piecemeal 'add-ons' rather than the result of a coherent, rational decision process. By the end of the process it had become clear that as a result the Act was now firmly pulling in two directions with the centralizing element of, for example, the compensation scheme being at odds with the autonomy of the SROs in other areas, and more than one participant commented that it would have been more rational to start with a statutory body and concentrate on increasing its flexibility, rather than with a self-regulatory one to which powers were constantly being added.[61] Indeed, there was an increasing feeling as the amendments piled up that the balance had shifted so far from that created in the White Paper that it was incoherent to leave SIB as a non-statutory body when it had all the powers associated with a statutory one.[62]

The changes made to the regulatory structure were the result of three main factors: the resistance of many MPs of both parties to fully-fledged self-regulation; the reluctance many felt to passing legislation cast in wide terms without knowing how those powers would be used, or even who would be using them; and the influence of SIB and the nascent SROs on the legislative process. The doubts indicated above concerning the effectiveness of self-regulation in providing adequate investor protection were enhanced by the broad terms in which the legislation was drafted. It was unclear as the Bill went through the Commons how many SROs

[61] See, e.g., HL Debs. vol. 479 c. 795 (Vct. Chandos); HL Debs. vol. 481 c. 19 (Lord Ezra).

[62] Vct. Chaldane commented, e.g., that '[t]he risk is that the SIB will resemble that ugly and awkward animal the camel, or a horse designed by a committee'. HL Debs. vol. 478 c. 602.

there would be, or what areas of the market they would regulate. One MP commented that the Bill was 'legislating for a mirage'.[63] Uncertainty as to what form SIB and particularly the SROs would take was exacerbated by the absence of subsequent accountability of the SROs and lack of control over SIB's rules. MPs therefore wanted to impose more detailed legislation to ensure greater control over the future operation of the structure. The Government resisted such attempts with the response that only broad rule making powers would provide the flexibility needed,[64] and that it would ensure that the rules were satisfactory before it delegated powers to SIB.[65] The Government would exert control over SIB's rule book at the recognition stage, not Parliament at the legislative stage. The Standing Committee was told 'to think very carefully before taking upon itself a rule drafting role'.[66] Nonetheless, amendments were sought to increase the specificity of the substantive provisions of the legislation, for example to elaborate on the meaning of 'fit and proper',[67] and to incorporate into the Bill as many as possible of the regulations and guidelines which were being left to SIB to formulate. This was particularly the case in relation to the disclosure of charges and commissions, 'which we do not want to leave to be drawn up after with a more lax and accommodating approach'.[68] The sense of 'legislating for a mirage' was exacerbated by the 'doublespeak' of the Act: although the powers were formally being conferred on the Secretary of State it was well understood that it was SIB who would be exercising them. To compound matters, SIB was not even named as the designated agency until the Government was forced to accept an amendment to this effect.[69] Yet proposed amendments, for example to impose an obligation to make rules by requiring 'the Secretary of State *shall* make rules' instead of the enabling provision '*may* make rules', were rejected by the Government on the grounds that it was 'unnecessary and unusual to impose such a mandatory requirement on the Secretary of State'.[70]

[63] 1985/6 HC Standing Committee E, c. 233, Austin Mitchell.
[64] Ibid., c. 440 (Michael Howard); HL Debs. vol. 480, c. 1013 (Lord Lucas).
[65] Ibid., cc. 425 and 439 (Michael Howard).
[66] Ibid., c. 425 (Michael Howard).
[67] And to provide that the Secretary of State 'shall' make rules instead of 'may': 1985/6 HC Standing Committee E c. 439 (Tim Smith); HL Debs. vol. 480 c. 768.
[68] Ibid., c. 167 (Austin Mitchell).
[69] 1985/6 HC Standing Committee E, c. 519–38.
[70] 1985/6 HC Standing Committee E, c. 439 (Michael Howard).

The frustrations of both Houses were summed up by Lord Tyron: 'the whole debate has seemed something like Hamlet without the Prince because the whole time we have been trying to guess what SIB might do, what their rules might be'.[71]

For their part, SIB and the SROs sought, and fought, a number of amendments, largely successfully. The unusual regulatory structure gave rise to the relatively rare situation of the agency itself being a powerful lobbyist in the formation of the legislation which would endow it powers.[72] SIB sought mainly to increase its power over the SROs, and amendments which it sought were tabled in Committee by MPs of all parties. In particular, it sought, successfully, for the provision of a central compensation scheme,[73] and for the power to revoke or amend the rules of the SROs without having to seek a court order if it considered that they failed to provide investor protection equivalent to that provided by its own rules.[74] Both proposals were fiercely resisted by the nascent SROs. Less successfully SIB also sought that it be clearly established that its rules would have precedence over the SROs',[75] and for the power to alter the practices as well as the rules of the SROs.[76] SIB also managed to exert a negative influence, and made it clear that it did not want certain powers. For example, as a result of an amendment by a Tory back-bench MP it was given the power to investigate unauthorized businesses,[77] but it stated that it did not want its enforcement powers to extend to the members of SROs without the SROs' request.[78] Most significantly, SIB made it clear that it did not want to be a statutory commission. There was a sustained attempt, headed by Tory MP Anthony Nelson and supported by Tory and Opposition MPs, for SIB to be a statutory commission. However SIB stated that if it was statutory it would be tied to civil service pay scales, which would seriously reduce the quality of staff which it could attract. Amendments to this effect failed, but Nelson did

[71] HL Debs. vol. 481, c. 102.

[72] This has in fact become increasingly common, e.g., the Rail Regulator was set up prior to the privatization legislation in order to commence the privatization process.

[73] See the debate at HL Debs. vol. 479 cc. 784–97.

[74] Ibid., cc. 235–42.

[75] Letter from Sir Kenneth Berrill to Mr Campbell Savours, HC Debs. vol. 89 c. 987.

[76] HC Debs. vol. 99, cc. 431–2.

[77] 1985/6 HC Standing Committee E, c. 513 (Anthony Nelson), later amended to be exercised in conjunction with the Secretary of State. See now ss. 106 and 114 FSA.

[78] Ibid., cc. 489–90.

succeed in passing his amendment, against the Government, that SIB be named in the Act as the designated agency that would receive the Secretary of State's statutory powers.[79]

The influence of the nascent SROs was also strongly felt. Only one body had so far formed and was promoting itself as a future SRO, the International Securities Regulatory Organisation (ISRO). A confederation of international bond and securities dealers, it had formed mainly due to concerns that the White Paper had failed to take any account of the impact of the proposed regulation on the professional investment market and on international operators in the UK, particularly the Eurobond market. ISRO turned itself into a highly effective pressure group and headed the campaign for legal immunity for the SROs. Initial Opposition proposals that the SROs and their officers be immune from liability to its members except for acts in bad faith were initially refused by the Government on the grounds that statutory immunity should only rarely be given to private bodies. Its response was that SROs should include it in their membership rules if they wanted it.[80] ISRO in particular argued that this would be impossible; SROs who did not seek immunity would have a competitive advantage over those that did, with the result that firms would only join SROs that did not have immunity. The nascent SROs therefore signalled that they would not be prepared to become SROs unless immunity was statutorily provided. Amendments made to SIB's powers enabling it to change their rules were also called to their aid: as SIB had now been given the power to amend their rules the SROs argued they should not be liable for acting according to rules over which they had little choice.[81] The Government thus agreed to amend the Act to grant immunity from action in respect of all persons, except for acts in bad faith.[82] In a counter move which illustrated clearly the fluidity of the situation and the nature of the bargaining process which characterized significant parts of the legislative process, the grant of immunity gave fuel to Opposition amendments to increase the SRO's accountability by requiring the governing bodies of SROs to be such as to secure a proper balance between interests of the different members of the organization and between the interests of the organization and

[79] Ibid., cc. 519–30. [80] Ibid., cc. 172–88.
[81] HC Debs. vol. 96, cc. 416–7. [82] Ibid., cc. 402–4.

the public. These amendments had failed in the Commons,[83] but due largely to the grant of immunity, were passed in the Lords.[84]

The Current Structure

The structure comprises three levels of regulators. At the top, Governmental, level are the Treasury, the Office of Fair Trading, the Bank of England, and the Secretary of State for Trade and Industry (who exercises some enforcement powers jointly with SIB). At the central level is the Securities and Investments Board (SIB), to whom the legislative, investigative, and enforcement powers conferred in the Act on the Secretary of State have been delegated. At the third, often referred to as the 'practitioner' level, are the self-regulatory organizations, and regulated professional bodies, exchanges, and clearing houses. The Act requires any person who conducts investment business to be either authorized or exempt.[85] Authorization is conferred through membership of an SRO,[86] recognized professional body[87] or through direct regulation by SIB.[88] Exemption is conferred by membership of a recognized investment exchange,[89] recognized clearing house,[90] if the person is authorized in an EC member state,[91] or falls within the specified list of exempted persons in the Act.[92]

The Chancellor, the OFT, and SIB

The Act gave legislative, investigative, and enforcement powers to the Secretary of State for Trade and Industry, and enabled the majority of these powers to be delegated to a 'designated agency'[93] subject, until 1989, to Parliamentary approval.[94] The agency was named in the Act as the Securities and Investments Board.[95] The powers could be delegated only if the body satisfied statutory conditions as to structure, Board membership, monitoring and enforcement, complaints and disciplinary procedures, and its rules complied with the principles set out in the Act.[96] SIB achieved

[83] 1985/6 HC Standing Committee E, c. 227. [84] HL Debs. vol. 480, c. 913.
[85] S. 3. [86] S. 7. [87] S. 15. [88] S. 26. [89] S. 36.
[90] S. 38. [91] S. 31. [92] Ss. 35, 43–5.
[93] S. 114. Responsibility for the Act was transferred to the Treasury in 1992.
[94] Via the affirmative resolution procedure (s. 114(11)). [95] S. 114(2).
[96] S. 114. The requirements are contained in Schs. 7 and 8.

designated agency status in May 1987, and the majority of the statutory powers, including all of the legislative powers, have been delegated to it.[97]

The Bank of England and the Chancellor jointly appoint the chairman and Board of SIB, although the initial Board appointments were made by the Bank.[98] The composition of the Board must be such as to 'secure a proper balance between the interests of persons carrying on investment business and the interests of the public'.[99] The Bank's role in these appointments reflects the influence which it exerted in the process leading up to the Act, and that which it wished to continue to exert over the development of the regulation. There was cross-party support for the removal of the Bank's role which it was argued was there simply to enable the Bank to exert a continuing influence over SIB,[100] but it was justified on the grounds that it would limit rivalry between the bodies and reflected the 'special authority' and 'established preeminence' of the Bank.[101]

Responsibility for supervision of financial services regulation was transferred to the Treasury in 1992, and so the Chancellor now exercises powers initially conferred on the Secretary of State for Trade and Industry.[102] SIB must report annually to the Chancellor and a copy of the report must be laid before Parliament. The Chancellor may make directions relating to SIB's accounts and their audit, with which SIB must comply,[103] although SIB is funded by the authorized firms and receives no public finance.

The Chancellor must ensure that SIB's rules do not restrict or distort competition to a significant extent, and can direct that its rules be amended if they do.[104] This power applies across the range of regulatory bodies: SIB, the SROs, recognized professional bodies (RPBs), recognized investment exchanges (RIEs), and clearing houses (RCHs).[105] In exercising this function he must consult

[97] Financial Services Act 1986 (Delegation) Order 1987. Powers were transferred which included several not then in force. Powers relating to authorized unit trust schemes were delegated by the Financial Services Act 1986 (Delegation) (No. 2) Order 1988. The system came into operation on 29 Apr. 1988, 'A Day'.

[98] Sch. 7 para. 1(2). [99] Sch. 7 para. 1(3).

[100] See e.g., 1985/6 HC Standing Committee E, c. 719 (Anthony Nelson).

[101] Ibid., c. 714 (Alan Howarth).

[102] Investigation and enforcement powers which the Secretary of State exercises in conjunction with SIB under s. 114 were not transferred. [103] S. 117.

[104] S. 119. [105] S. 119.

the Director General of Fair Trading, who is under a continuing duty to review the rules for their competitive effects.[106] In addition, SIB has to have leave from the Chancellor that the competition provisions have been complied with before it can recognize a body.[107] These powers of the Chancellor and OFT replace the general competition legislation, from which the rules and practices of these bodies are exempt.[108]

It is important to note that it is only in relation to the competitive effects of the rules that the Chancellor has any power to order SIB to alter or revoke its rules.[109] If SIB's rules are failing to provide adequate investor protection or SIB is not otherwise meeting the required conditions, then the Chancellor has only the power to resume any of the transferred functions in whole or in relation to any aspect of investment business.[110] As this would involve a radical restructuring of the present regulatory edifice it is has been more aptly described as a 'nuclear deterrent' than an effective continuing control mechanism. In practice, the most rigorous public form of accountability is to Select Committees, which are not given any formal supervisory or accountability role in the Act. Since 1990 the SIB chairman and other officials have been called before the Trade and Industry Select Committee, and, following the transfer of functions to the Chancellor in 1993, the Treasury and Civil Service Select Committee, to given an annual account of the operation of the system.

SIB and the SROs

The Securities and Investments Board

The current chairman of SIB is Sir Andrew Large, who was the first chairman of the SRO TSA (the Securities Association) and subsequently the chairman of the London Futures and Options Exchange,

[106] S. 122. [107] Ss. 119–21.

[108] Ss. 124–6 (Fair Trading Act 1973, Restrictive Trade Practices Act 1976, Competition Act 1980). These provisions stem from the case against the Stock Exchange brought by the OFT under the Restrictive Trade Practices Act 1956, which was settled in 1983. See Gower Report, Part I, paras. 5.02–5.07 and 6.17–6.34. The role of the OFT in supervising has been said to have been the *quid pro quo* for the OFT being told to drop the case against the Exchange: Reid, *All Change in the City*.

[109] The same provisions and powers lie in relation to RIEs, RCHs, RPBs, and SROs.

[110] S. 115. If done at the request or with the consent of SIB, the order is subject to a negative resolution procedure, otherwise the affirmative resolution procedure applies: s. 115(6).

a recognized exchange under the Act. SIB is funded by the recognized bodies, directly authorized firms, and collective investment schemes, although it has expressly stated that it does not regard this factor as making it accountable to them.[111] Initially it operated on an advance facility from the Bank of England, which by 1988 was nearly £9 million,[112] and its net costs for the year ending March 1995 were just over £20 million.[113]

The SROs

The organization and number of the SROs is not prescribed in the Act, but the understanding has been since the inception of the regulation that they should be organized on a functional basis.[114] There are currently three SROs: the Personal Investment Authority (PIA), the Securities and Futures Authority (SFA), and the Investment Management Regulatory Organisation (IMRO). Only IMRO still exists in its original form, the others are the results of regulatory mergers and restructuring.

The most recently recognized is the PIA, formed in 1994. This effectively took over the regulatory function of Lautro[115] (which regulated the marketing and sales of life assurance and unit trusts through the direct sales forces and company representatives of life offices, unit trust companies, and a small number of friendly societies)[116] and Fimbra[117] (which regulated independent financial advisers, and managers and brokers who act principally for individual investors).[118] It also regulates the majority of banks and

[111] See comments of Sir David Walker (SIB's chairman 1985–8), 1990/1 Trade and Industry Select Committee, Securities and Investments Board, Minutes of Evidence, HC Paper no. 131, para. 6.

[112] SIB, *Annual Report 1987–8*, 79.

[113] SIB, *Annual Report 1994/5.*

[114] See Gower, *Discussion Document.*

[115] Life Assurance and Unit Trust Regulatory Organisation.

[116] Although most of its members were automatically authorized under ss. 22–4 of the Act, Lautro was formed as the result of an initiative of the main life and unit trust trade associations to regulate the direct selling of these companies, who did not want to join NASDIM (below, n. 118) as they felt they were of a different nature and scale to the intermediaries which comprised its membership. Its principal initial function was the administration of the Maximum Commissions Agreement, introduced in its 1988 rules but abolished in 1990: see Ch. 4.

[117] Financial Intermediaries, Managers and Brokers Regulatory Association.

[118] Fimbra was the product of two groups, NASDIM and Lutiro. NASDIM (National Association of [Licensed] Securities Dealers and Investment Managers) had been formed and recognized in 1983 under the 1958 Prevention of Fraud (Investments) Act, after persuasion by the Bank of England, and was seen as a prototype SRO: Gower, *Report, Part I*, para. 6.05. Its members were generally small firms advising private investors and managing only small portfolios. Lutiro (Life insurance and Unit Trust Intermediaries Regulatory Organisation) was formed in 1985

building societies who have activities in these areas, and who were previously regulated directly by SIB.[119]

SFA regulates brokers, dealers, and market makers in securities and those operating on the futures and derivatives markets, including the Eurobond market. It was formed in 1991 as a result of a merger between the Association of Futures Brokers and Dealers (AFBD) and the Securities Association (TSA). TSA was itself formed in December 1986 as a result of a merger (reluctantly undertaken on the Exchange's part) between the Stock Exchange and the International Securities Regulatory Organisation (ISRO). ISRO represented international securities dealers, including members of the Association of International Bond Dealers, and was formed as a prototype SRO in 1985 mainly because of their concerns at the omission of consideration of the impact of the regulation on international operators in the UK in the White Paper.

IMRO regulates investment managers acting for institutional clients, and the management activities of life and unit trust companies and pension fund managers. It was a creature of the accepting houses, formed in the spate of activity, prompted by SIB, to form SROs which occurred in the autumn of 1985. The impetus for creating an organization separate from life offices and small investment managers on the one hand, and large conglomerates on the other, was twofold. Accepting houses felt themselves to be of a different status to the small managers and advisers who were members of another association, NASDIM, and the scale of their fund management was far larger. However, they also wanted to disassociate themselves from the conflicts of interests involved in large conglomerates and emphasize their independence from the integrated houses (who were members of SFA's predecessors, TSA and AFBD) through a separate regulatory organization. Their membership base widened as life insurance and unit trust offices joined them in order to gain authorization of their fund management

by a second group of intermediaries, essentially those regulated under the Insurance Broker's Registration Act 1977, with a view to becoming an SRO. In Apr. 1986 the two joined to become IBRO, the Intermediaries, Managers, Dealers, and Brokers Regulatory Organisation, subsequently changed to Fimbra.

[119] Although the banks and building societies have their own retail products and act as both direct sellers and representatives for life offices, they preferred to seek direct regulation through SIB rather than Lautro for two reasons: the dominance of Lautro by the life offices, and the disadvantageous effects of its initial rules on their operation. On the latter see below, Ch. 4.

activities, and although SIB urged the merger of IMRO with Lautro in December 1985, this was resisted.

SIB's Regulatory and Supervisory Functions

SIB has two roles within the system, which many are beginning to suggest conflict. It is both a direct regulator, and a supervisor of the other regulatory bodies. The Act provides that if anyone is to conduct investment business they must first be authorized or exempt. Authorization derives from membership of an SRO, or direct regulation by SIB. Exemption is conferred if the person is a member of a recognized professional body, exchange or clearing house,[120] or the branch office of a firm registered in a member state of the EU.[121] SIB is responsible for recognizing these bodies, and for conferring the EU exemptions.

Before SIB can recognize each body, it must ensure that it complies with the statutory requirements. These vary, and are most detailed with respect to SROs. The Act requires that all bodies must have 'adequate arrangements' and resources for monitoring and enforcement, for the investigation of complaints and the promotion and maintenance of high standards of integrity and fair dealing.[122] With respect to SROs only, it requires that members be 'fit and proper persons to carry on investment business of the kind with which the organisation is concerned',[123] and for the membership of the governing bodies of the SROs to be such as to secure a 'proper balance' between the interests of different members of the organization and between the interests of the organization and the interests of the public.[124]

If a professional body, exchange or clearing house meets the criteria SIB still has a discretion whether or not to recognize it,

[120] It is also responsible for the Recognized Investment Exchanges (RIEs) and Recognized Clearing Houses (RCHs), but these are not considered here.

[121] S. 31.

[122] They are set out in Sch. 2 (SROs), Sch. 3 (RPBs), Sch. 4 (RIEs), and s. 39 (RCHs).

[123] Sch. 2 para. 1. This does not apply to insurance companies and friendly societies, and others who are members of the organization but do not gain their authorization through that membership (Sch. 2 para. 1(4)). It was presumed that RPBs would have similar requirements in their own membership rules.

[124] Sch. 5 para. 5. In relation to RPBs the Act requires that the arrangements for enforcement must be such as to secure a proper balance between the interests of persons certified by the body and the interests of the public. Sch. 3 para. 4(5).

although it must give reasons for refusal.[125] However, if an SRO applicant meets the criteria then that discretion is restricted. SIB must recognize that SRO applicant unless it considers that there is no need for such an SRO as one already exists which regulates that area of business.[126] The provision was an attempt both to limit the 'club factor' in the operation of the regulation and ensure that any eligible organization would not be refused authorization, and yet also to prevent regulatory arbitrage, or a situation in which there were a number of different SROs which a firm could join to gain authorization for a particular type of business, each competing on the basis of minimum standards.[127] A contrary attitude to regulatory competition is evidenced in the absence of any such provision in relation to exchanges and clearing houses: an amendment moved at the Committee stage to permit SIB to refuse to recognize eligible exchanges on the same grounds was rejected on the basis that this would amount to restricting markets, antithetical to the Government's competition policy.[128]

The focus here is primarily on the relationship between SIB and the SROs. SIB monitors the rules and practices of the SROs. The rules of the SRO must, together with those principles, rules or codes of practice of SIB to which its members are subject, provide adequate protection for investors. In judging adequacy, regard is to be had to the nature of the investment business carried on by members, the nature of investors, and the effectiveness of the organization's enforcement arrangements.[129] Monitoring of compliance used to be through a series of 'self-assessment' exercises undertaken by the SROs and then sent to SIB, who would then consider the report and discuss its contents with the SRO. Since the activities of the Maxwell pension fund managers came to light, throwing into question IMRO's regulatory activities, SIB's monitoring activities have become more formalized.[130]

SIB has no 'system management' powers beyond its ability to refuse recognition to an SRO on the basis of need. It cannot require

[125] Ss. 18, 37, and 39. [126] S. 10.

[127] 1985/6 HC Standing Committee E, c. 335.

[128] 1985/6 Standing Committee E, c. 334–6.

[129] Sch. 2 para. 3 and Sch. 3 para. 3, as amended by s. 203 CA 1989.

[130] For details see A. Large, *Financial Services Regulation: Making the Two Tier System Work*, SIB, May 1993, Ch. 4; SIB, *Review Implementation*, Nov. 1993, SIB, *Annual Report 1994–5*.

those who sought membership through it to apply to an SRO, nor can it force SROs to disband or restrict their area of regulation in the absence of a breach of the recognition requirements, powers which were viewed in 1986 as encroaching too deeply into the autonomy of the SROs.[131] However the relationship between the rule making bodies has evolved to a point where in his report on the regulatory structure in 1992 Sir Kenneth Clucas recommended that SIB be given the power to make these changes in the interests of the regulatory system as a whole.[132] Conferring on SIB the power to direct its members to move to an SRO, and even to cease its role as a direct regulator was also recommended in the same report. SIB has declined to seek these statutory powers immediately, but has indicated that should persuasion fail, it may ask for an amendment in its powers to this effect.[133]

SIB's Enforcement Powers

SIB has powers to require such information as it may reasonably need for the performance of its functions[134] and has extensive investigation powers akin to those of the DTI which enable it to call for persons and documents, and information given by a person may be used in evidence against him.[135] These powers, which must be exercised concurrently with the Secretary of State for Trade and Industry,[136] are not exercisable in relation to RPB or SRO members unless that body so requests, or appears to SIB to be incapable or unwilling to investigate them in a satisfactory manner. They are, however, exercisable in relation to appointed representatives.[137]

SIB has power to apply to the court for an injunction if there is a likelihood that any person will contravene SIB's rules and apply for the payment into court of a sum representing profits earned as a result of the contravention and/or loss or damage suffered by investors.[138] These injunction powers are extended to members of SROs or RPBs only if that body appears unwilling to

[131] 1985/6 HC Standing Committee E, cc. 227–8 (revocation of recognition), cc. 303–6 (directing firms to SROs).

[132] *Retail Regulation Review: Report of a Study by Sir Kenneth Clucas on a new SRO for the Retail Sector*, SIB, Mar. 1992 (Clucas Report).

[133] Large Report, Foreword, para. 22.

[134] S. 104.

[135] Ss. 95, 105, and 106.

[136] S. 114.

[137] S. 105(2).

[138] S. 61.

restrain the contravention,[139] but the power to order restitution is not so limited.[140] SIB's powers to issue disqualification directions prohibiting the employment of a particular person[141] and issue public statements as to a person's misconduct[142] also apply to all authorized persons.

SIB's and the SROs' Rule Making Powers

Whereas SIB's enforcement powers operate largely in parallel to those of the SROs, its rule making powers have been extended by amendments made to the Act in 1989. The Financial Services Act 1986 initially conferred wide rule making powers on the Secretary of State, all of which have been delegated to SIB.[143] These comprise powers to make rules relating to a firm's financial resources,[144] protection of clients' money,[145] conduct of business,[146] cancellation,[147] unsolicited calls,[148] notification regulations,[149] indemnity rules,[150] and a compensation fund.[151] Initially these applied principally to those regulated directly by SIB. SIB's conduct of business rules and notification regulations,[152] and its financial resources rules applied only to firms regulated directly by it or who operated under the 'Euro-exemption'.[153] Indemnity rules applied to SRO and RPB members only at the body's request, and rules concerning the compensation fund applied only to SROs after consultation with them. Client money, unsolicited call, and cancellation rules were capable of applying to all authorized persons; but with respect to client money and unsolicited call rules the Act provided that if the SRO had made rules dealing with these issues, or aspects of them, the authorized person was to follow those. In contrast, there was no provision as to the relationship between SIB's cancellation rules and those made by SROs.

The Companies Act 1989 altered the application of SIB's rules. In amendments which were part of what was commonly known as the 'New Settlement', the Act significantly extended SIB's rule

[139] S. 61(2). [140] S. 61(3). [141] S. 59. [142] S. 60.

[143] Powers delegated under s. 114. See below. The powers will thus be referred to as SIB's, although technically they are the Secretary of State's, and although delegated to SIB may be resumed under certain conditions. [144] S. 49.

[145] S. 55. [146] S. 48. [147] S. 51. [148] S. 56. [149] S. 52.

[150] S. 53. They also apply to members of RPBs only if these bodies have requested that they do so.

[151] S. 54. RPBs may request to join, but none has done so.

[152] S. 48(1). [153] S. 49(1).

making powers and altered the relationship between SIB and the SROs' rules in two respects: first the scope of SIB's rules altered; second the measure for assessing SRO rules was changed. SIB was granted the power to issue statements of principle 'as to the conduct and financial standing' of firms, which apply to all authorized persons (i.e., members of SROs and RPBs).[154] The scope of some of its rules was extended by the designation provisions which enable SIB to designate rules regulating financial resources, conduct of business, clients' money, and unsolicited calls as directly applicable to members of SROs, but which may take effect subject to the rules of the SRO of which it is a member.[155] Finally SIB has the power, as yet unutilized, to issue codes of practice with respect to any of the rules which it is enabled to make.[156] Breach of these rules is to be treated as a breach of the rules of the organization itself,[157] and SROs are therefore responsible for enforcing the principles, core rules (and codes of practice, if issued) in relation to their members,[158] although SIB may still seek injunctions to prevent a breach of its or an SRO's rules.[159]

The second aspect of the change was to the benchmark for assessing SRO rules. SIB is now to ensure that the SRO rules, taken together with its own principles and rules to which the SRO members are subject, provide 'adequate investor protection'.[160] The initial requirement was that the rules provided a level of investor protection which was 'equivalent' to that provided by SIB's. The equivalency requirement proved to be a source of considerable friction between SIB and the SROs, and the effect of this requirement and the reasons for the amendment are explored in the following chapter.

Provisions on SIB's powers for making conduct of business rules are found in two places in the Act: those sections which conferred rule making powers on the Secretary of State which have been delegated to SIB, and the Schedules which set out the criteria

[154] S. 47A, inserted by s. 192 CA 1989.
[155] S. 63A, inserted by s. 194 CA 1989.
[156] S. 63C, inserted by s. 195 CA 1989.
[157] S. 63A FSA 1986, inserted by s. 194 CA 1989.
[158] Sch. 2, para. 4(1), as amended by s. 206 CA 1989.
[159] S. 61. SIB's power to issue and enforce rules or guidance against members of SROs was considered in *R* v. *Securities and Investments Board & Anor. ex p. Independent Financial Advisers Association & Anor.* [1995] CLC 872.
[160] Sch. 3, para. 3, amended by s. 203(1) CA 1989.

which SIB has to meet as a designated agency. The first group of powers are expressed in general terms and are enabling rather than mandatory, providing merely that SIB may make rules rather than requiring it to do so. There are exceptions, notably the unsolicited call provisions: cold calling is an offence unless the rules are complied with. The conduct of business rules also contain an uncharacteristically specific limitation: that SIB may not make rules which place limits on the amount of commissions or other inducements paid in connection with investment business.[161]

The second group of powers are mandatory provisions as to the content of rules set out in the statutory conditions for SIB receiving and retaining designated agency status.[162] These provide that the rules have to provide an 'adequate' level of protection for investors,[163] adjust the standard of conduct required to that appropriate for different types of customer that a firm may be dealing with,[164] 'promote high standards of integrity and fair dealing', and 'make proper provision' for the following:

1. authorised persons to act with due skill, care, and diligence;
2. firms to subordinate their interests to those of their customers;
3. firms to act fairly between customers;
4. firms to have due regard to the circumstances of their customers;
5. the disclosure of material facts (including the firm's own interests, commissions, and inducements);
6. the disclosure of capacity (for example principal or agent) and terms of business by the firm;
7. the provision of sufficient information about the investment and its implications to enable the customer to make an informed decision;
8. the protection of property entrusted to a firm;
9. the keeping and inspection of records.[165]

In exercising its rule making powers, SIB is required, as a result of amendments made to the Financial Services Bill, to publish its proposed rules and regulations, together with a statement that representations can be made within a specified period, and SIB must have regard to any representations made.[166] The provision

[161] S. 48(3).

[162] It is notable that the Secretary of State, were he or she ever to resume the rule making functions designated, would not have to comply with these principles.

[163] S. 114(9). [164] Sch. 8, para. 12. [165] Sch. 8, paras. 2–7 and 9–11.

[166] Sch. 9, para. 12(1).

does not apply where SIB considers that the delay in complying would be prejudicial to the interests of investors,[167] and did not apply to the initial rules which SIB made in order to have the powers transferred to it under the Act.[168] There is no requirement, following the underlying philosophy of the Act, that the Chancellor should be consulted in the formation of the rules, and subject to the competition requirements, his or her approval is not required. The constitutions of the SROs require them to undertake a similar consultation exercise with their own members. Amendments made by the 1989 Companies Act also require SIB and the SROs to have 'satisfactory arrangements' for taking account of the costs of compliance when forming rules.[169]

Finally, the effects of breach of SIB or SRO rules has also altered since the initial Act. Under section 62 of the 1986 Act any person who suffered loss as the result of contravention of the rules of SIB or an SRO had an action for damages.[170] In 1989 this right was restricted to private investors,[171] and the statements of principle were excluded from its scope.[172] The reasons for these changes and the effect which they had on the rule making function will be explored in the following chapter.

Characterizing the System—'Self-Regulation within a Statutory Framework'?

The White Paper described its proposed structure as 'self regulation within a statutory framework'. The regulatory structure has, as we will see, been difficult to manage, and calls have increased recently for the system to be put on a statutory footing. The structure has had a significant impact on the rule making process; just as significant as the organization of institutional power, however, has been the rhetoric of 'self-regulation' which surrounds the system, and the assumptions which have accompanied it as to the nature of regulation which a 'self-regulatory' system should deliver; assumptions which as we have seen dominated debates surrounding

[167] Sch. 9, para. 13(2). This has as yet not been used.
[168] Sch. 9, para. 12(3).
[169] Sch. 2, para. 3A (SROs) and Sch. 7, para. 2A (SIB), inserted by s. 204 CA 1989.
[170] S. 62. [171] S. 62A, inserted by s. 193(1) Companies Act 1989.
[172] S. 47A(3), inserted by s. 192 Companies Act 1989.

its formation. An adequate characterization of the system is necessary both for the wider considerations of its reform, and for the more immediate concerns of this study, notably the context in which rule making occurs.

The system does combine statutory elements with a reliance on non-statutory, associational, and contractual methods of regulation. The statutory framework is present in the conditions for recognition of SIB and in turn the SROs, RPBs, and RIEs. It prescribes the broad rule making procedures of SIB and the SROs, outlines the composition of governing boards requiring them to maintain a balance between the interests of their members and of the public, and sets out principles to which their rules should conform. The statutory framework has not only enabled and facilitated regulation, it has also restricted SIB and prevented it from adopting certain courses of action that it may have otherwise taken. SIB, as we have seen, has no system management powers, it cannot order firms to join one SRO rather than another, or require an SRO to form; it is the sole recipient of the statutory powers, which it cannot delegate. This has prevented it from delegating to IMRO, for example, the responsibility for regulating unit trusts. Moreover, SIB cannot, unlike the SROs, give itself enforcement or other powers, for example the power to impose fines.

The SROs operate on the basis of a contractual relationship with their members, and so although their rules and enforcement procedures have to meet broadly defined requirements, it is through their corporate form and the contracts with those they regulate that they acquire their powers. They can thus determine the scope of their regulation, their enforcement powers, and operational practices. However, the statutory framework also imposes limitations: their ability to determine their rules is subject to the statutory requirement of adequacy, and as we will see, their freedom to write the rules they want is further circumscribed by the position of those rules in a complex rule system. Statute also endows their regulation, indirectly, with a compulsive element: anyone wanting to conduct investment business has to be authorized, either by virtue of membership of an SRO, an RPB or direct regulation from SIB. Thus a large part of the power, authority, remit, and indeed the reason for the existence of the SROs stems from statute.

Such meshing of statutory and self-regulatory aspects suggests that the description of the SROs as 'self-regulatory' fails to capture the true nature of these bodies. Moreover, there have recently been moves by the SROs themselves to disassociate themselves from the label of 'self-regulation'. When TSA merged with AFBD the new body replaced the word 'Association' with that of 'Authority'. SFA recently renamed its membership department (dealing with applications) to 'Authorisation'. That such changes are more than semantic is reinforced by an internal SFA memorandum relating to the latter change:

> This reflects a new general policy to seek to minimise the profile of SFA as a self regulatory organisation, and instead to seek to project an image of an independent regulator. Identification with self regulation is becoming increasingly unattractive and, in the Board's view, detrimental to our projection as an effective regulator.[173]

PIA and IMRO have both expressed similar sentiments, and the TCSC concluded in its 1995 Report, '[t]he evidence we have received from the regulators has . . . stressed that the term "self regulation" is a misnomer and fails to reflect their independence or the statutory basis of their authority'.[174]

In seeking to characterize the system the TCSC, however, simply reaffirmed the White Paper's description of the system as 'self regulation within a statutory framework'. A better characterization is that the system is in fact a particular type of self-regulation, what may be termed mandated self-regulation, in which a collective group is required or designated as competent by government to formulate and enforce norms within a broadly defined framework set by government.[175] This type of self-regulatory system is essentially a corporatist arrangement: the state endows self-interested groups or associations with governmental power, and those groups in turn both develop and implement public policy objectives.[176] Streeck and Schmitter define such bodies as associations of 'private interest government': the 'self-"government" of categories of social actors defined by a collective self-regarding interest . . . under which an

[173] Unprinted SFA memorandum, cited in the Treasury and Civil Service Select Committee Sixth Report, *The Regulation of Financial Services in the UK*, Volume I, HC 332-I, (London, 1995), xi.

[174] Ibid.

[175] For further analysis of self-regulation see J. Black, 'Constitutionalising Self-Regulation' (1996) 59 *MLR* 24.

[176] The corporatist analysis is applied in depth to the financial services regulatory system by Moran: M. Moran, *Politics of the Financial Services Revolution: The USA, the UK and Japan* (London, 1991), who further argues that financial services exhibit a bias towards corporatism, 15–19.

attempt is made to make associative, self-interested collective action contribute to the achievement of public policy objectives.'[177]

Why does the characterization of the system matter, however? The concern of SROs to move away from the label 'self-regulation' and the constant debates over what the system should be indicate that it clearly does.[178] The reason why lies in the perceptions held of self-regulatory and statutory regulatory systems. These perceptions have had a historical significance, as we have seen in the formation of the Act. Self-regulation was perceived to provide flexible regulation, expertly designed and sensitively enforced, which would lead to an environment in which investors were confident to enter the markets and so both contribute to, and certainly not endanger, London's international competitiveness. Some element of supervision was seen to be necessary, even by self-regulation's most ardent adherents, to prevent the repeat of cartelization and anti-competitive practices, and a degree of compulsion to ensure firms became part of the system to prevent against fragmentation and the conferring of unfair competitive advantage on those who decided not to opt in. Those adherents of self-regulation resisted any greater statutory element on the ground that it would lead to bureaucratic regulation, inexpertly designed and rigidly enforced which would lead to ossification, stifling market innovation and cause firms to flee London for more appealing regulatory climes. For its opponents, self-regulation was seen to lead to lax and self-interested regulation, which would provide a fertile ground for fraud and provide inadequate protection for investors; and statutory regulation to provide the standards of regulation and compulsion necessary to stamp out fraud and protect investors. As the experience of rule making in the regulatory system indicates, these assumptions have continued to have an effect on the operation of that system and the light in which it is viewed.

177 W. Streeck and P. C. Schmitter, 'Community, market, state—and associations? The prospective contribution of interest governance to social order' in W. Streeck and P. C. Schmitter (eds.), *Private Interest Government, Beyond Market and State* (New York, 1985), 17, italics omitted.

178 Most recently the Treasury announced that it would review the entire structure, possibly with a view to creating one regulator and bringing regulation within the Department: the *Independent*—Feb. 1996.

3 The Regulatory Policy of Rule Use

The regulatory structure provided for by the Financial Services Act 1986 bore the stamp of Gower's proposed model, but that model had been appropriated to resolve problems not envisaged when Gower wrote, namely the restructuring of the wholesale markets precipitated by the Goodison-Parkinson agreement. As we have seen in the previous chapter, in the course of the policy process leading up to the Act the structure proposed became somewhat distorted and was ultimately the product of a compromise negotiated incrementally as the Bill passed through Parliament. The result was a complex structure with the respective roles of the different bodies being ill-defined. There are strong centralizing tendencies: SIB's rule making powers, outlined in the previous chapter, are extensive and as recipient of the legislative powers it also has the monopoly on the formation of particular sets of rules. It has extensive powers of investigation and enforcement, and responsibility for administering the central compensation fund. It is also responsible for recognizing and monitoring SROs, professional bodies, exchanges, and clearing houses, and can amend rules of SROs without their consent. It combines this supervisory function with that of acting as a regulator of firms itself: it is open to any firm to seek recognition from SIB, and SIB has no statutory power to refuse authorization on the grounds that there is a suitable SRO which that firm could join.

Against this lies the position of the SROs. The role envisaged by most was that they would be the regulators of the majority of firms conducting investment business and would be responsible for forming and enforcing rules tailored to their particular areas of the market. It was anticipated by most observers that they would have a considerable amount of flexibility in forming rules and would be engines of policy change. It was through them that the advocates of self-regulation anticipated that the benefits of effectiveness and flexibility would be achieved. That there was a considerable lack of clarity as to whether or not the SROs were in fact to perform this role is evident from reading the Act. Their role as rule making powerhouses is not apparent on its face. Indeed, the requirement that their rules provide investor protection equivalent to that provided by SIB's rules and the power of SIB to alter SRO rules suggest that SIB was intended to have a considerable say in the form and substance of SROs' rules. This ambiguity has been of critical significance in the rule making process. What was to be the relationship between SIB's rules and those of the SROs? Was SIB to form rules which were general standards, or detailed rules to regulate comprehensively the entire area? Were SROs to write rules tailored to their own areas in the ways they wished, or were they to follow SIB's lead in every respect?

Attempts to resolve these questions have had a particular impact on the rules used in the regulatory system: the institutional structure provides in part the reason both for the form of the initial rules and for the subsequent changes in the uses of rules. The institutional structure, its history, and the rhetoric of 'self-regulation' which surrounds it have shaped the goals of the regulatory system, goals which rules have been used to achieve. The use of rules, particularly in the New Settlement, has been a tactical and strategic exercise; rule type has been a regulatory policy in its own right. Both the definition of this policy and the rule making process itself have been affected by the institutional structure and legal framework, by the role each set of rules played in the regulatory system, the continuing impact of the tensions between 'statutory' and 'self-' regulatory systems which had so marked the formation of the Act, changes in the political environment, and the perceptions of the regulators themselves as to their respective roles.

This chapter examines the three main phases of rule making which have occurred thus far: the formation of the initial rules, the revision of the rules and statutory amendments to SIB's rule making powers which formed the New Settlement, and the subsequent changes in the uses of rules following the report of SIB's current chairman, Sir Andrew Large. It explores the reasons for the detailed and complex nature of the initial rule books, the factors underlying the restructuring of the rules which occurred three years later under the label of the New Settlement, and the shift in the role of rules following the Large report. It shows the manner and extent to which rules have been used to define the respective roles of SIB and the SROs in the regulatory structure and have been deployed in attempts to gain legitimacy for the regulatory system as a whole, to change the light in which the regulation is viewed by the regulated and other political and media observers. Associated with this, attempts have been made, through changing the type of rule used and the associated development of interpretive communities, to induce compliance, to replace creative compliance with instinctive compliance, and to build understandings as to the requirements of rules which can then replace detailed rules. Not all uses of rules have been so strategic, however, and the formation of the initial rules in particular demonstrates the confluence of pressures which can lead to highly detailed, complex sets of rules. The chapter examines this process, before turning to explore the reasons for the New Settlement and analyse the three tiered rule system and to discuss the subsequent changes in the uses made of rules.

The Formation of the Initial Rules

The conduct of business rules were only one of the eight sets of rules which SIB had to form before it could meet the statutory criteria and before the regulation could come into effect. The task facing SIB was enormous: one initial Board member likened it to 'mapping a continent: you had to find out where the rivers and mountains were'.[1] As we have seen, many of the activities covered by the Act had not been subject to regulation. There was thus little experience of regulation on which to draw, and no model of rules to follow. The rules had to embrace the statutory requirements for delegation of powers, and the statute did specify some issues which the rules could cover. These statutory provisions were however less detailed than those contained in the White Paper,[2] which were themselves based on the draft codes of the CSI,[3] the Stock Exchange,[4] and a joint working paper of the DTI and Bank of England.[5] However, although these codes could be

[1] Interview, May 1992.

[2] *Financial Services in the UK: A New Framework for Investor Protection*, Cmnd. 9432 (London, 1985), Ch. 7. This had, e.g., included a provision as to best execution, not contained in the Act.

[3] CSI, *Draft Code of Conduct on the Management of Conflicts of Interest*, CSI *Annual Report* 1985, App. B.

[4] Stock Exchange, *Conflicts of Interest and their Regulation: Discussion Document*, Nov. 1984, in 1985 *SEQ* 18.

[5] L. C. B. Gower, *Investor Protection in the UK, Report, Part II* (London, 1984), Ch. 4.

drawn on in forming the rules, none had ever been implemented, and so they were untested in terms of their workability and effects. The Licensed Dealers' (Conduct of Business) Rules, which were operational, had been revised in 1983 but the experience of their operation was limited: they had only been in force just over two years, and relatively few persons were subject to them. They were also not as extensive in their requirements. The regulators thus had to look further afield, to the SEC, for a prototype rule book. The lack of regulatory experience was further exacerbated by the changes occurring in the regulated industry. The radical restructuring of the City meant that even if there had been regulation prior to the 1986 Act, much of it would have had to be revised to meet the changing market structure and operations. Moreover it was not clear exactly what new activities would be emerging which would need regulation.

SIB in fact began drafting its rules prior to the legislation being passed in Parliament; the first draft of conduct of business rules was published in March 1986, the next in September.[6] In February 1987 SIB produced a further draft which it submitted to the Department of Trade and Industry in its application for designated agency status and the transfer of statutory powers. The DTI requested further amendments, and finally granted the delegation order in May 1987. SIB's rules were published in final form in October 1987 and came into force on 29 April 1988 ('A Day').

The rule books which emerged were far more detailed and complex than had been anticipated by many of those involved in the drafting of the White Paper, and by those to be subject to them. They were greeted with a considerable degree of hostility, well described by SIB's current chairman, Sir Andrew Large, as 'a sense of outrage'.[7] Criticism focused primarily on their precision, complexity, and their lack of clarity. There was a certain amount of truth in this. Many of the rules, particularly those setting out information to be contained in documents, were highly detailed, specific, and precise. Whilst many of these were nonetheless clear on their own, the sheer number of requirements or conditions imposed by the rule book as a whole made them highly complex. This

[6] SIB, *Draft Rules and Regulations*, 1986.

[7] Treasury and Civil Service Select Committee, Financial Services Regulation, Minutes of Evidence, 1992/3 HC no. 733-i, para. 7.

complexity was exacerbated by an extended use of cross-references to other rules and long definitions sections. In addition, the rules were subject to frequent amendment, due to reconsiderations or requests for exemptions. Many of these were drafting or technical amendments, but a substantial number were substantive changes to the rules, either their requirements or their scope.[8]

The form and structure of the initial rules were the product of a number of interacting factors. Some of these, such as the statutory provision for a right of action for breach of the rules, SIB's own experience and attitude to its regulatory function, were on their own significant, and perhaps determinative. Others, such as the role of SIB's rules in the regulatory structure, the statutory powers of the DTI, need not perhaps of themselves have led necessarily to the complex rule book which emerged. However, when coupled with other extraneous factors: the extreme state of flux within the industry, the need for speed, the political pressure for tough regulation, and, above all, the considerable degree of uncertainty which prevailed as to the shape of the industry and the nature of the regulators, they together exerted a strong influence in favour of detailed rules.

The statutory provision in section 62 of the Act of a right of civil action for breach of the rules is noted by many of those involved in the process as one of the significant factors which increased the pressure for detailed provisions and exemptions. There was a strong perception, particularly in the City, that the restructuring would be accompanied by an increasingly litigious atmosphere in which firms would be suing each other almost as a matter of course. This fear was prompted by several factors: the 'consciousness raising' of the duties that firms were under which came from the Act and the rules generally, the changing nature and increased competitiveness

[8] Between Feb. 1987 and Oct. 1987 there were two major sets of amendments; in Mar. and Apr. 1988 (the rules came into effect on 29 Apr.: 'A Day'), SIB issued six rule releases containing over fifty amendments; in the following two months it issued three releases containing nearly thirty amendments, over half of which were substantive: The FS (Conduct of Business) (Amendment) Rules 1988 (No. 8); The FS (Oil Markets) Rules and Regulations 1988 (No. 11); The FS (Misc. Amendments) Rules and Regulations 1988 (No. 13); The FS (Transitional) Rules and Regulations 1988 (No. 14); The FS (Conduct of Business) (Amendment No. 2) Rules 1988 (No. 21); The FS (Interim) Rules and Regulations 1988 (No. 22); The FS (Conduct of Business) (Amendment No. 3) Rules 1988 (No. 23); The FS (Conduct of Business) (Amendment No. 4) Rules 1988 (No. 26); The FS (Misc. Amendments) (No. 2) Rules and Regulations 1988 (No. 27).

of the City environment, and the entry of American firms, seen as highly litigious, into the market. Evidence used in support of these fears was the then recent litigation against the Takeover Panel, taken for the first time in 1987, when it was held that the Panel was susceptible to judicial review.[9] Firms were therefore concerned to ensure that their duties were clearly defined and their liability to other professional firms was limited. They demanded rules which were certain, but not too detailed.

The pressure for detail which section 62 exerted was one which was largely industry driven: section 62 had not initially been a major consideration for SIB in its drafting. Indeed, actions in common law for breach of agency or fiduciary duties had not figured prominently in the history of investment business. The actual likelihood of actions did not matter, however, what was significant was the perception that litigation would increase dramatically. This led to increased demands for specification as to what exactly a particular rule required, and pressure for exemptions from their scope. As a chairman of SIB subsequently commented:

> [Section 62] had a serious adverse effect on the SIB rulebook . . . The problem was that it focused the attention of practitioners, and more particularly their lawyers, on amending the rules, not to improve them generally, but simply to minimize the possibility of claims. This led to long and complicated provisions, attempting to draw fine distinctions to provide safe harbours for legitimate industry practice, while maintaining the essence of the original objective of the rule.[10]

In providing a private right of action for breach of the rules, the section meant that the courts, and not just the regulators, would be involved in the enforcement of the rules. The regulators would not have a monopoly in their application, and so could not rely on the exercise of their own discretion in enforcement to remedy any over- or under-inclusiveness of the rule, for example. Indeed, section 62 almost negated any possibility that the rules could have the 'flexibility' which had formed such an important part of the rhetoric surrounding the genesis of the Act, as it meant that

[9] *R* v. *City Panel on Takeovers and Mergers, ex p. Datafin* [1987] 1 All ER 524 (CA).

[10] D. Walker, 'Financial Services: The Principles Initiative' (1989) *BJIBFL* 51. See also K. Mortimer, 'The Securities and Investments Board', in A. Seldon (ed.), *Financial Regulation—or Over Regulation?* (London, 1988), at 50. Mortimer was Policy Director at SIB, 1985–7.

enforcement and application of the rules was not in the hands of the regulators alone. Section 62 provided a mechanism for private enforcement of the rules, which paralleled the public enforcement responsibilities of the regulators. The regulators thus had no monopoly either over the interpretation of the rules nor the enforcement strategy to be adopted. Reliance on vague, purposive (but over-inclusive) rules could not be placed: the regulators could not control their interpretation, and nor could they rely on mitigating the over-inclusive rule through selective enforcement, along the lines of a 'conversational model' of regulation.[11] Any firm who breached a rule was open to civil action on the part of the person who suffered loss; the regulator could not prevent enforcement. On the part of the regulated, the lack of knowledge of how the rules would be interpreted by the courts, together with the fact that enforcement could not be negotiated with the regulator but would have to be defended in the courts, meant that they wanted to be absolutely sure what was covered by the rule and what was not. This certainty was sought through increased precision and specification.

The private right of action thus provided a pressure for detailed rules. The private right of action, SIB argued, meant that the rules had to be drafted in 'legal language' precise enough to enable both the regulators and the courts to establish whether they have been broken: '[r]ules of this sort cannot be as "user friendly" as the Highway Code or CSI codes'.[12] Section 62 also provided a justification for such rules, however, and SIB used it to counter criticisms that the rules should be more general. For SIB's own approach to its statutory responsibilities also tended towards the formation of detailed rules imposing high standards of conduct. Gower had urged against 'moral exhortations' in his Report,[13] and SIB showed no inclination to use them. SIB's idea of what regulation should provide was expressed clearly in the overview to its rule book. SIB stated that when drafting the rules to implement the statutory principles 'whilst fully appreciative of the appeal of simple relatively general rules', it had felt bound to give weight to three important considerations:

[11] See Ch. 1.

[12] SIB, *The Securities and Investments Board's Application for the Designated Agency Status under the terms of the Financial Services Act 1986 and the Revised Rule Book*, Feb. 1987, para. 5.

[13] Gower, *Report, Part I*, para. 8.52.

certainty: the need for firms to know what they must do, can do or cannot do; for customers to know what to expect and to what they are entitled; for the rules to be capable of being monitored effectively and efficiently; and for the sanctions under the Act, whether discipline of firms or of individuals or redress by the courts for individuals who have suffered loss, to operate effectively;
consistency: the risk that rules drafted in general terms will be interpreted too diversely by different firms in a huge, competitive and diverse industry, penalising firms who take a strict interpretation and the customers of other firms;
standards: the difficulty, given a starting point of considerable variations in standards of competence and honesty, and given the highly competitive environment, of assuming that without specific guidance all firms will operate to the standards of the best.[14]

These considerations illustrate a particular set of assumptions underlying the use of rules. Although the provision in section 62 gave the requirement of certainty a particularly exaggerated hue, certainty was seen by SIB and others as a virtue in its own right: it embodies many of the positive rule of law values. It was assumed that certainty could be conferred through precision. A rule, for example, that 'sufficient information' be provided was rejected as giving too little guidance as to what would be considered sufficient.

The other two considerations which SIB highlighted, consistency and standards, have a different rationale, not one of certainty but of control. The issue here is not that 'sufficient information' provides too great uncertainty for the firm, but that it provides too little control for the regulator. It leaves the interpretation of 'sufficient' to the firm. Given the context in which the regulation was to operate, the uncertainty and flux in the regulated industry, the heterogeneity of participants, and the lack of previous regulatory experience providing customary interpretations, SIB could not rely on the firm taking the interpretation that SIB might want. SIB's response was thus to attempt to control the operation of the rule through increased precision.

The institutional structure of the regulation also exerted particular pressures on the rule making process. SIB was conscious of the role its rules played in the regulatory system. They were the benchmark against which the SRO rules were to be assessed, and had to be capable of being a regulatory system in their own right,

[14] SIB, *The SIB Rulebook: An Overview*, Oct. 1987, para. 10 (emphasis provided).

regulating those who sought direct authorization from SIB. In particular, SIB felt that the requirement that the rules of the SROs provide a level of protection equivalent to that provided by SIB's meant that its rules had to be the exemplar, providing a very high level of protection.[15] This was equated with detailed rules largely due to the uncertainty as to what the SROs would be like as regulators. At the time, the SROs were unknown quantities. They were in the process of forming, of recruiting staff, ensuring that their organizational structures, membership, and disciplinary processes satisfied the statutory conditions, and setting up procedures for handling the vast numbers of firms that would seek authorization through them. With the exception of those who had worked in the Stock Exchange or been members, none had experience either in regulating or being regulated, or had been subject only to very general codes of practice. No one, including SIB, was sure what form of regulation the SROs would produce of their own initiative.

In addition, SIB's rules were the test for the delegation of statutory powers and the initiation of the whole system of regulation. Again, of itself, this need not have been a significant factor. The statutory criteria that the rules had, and still have to meet is generally expressed and the rule making powers are widely defined. Moreover, provisions as to its rules are only one of the criteria that SIB had to meet in order to receive designated agency status. That the rules had to be approved before powers were delegated nonetheless was a significant factor in their formation, in particular in their level of detail. The reason why lies in the role and approach of the approving body, the DTI. Although there was never a real threat that the statutory powers would not be delegated to SIB, the fact that SIB had to meet the DTI's approval that it satisfied the statutory criteria gave the DTI a crucial role in the formation of the initial rules. If SIB was unsure of what the SROs would be like as regulators, the DTI was unsure of SIB. Moreover, under the Act the DTI had no subsequent powers over the SIB rule book other than under the anti-competitive provisions. If it wanted to affect the shape of the regulation, this was its only time to do so. Again, an attempt to exert control was manifested in detailed rules. Indeed, responsibility for the growth of the rule book between the first drafts of 1986 and the final draft

[15] Ibid., para. 5.

of 1987 is laid firmly at the feet of the DTI by those at SIB during that period. In the words of one senior official:

> [t]hey insisted that it [the rule book] be comprehensive, and told SIB that it would not have powers delegated to it unless they could see what it would do with them.[16]

And in the words of another senior executive,

> [w]hen the Bill became an Act the DTI lawyers especially were very proprietorial over it—it was their baby . . . They were very insistent on a strict interpretation of the views of Parliament as expressed in the debates and text, and those views were very restrictive. The pressure was to be watertight, not user friendly. The DTI did not really care if the rules worked, they just had to be legally correct and precise.[17]

The wider political context also required an indication from the rules that SIB would be a tough regulator. As we have seen, during the initial stages of the Act, the need for strong regulation to combat fraud and sharp practice had been at the forefront of debates. Although this had subsequently been subsumed by concerns to ensure that professional investors were not too constrained by the Act's requirements, prompted mainly by the professional investors themselves,[18] the desire for strong regulation was still great. This pressure was enhanced by the issue of SIB's legitimacy as a regulator. Critics of self-regulation argued that it was no more than a cartel system in which regulation was provided to meet the demands of the regulated rather than a wider public interest. Strong regulation, again perceived to be manifested by detailed regulation, would be a sign that the system would not be simply regulating in the interests of the regulated.

The lack of any domestic history of regulation on which to draw, the considerable uncertainty as to what the regulated industry would in fact look like, the requirement that the regulatory system be implemented as quickly as possible, and the preoccupation of those to be regulated with the restructuring occurring in the industry were the final contributory factors influencing the structure of the initial rules, and indeed exacerbating the likelihood that they would be significantly under- or over-inclusive. The rules were being formed in anticipation of a new market

[16] Mortimer, 'The Securities and Investments Board', 50–1.

[17] Interview, Apr. 1992.

[18] See above.

structure and new business practices, a situation which, as noted in chapter 1, is likely to enhance the problems of inclusiveness. There was no previous regulatory history on which to draw, even if the information this could have provided may have been limited, and in addition the pressures for speed in drafting were great. The new dealing system on the Exchange (Big Bang) was to be introduced on 27 October 1986. Firms would then be dealing without restraint of rules other than the CSI's Code of Conduct and the Stock Exchange rules (for those who were members of either) until the Act and rules came into force. The Government was keen that this should be as short a time as possible and the initial timetable for implementation was 1987, although in the event the system did not come into effect until April 1988, eighteen months after Big Bang. The City's attention was occupied by the restructuring of industry and the bull market, which prevailed until the crash of October 1987. Responses to consultations thus tended to come at the end of or after the consultation process and be particular to each firm's or sector's problems. This in itself exerted a particular impact on the structure of the rules. The dominant style of the initial rules was a general statement or provision which was followed by a long list of exceptions. This was explained by one official as being specifically designed to accommodate the frequent requests for 'carve outs' or exemptions from the rules which came from the regulated. The extensive use of cross-references was also deliberate as it facilitated amendments: changes made in one part could be automatically reflected in another. Finally, the pressure of time meant that there was subsequently little time to stand back and review the rule books as a whole, either on the part of the regulated or SIB, with the consequence that they were, in the words of one official, produced in a 'fairly raw form'.

The New Settlement

Overview

The 1987 rule book did not last long, and the replacement for SIB's chairman, Sir Kenneth Berrill, was announced before the rules even came into effect. The new appointee, Sir David Walker, quickly announced a revision of SIB's rules. From comparatively small beginnings the process snowballed and resulted in a change far more radical than was initially anticipated. Dubbed the 'New Settlement' it had three main elements: the restriction of the private right of action to a particular class of investors, private investors; the change in the criteria for assessing SRO rules from that of whether they provided a level of protection equivalent to that of SIB's rules, to whether their rules, together with other elements of their regulatory function, provided adequate investor protection; and a change in the rule making powers of SIB. SIB was now given the power to make principles which would apply directly to members of SROs and RPBs, to designate rules as directly applicable to members of SROs, and to form codes of practice of evidentiary status. In 1990 SIB formed ten principles and in 1990–1 forty Core Rules (designated conduct of business rules). It also used the powers to form a comprehensive set of designated client money, financial resources, and unsolicited call rules.[19]

By the admittance of many involved in their formation, the initial rule books needed considerable revision. That such revision required the changes in the statutory powers which comprise the New Settlement is not self-evident, and indeed was not immediately seen as the obvious step to take. The process leading up to the change and the reasons for it reveal that it was changes in the context in which the regulators were operating which were responsible. Some elements of the context in which the initial rules were formulated had now gone. Part of these were legal and so structural, others more transitory. Structurally, after delegation the DTI had no further statutory control over the SIB rules other than via the anti-competitive provisions; any pressure which it had exerted for detail had correspondingly less force. Changes had also occurred in the political and regulatory climate: the pressure of speed was lifted; at least some operational regulation was now in place. Further, politically the demand was now for greater flexibility, and more importantly, for a different role for SIB. The new Secretary of State, Lord Young, publicly acknowledged the concern over reports of 'excessive legalism' of SIB and some of the

[19] Financial Services (Client Money) Regulations 1991; Financial Services (Client Money) (Supplementary) Regulations 1991; Financial Services (Financial Resources) Regulations 1991; Financial Services (Common Unsolicited Call) Regulations 1991.

SROs[20] and as part of the 'Releasing Enterprise' initiative[21] expressed his intention to ensure that small businesses were not burdened with excessive demands under the Act. Officials at the Bank of England also wanted changes, principally a repeal of section 62 and a rewriting of the rulebooks. More fundamentally, the Bank also sought a revised approach by SIB to its regulatory role, one which fitted better with the self-regulatory model which the Bank had intended. In furtherance of this, the suggestion endorsed by leading Bank officials was that the SIB rule book should confine itself to stating general principles rather than detailed provisions, giving more discretion to the SROs.[22]

Changes in personnel, notably in the chairman of SIB, were also of key significance. The hostility expressed towards the initial rules was focused on the first SIB chairman, Sir Kenneth Berrill. Responsibility for appointing the SIB chairman lies with the Secretary of State and the Governor of the Bank. There had been reports of a growing discontentment with the SIB chairman in the City and Bank of England for many months prior to the announcement, and it emerged that the Bank and Lord Young had decided as far back as October 1987 that he would be replaced.[23] When in February 1988 it was announced that Sir Kenneth Berrill's term of office as chairman of SIB would not be renewed, despite his publicly stated wish to remain,[24] many in the City were delighted. That his successor was a Bank of England executive director, David Walker, was seen as a victory for the City establishment in the battle against the regulators: one commentator described 'Sir Kenneth's scalp' as 'the City's biggest prize',[25] another called it a 'slap in the face for SIB'.[26] The expectations attached to Walker's appointment were clearly expressed by the Governor in his speech at the Lord Mayor's Dinner subsequent to Walker's appointment, where reflecting on the experience of regulation thus far he stated that the 'practitioners' contribution had been overshadowed' and expressed the hope that 'we are now moving into a phase of application and refinement in which practitioners can be allowed a greater part'.[27]

20 *FT*, 11 Feb. 1988.
21 DTI, *Releasing Enterprise* (London, Feb. 1988).
22 Clive Wolman, 'Bank's hopes for SIB Chairman', *FT*, 31 May 1988.
23 Richard Waters, 'Decision to appoint Walker', *FT*, 27 Feb. 1988.
24 *FT*, 29 Feb. 1988, Leader.
25 *The Economist*, 10 Apr. 1988.
26 Waters, 'Decision to appoint Walker'.
27 R. Leigh Pemberton, 'The Markets, the City and the Economy' (1988) *BEQB* 59.

Structural elements which had always been present also began to exert an influence in a way in which they had not in the formation of the initial rules. In particular, the SROs began to raise their objections publicly and to become vocal participants in the debate as to the appropriate nature of the SIB/SRO relationship. The issue was inevitable given the regulatory structure; that it had not been raised before was largely because the SROs had not been in a position to participate in the forming of the initial rules. As we have seen, SIB started forming its rule book before the legislation was passed; most SROs were not yet formed and their attention was subsequently focused on getting their own organizational structure and rule books in place. Now they had done that, they were in a position to focus on the question of their relationship with SIB. The process of being recognized and of forming their rules had been dominated by the statutory requirement that their rules provide protection equivalent to that provided by SIB's, a provision which SIB had interpreted strictly. The SROs consequently felt they were being given insufficient opportunity to draft their own rules. IMRO publicly urged SIB to adopt a lower profile, threatening that self-regulation would otherwise come to an early end: 'SROs must be allowed to develop personalities without being over-restricted by the school-marmish SIB . . . SIB should allow SROs scope to vary their rulebooks and apply flexible, practitioner based regulation'.[28]

Questions which remained constant, such as how to provide certainty and flexibility and ensure high and consistent standards of regulation, also began to receive different answers. Within weeks of taking office, Walker publicly agreed with the need for simplification of the rule books, later stating that they were 'over-long, over-complicated and over-specific'.[29] Although he resisted calls for substantive modifications of the regulation,[30] he did see a different role for regulation and rules from that manifested in the initial rule books. Instead of 'detailed prescription of when and how things should be done', he argued, rules should merely 'prescribe that they be done'.[31]

[28] Speech of John Morgan, chief executive of IMRO, to the National Association of Pension Funds, quoted in *FT*, 27 Feb. 1988.

[29] D. Walker, 'Financial Services: The Principals Initiative' (Feb. 1989) *BJIBFL* 51.

[30] Principally of the polarization regime and client agreement requirements.

[31] *FT*, 6 July 1988; *The Economist*, 30 July 1988.

Defining Roles through Rules

The motivations for the New Settlement are a remarkable study in the implicit, and often explicit, assumptions which are made as to rule type. Rule type has a symbolic value, contributing to, but extending far beyond, functional questions of efficiency, effectiveness or enforceability. As we saw in the debates surrounding the formation of the regulatory structure, rule type is not only associated with particular institutional structures, but with particular styles of regulation. Rule type was used in the New Settlement to achieve a range of regulatory goals. It was used as a regulatory technique to improve regulatory effectiveness, not by aiding enforcement, but by inducing compliance through attempting to change the regulated's attitude towards regulation. Rule type was used to address the pervasive questions of certainty and flexibility, consistency and regulatory control in a different way to that used hitherto. Different elements of the New Settlement were used to achieve these different ends. One of the most pressing concerns however was to define the respective roles of SIB and the SROs and so to address the tensions between them inherent in the regulatory structure. The New Settlement was in large measure directed at this issue, which pervaded the reforms. It is worth thus focusing on this aspect of the reforms before moving to consider each of the different tiers of rules, Principles, Core Rules, and third tier rules, in more depth.

The New Settlement shows that rule type can be in a reflexive relationship with the rule making body: rule type can define and be defined by the role of the rule's issuer in the regulatory system. The reactions which greeted the initial rules illustrate clearly the role of the symbolic or signalling element of rules in defining the institutional position of their issuer. The criticisms of the detail and complexity, the uncertainty and inflexibility of the initial rules were aimed not simply at their workability. In part they stemmed from the shock felt by many of being subject to regulation for the first time. However, underlying many of the complaints about the rules was the more fundamental criticism directed at the role the rules demonstrated SIB was playing in the regulation. SIB was not laying down the minimum standards many had expected, rather it appeared to be setting out, in great detail, what best practice should be. This was a more dominating role than many had anticipated and critics argued that the self-regulatory ideals of the regulatory system were being betrayed. The practitioner input expected from the regulatory structure was not being allowed to be felt and SROs could not tailor the rules to suit their own market sector.

The root of the issue lay in the ambiguity inherent in the institutional structure. As we saw in the previous chapter, the structure is essentially federal and exhibits consequent tensions between the centre and the outlying bodies as to what should be their appropriate roles. The 1986 Act envisioned a strong initial role for SIB in the establishment of the regulatory structure, and a continuing role of monitoring and oversight. In that SIB's rules set the standard for investor protection, a leading policy role was also envisaged. Crucial ambiguities remained, however, as to the extent to which SIB should become involved in the detail of policy formation, and indeed this is still undefined by the 1989 Companies Act amendments.

The appropriate division of roles between the two tiers of SIB and the SROs was thus left for them to work out. As became manifestly apparent, SIB's initial approach, detailed above, differed from the SROs' view of what the regulatory approach should be. This difference, and the dominant role SIB was felt to be playing, meant that this structural ambiguity became a source of severe friction between the two tiers, and relations between them were extremely strained. The primary motivation for the New Settlement was to resolve this tension. This was clearly expressed in a working document produced in October 1989 and initially unpublished, which stated that the aim was:

> to create a more satisfactory set of relationships in which there is a greater sharing of responsibility for the successful operation of the FSA system, greater clarity of role as between SIB [and the SROs] and more room for the other bodies to develop their own style and approach.[32]

The way that this was achieved was twofold: changing the criteria which the SRO rules had to meet from one of providing a level of investor protection equivalent to that provided by SIB to a requirement to provide adequate investor protection; and changing the nature of SIB's rules, facilitated by a statutory change in its rule making powers.

[32] SIB, *A Forward Look*, Oct. 1989, para. 5.1.

The change from equivalency to adequacy appears the most technical and minor change. It had huge symbolic significance, however. Although the tension between SIB and the SROs is inherent in the institutional structure, it was the interpretation of the equivalency requirement which had become the focus of the SROs' frustration. The provision was ambiguous: was it the overall protection provided which had to be equivalent, or the precise requirement of rules? SIB took the latter interpretation and required that the rules be 'equivalent in each separate respect', so locking the SROs' rules into to SIB's rule book. The operation of the requirement had caused such a degree of friction between SIB and the SROs that relations between them were strained almost to breaking-point. The simplest way of signalling a change in this relationship was seen to be a change in the requirement itself. However, if SIB was to be able to supervise the rules of the SROs it needed some benchmark of assessment; the substance of the equivalency requirement could not therefore be radically altered. The solution was to change the statutory requirement from one of equivalency to one of adequacy. To prevent recurrence of the bitter disputes which had occurred over the appropriate interpretation of equivalency, adequacy would be defined and would be assessed on a wider basis, taking into account the nature of investment business carried on by their members and the kinds of investor involved, the effectiveness of arrangements for securing compliance, and other controls to which the members were subject.[33]

The motivation for the amendment was thus primarily political in nature, and it was an attitudinal and psychological move rather than a substantive change. It was nonetheless viewed by many participants as the key change, facilitating the rest. Its purpose was to signal a difference of approach, to indicate the anticipated form of a new relationship. In an accompanying statement, the New Approach, SIB emphasized that the test was 'a major step on the way to establishing more satisfactory and durable regulatory relationships', recognizing that the equivalency requirement, despite its provenance and intention, 'has involved an unsustainably intrusive role for SIB'. The paper stressed the more flexible approach the

[33] Sch. 2, paras. 3(1) and (2) FSA, amended by s. 203 CA 1989 and s. 128A, inserted by s. 196 CA 1989.

adequacy test permitted, taking into account an SRO's monitoring and enforcement arrangements as well as its rules, although SIB would also take into account the consistency of the SRO's rules with those of other recognized bodies.[34] It emphasized the responsibility SROs would take for their own rules, stating that 'as a deliberate counterbalance to the diminution in the autonomy of recognized bodies inherent in [the designation] . . . SIB will stand back . . . from third tier rule-making'.[35]

Changing the equivalency requirement to one of adequacy may have been necessary but it was not felt to be sufficient, however, to redefine the respective roles of SIB and the SROs. Arguably the more important change, certainly from the point of view of rule formation, was the introduction of the power for SIB to form principles which would apply directly to members of SROs and RPBs and to designate rules as directly applicable to members of SROs. SIB could thus alter the scope and application of its rules to regulate firms who were not directly authorized by it. This enabled SIB to control more directly the standards of regulation. Previously, SROs had to follow SIB's rules simply because of the requirement of equivalency; following the New Settlement SROs were effectively bound by SIB's rules because their members were. SIB's rules became more clearly legislative in nature and centralizing in their effect.

Indeed, the statutory amendments are potentially far-reaching. The power to designate rules applies to conduct of business, financial resources, client money, and unsolicited call rules, and gives no indication of what the nature of the 'principles' which apply to members of SROs and RPBs should be; the provision simply states that they should relate to a firm's conduct and financial standing, giving no indication of their number or level of detail.[36] Potentially, then, the principles could have a centralizing effect which is far more dramatic and stifling for the SROs than SIB's initial rules. Indeed in relation to client money and unsolicited calls SIB has used the power to designate a comprehensive set of rules replacing those of the SROs. With respect to the conduct of

[34] SIB, *A Wider Basis for SIB's Principles of Conduct: The Next Stage of the New Approach*, Mar. 1989, 8, and see also SIB, *Regulation of the Conduct of Investment Business: A Proposal*, Aug. 1989, paras. 21 and 24.

[35] Ibid., echoing *A Forward Look*, para. 4.11. Financial supervision rules would be an exception.

[36] S. 48A, inserted by s. 192 CA 1989.

business rules, however, the powers were used with the deliberate strategy of redefining SIB's role as a regulator in this crucial area. The ten principles and forty Core Rules operate at what SIB describes as 'high and intermediate levels of generality'.[37] The aim in forming far more general rules, SIB stated, was to retreat from detailed rule making, handing 'the baton of adaptation and innovation' to the SROs:

> [t]he essence of the new settlement is that greater unanimity and cohesiveness at the level of principles and, where applicable, Core Rules, makes it possible for the SIB to be more flexible and less intrusive at the level of detailed support. . . . its new power to write the essential elements of regulation in a clear and enforceable way by designation rules means that it can, without impairment to investor protection, properly stand back from the detail of an SRO's own rules.[38]

In forming less specific and precise rules, SIB aimed to redefine its relationship with the SROs. The New Settlement represents an attempt to resolve the tensions between the role of SIB and that of the SROs arising from the institutional structure through the adoption of a particular rule type. SIB could define its role as the body responsible for the high-level policy by forming rules of a high and intermediate level of generality. The detailed application of this policy would be by practitioners, whose expertise and knowledge could thus be felt in the day-to-day operation of the rules. However, the greater discretion given through the change in structure of the rules was mitigated by the change in their scope and application. By designating rules as directly applicable to their members SIB could still achieve the aim of exercising control over the standards of regulation set by SROs and ensuring consistency between them.[39] This control no longer had to come from a requirement that SROs follow literally SIB's own detailed rules. The formation of the more general Principles and Core Rules enabled

[37] See further below.

[38] D. Walker, 'The New Settlement in Financial Services', *Law Society Gazette*, 26 July 1989.

[39] The SROs' rules had also been criticized on the basis that there was too much diversity between them. As the SROs are organized on a functional basis, one firm may be member of more than one SRO. The need for a firm to digest each rule book, and conform to the slightly different requirements of each served only to exacerbate the complexity of each individual rule book.

SIB to set out the central elements of regulatory policy and act as a high-level regulator, whilst leaving the detailed working out of that policy to the SROs 'in the confident expectation that the essential elements of investor protection can be fully safeguarded in the overall result'.[40] Thus was rule type used to define the nature of the new regulatory relationship.

Analysing the Three Tiers: The Principles

As we have seen, the New Approach sparked a debate as to the proper nature and role of principles, with IMRO and TSA particularly having clear ideas as to what the principles should be. In the period following publication of the New Approach, SIB and the SROs established working groups to negotiate a set of principles which was then sent out for consultation.[41] The Principles, which came into effect in April 1990, were largely derived from a distillation of the most important of the ninety-three Principles contained in the New Approach, including the Introduction to the 1987 Rules, and the principles set out in Schedule 8 to the FSA 1986.[42]

The motivations behind the introduction of the Principles were complex. As we have seen, they were to give a clear statement of the aims of the regulatory regime, setting out the essence of the duties in an attempt to instil a less formalistic approach to the regulation by those subject to it. They were expected to provide consistency and cohesiveness of standards, and to be readily applicable to changing circumstances so avoiding the need for frequent updating, be readily understood by all involved in financial markets, and underline the need for compliance with the spirit rather than the letter of the rules.[43] In particular, three main themes in the motivations for their introduction can be identified, themes which were not always articulated: the attempt to change the attitude of the regulated towards the regulation, the attempt to resolve

[40] SIB, *Proposal*, Aug. 1989, para. 11.

[41] Ibid., Annex B and SIB, *The Proposed Principles for Investment Business*, CP 33, Jan. 1990. The statutory consultation process had been extended to apply to the statements of principle.

[42] The *Statements of Principle* came into effect on 30 Apr. 1990.

[43] For statements as to aims, see e.g., CP 33, para. 14.

the tension between certainty and flexibility, and the attempt to create and develop an interpretive community between regulator and regulated.

Altering Perceptions; Inducing Compliance

Whilst the desire to address the tensions in the institutional structure was the dominating motivation for the formation of the Core Rules, the formation of the Principles had a separate and additional rationale. Indeed, the idea that SIB should form principles preceded the idea that the Core Rules should be formed, indeed that there should be any change in SIB's statutory powers. When Walker arrived at SIB he immediately commissioned SIB's chief legal adviser, Michael Blair, to redraft the rules. The result, titled 'the New Approach' was essentially a recasting of the rules, reorganizing and simplifying them but leaving their substantive content intact.[44] The stated aims were to 're-fashion the . . . requirements so as to enable the principles underlying them to be more readily discerned',[45] and to 'infuse a degree of willingness to comply with the rules, instead of mere literal observance of the detail'.[46] To this end, 'principles of conduct' were introduced which had the detailed requirements set out beneath them. Walker stressed five qualities which he felt principles had:

—consistency and cohesiveness in the standards applying, as a backbone which draws the rules together;
—intellectual rigour on the part of the regulators, in ensuring that the new requirements really are justified;
—practitioner understanding of and support for the provisions made;
—emphasis on the spirit, rather than the letter, of what is prescribed; and
—a dynamic quality in the rule books, enabling them to apply to new situations without constant reformulation.[47]

This sentiment was widely supported, but its execution in the New Approach and SIB's subsequent revisions were criticized by

[44] SIB, *Conduct of Business Rules: A New Approach*, Nov. 1988. For details of the changes, see Commentary, paras. 11–42.

[45] Ibid., para. 10. See also A. Whittaker, 'Financial Services, Developing the Regulatory Structure' (Jan. 1989) *BJIBFL* 5.

[46] SIB, *A New Approach*, para. 1.

[47] Walker, 'Financial Services: The Principles Initiative'.

the SROs and the regulated as a misunderstanding of the role and nature of principles.[48] In total there were ninety-three principles. Some were quite general but others more detailed in structure. Some stood alone and had to be observed according to their terms, most were followed by more detailed rules and were an 'indication of purpose and a general guide' for the interpretation and application of the rule.[49] However, some of the principles were more explanations than statements of fundamental obligation.

The idea of principles was nonetheless seen by SIB and the other SROs, principally IMRO and TSA,[50] as the key to a revision of the rule books. The question lay as to the appropriate function of principles within the rule and regulatory system. Their function was seen as the determinant of their structure, substance, and status. The SROs appeared to have a clearer conceptualization of the problem than SIB. The chief executive of IMRO, John Morgan, argued that SIB was confusing the role of principles with that of rules. Principles, he argued, 'require observance at all times of high standards of conduct, when there may not be relevant rules to follow, and infringement may mean unfitness to practice . . . [they] serve a vital purpose in helping to enforce the standards of conduct which underlie authorisation'. Rules, on the other hand, 'tell members how to behave in certain circumstances'. A short list of fundamental principles, therefore, should be segregated from the rest. These few principles should be an agreed statement of the essential requirements of fitness and properness. The remainder, 'which are really rules masquerading as principles, should be redrafted for what they really are, and be used as benchmarks for SROs in drafting their rulebooks'.[51]

Both the exact form of the final principles and the motivations behind them evolved over the period from the publication of the New Approach in November 1988 to the final draft of the Principles

[48] The Law Society's Committee on Company Law, e.g., concluded that 'the New Approach would not only create new problems but also do nothing to solve the fundamental problems in the old system'. Law Society's Committee on Company Law, *Law Society Gazette*, 22 Feb. 1989.

[49] SIB, *A New Approach*, r. 2.01.

[50] The Securities Association, which merged in 1991 with the Association of Futures Brokers and Dealers to become the Securities and Futures Authority (SFA).

[51] John Morgan, 'The Difference between Rules and Principles', *FT*, 29 Mar. 1989.

in March 1990. The most clearly expressed motivation was to improve regulatory effectiveness, in two respects. First, to use general statements of principle to widen the application of the rules: 'to remove the unmeritorious technical defence of a lacuna in the rules'.[52] Secondly, to attempt to thwart creative compliance behaviour by emphasizing that mere observance of the literal meaning of the rule, while flouting its purpose, would not be accepted as compliance. It was now argued, by SIB and others, that rules which were more general could ensure compliance and high standards of conduct better than detailed rules. This represents a shift from SIB's initial approach, which as we saw above, relied on detailed rules to achieve the same aim. This difference is clearly expressed by the chairman of TSA, who stated:

> [w]e do not believe that complexity ensures better regulation, on the contrary it encourages loop-hole hunting and excessive reliance on legalistic interpretation rather than common, practical sense.[53]

Rather than use detailed rules, Walker argued:

> in giving high level guidance to firms, [general rules] weaken the inducement to firms, often using their legal advisers, to explore the detail of complex subordinate rules to find ways around the letter. By making clear, as the 10 principles do, the spirit of regulation, high level compliance should be more readily achieved.[54]

The very properties of brevity, simplicity, generality, and scarcity (there would be only ten Principles) would also improve compliance, it was argued, simply because they would be easier to understand and to remember. Moving from detailed rules to Principles was an attempt to raise the profile of the regulation within particular firms, lifting it from the attentions of compliance officers and into the boardroom. The Principles would thus serve to remind chief executives that there were basic principles that should govern the conduct of their business. Literal compliance could not be a substitute for management complexity: the Principles would help chief executives to see the moral wood for the technical trees. 'Self-regulation' it was argued, meant 'regulation of the self'. Management had an essential role to play in maintaining

[52] SIB, *A New Approach*, Commentary, para. 10. [53] *FT*, 23 Nov. 1989.

[54] D. Walker, 'Some Issues in Regulation of Financial Services', Lecture at the Irish Centre for Commercial Studies, University College, Dublin, 14 Nov. 1991.

a high corporate ethos of what was right or wrong, and so provide a base for the efforts of regulatory authorities, 'which provide systems and rules but cannot be a substitute for high standards in the firms themselves'.[55]

The move to more purposive rules was not only a hard edged concern for regulatory effectiveness, its underlying motivations were more subtle. The change in the structure and status of the rules was addressed not only at failings in compliance, but at what creative compliance behaviour symptomatized, namely a loss of regulatory goodwill, and a breakdown in relations between the regulator and regulated which the system had been meant to foster. It was feared that the mass of detailed rules was alienating the regulated and as a result undermining the legitimacy of the regulation.[56] In particular, both the detailed rules and the creative compliance behaviour represented a betrayal of the self-regulatory ideal which many, particularly the Bank from whence Walker came, had advocated so strongly. Compliance with the spirit of the rule had been emphasized as one of the benefits of self-regulation when the structure was being formed. Practitioners, it had been argued, would not be tempted to adopt a formalistic and legal approach to the rules, as under a statutory system, but would comply with the purpose of the rule. Compliance with the spirit of the rules, in other words, was seen to be of the essence of self-regulation. It was the approach encouraged by that highly respected self-regulatory body, the City Panel on Takeovers and Mergers, and echoed the traditions of City regulation of 'my word is my bond'. Moving to more general and purposive rules was an attempt to adopt that regulatory style, and so to change the internal attitude of the regulated towards it by gaining legitimacy and acceptance of the regulation.

Certainty and Flexibility: Combining Rule Types, Creating Interpretive Communities

It is the continual requirement of those subject to the regulation that rules should be sufficiently certain to enable the regulated to know what is expected of them, and yet sufficiently flexible to

[55] R. Leigh Pemberton, 'Takeovers and Standards in the City', Speech to the Association of Corporate Trustees (1989) *BEQB* 545.

[56] See, e.g., D. Walker, 'Financial Services Regulation, Mid-1988, and Some Elements in Prospect', Speech to the Financial Times/Deloittes Conference, 5 July 1988.

allow business practices to develop. Forming regulation which meets the twin demands of certainty and flexibility is the regulatory equivalent of the Holy Grail. SIB's initial approach, as we have seen, was to use detailed rules to provide certainty. Those rules were however criticized on the basis that their complexity, and the difficulty of understanding how and whether a rule applied to any particular circumstance rendered them too uncertain.

It was a desire to improve certainty by clearly stating the underlying rationale of the individual rules which was the initial impetus for the formation of the Principles. Although, as we have seen, the principle of the Principles was subsequently refined and the Principles later adapted to meet further objectives, the idea remained that different types of rules could be combined within one system to achieve the elusive balance between certainty and flexibility.

The Principles which were issued in 1990 were a radical departure from the initial style of regulation expressed by, and required of, SIB. One of the main concerns in their drafting was therefore not so much their wording but to enable people to believe that it was possible to draft ten general guiding rules which would be effective. What was seen as important was to sell the idea that the rules did not have to be as specific as those of the old rule book to work. It was therefore crucial to keep the Principles 'short and sweet', and to indicate to firms and customers that there was more than one approach possible to regulation.

This led to a variety of drafting techniques being used. For example there is no definitions section attached to the Principles apart from the meaning of the word 'customer', and certain phrases were deliberately avoided to escape the need for definition.[57] On first reading the Principles appear vague and open-ended, with frequent use of words such as 'reasonable', 'proper', 'adequate', 'fair'. Certain definitions have been chosen in such a way as to enable SIB to postpone a decision on the principle's application in uncertain areas,[58] and the regulators have preferred to err on the side of over-inclusiveness and to use the fact that they have the monopoly over enforcement to mitigate this effect through flexible

[57] One example given in interview was of the phrase, 'customer that the firm advises', used instead of 'advisory customer' as the latter was felt to need a definition. Interview, Mar. 1992.

[58] e.g., the phrase 'universal' in para. 1 of the Introduction.

application to individual situations.[59] The phrasing of the Principles is very deliberate, however, and they are not simply generalized appeals for honesty, integrity, and fair dealing. Certain words and phrases have been carefully chosen to impart a particular meaning,[60] and they do not always stop at prescribing that things be done, going on, for example in Principle 6, to set out the manner in which they should be done.[61]

The interaction of the Principles with the other rules in the rule system, in particular the third tier rules of the SROs, addresses the problem of providing for both certainty and flexibility within a rule system. The Principles override the SRO rules, so that issues of application and interpretation are to be resolved in the light of their provisions. This interaction thus confers the purposiveness of imprecise, evaluative rules with the greater certainty which can be provided by more precise rules, whilst going some way to avoid the problems of under-inclusiveness and creative compliance to which precise and complex rules can give rise. This combination of rule types within a system of rules also assists the rule maker. The Principles reduce the pressures for precision which arise out of a fear of creating gaps in the rules. One SRO official in interview described the Principles as a 'safety net', relieving the pressure for the SRO to ensure that all situations were covered in the SRO rules.

The tension between certainty and flexibility has also been addressed through changing the status of the rule and the sanction attaching to it, both with respect to the Principles and the third tier rules. In the case of the third tier rules it has been through changing the status of detailed rules from rules to guidance. In the case of the Principles, it is the change of sanction on rule structure which performs this function. Further, as will be explored below, rule type has been used in conjunction with the attempt to develop interpretive communities, both to address this tension, and to achieve wider regulatory goals.

When the Principles were first introduced in the New Approach, one of the main criticisms which they attracted was that the private

[59] See Ch. 1.

[60] e.g., the phrases 'universal' and 'not exhaustive' in the Introduction.

[61] For a detailed analysis of what these terms are in fact intended to mean see M. Blair, *Financial Services: The New Core Rules* (Oxford, 1993), Ch. 1. Although writing in his personal capacity, Michael Blair was head of SIB's legal division during the New Settlement era and closely involved in the formation of the principles.

right of action could not attach to such vague and imprecise rules. Although SIB did not initially propose changing the sanction attaching to them,[62] their structure was not considered by the SROs and regulated to be acceptable unless they were subject to discretionary disciplinary action only.[63] It was the restriction in the application and availability of the right of civil action for breach of the rules, and its removal altogether for breach of the Principles,[64] that enabled the refinement from the ninety-three Principles to ten. As Walker later explained:

> the essential purpose [of not providing a right of action for breach of a Principle] is to enable the nature of these statements of Principle to be different from that of rules, and for the general standards expected which they express to be reiterated less precisely than is necessary in a rule.

Why should the change of sanction matter? Why were opaque rules perceived to be too uncertain and so unacceptable unless there was no possibility of court action for their breach? The conviction was strong, but the reasoning for it was not well articulated. The reason why general rules may have been perceived to gain certainty when subject to disciplinary action only, and to lose that if a court were to be involved in their enforcement, it is suggested lies in the deliberate creation of an interpretive community. To understand how that was created, and what it means, we need to step back briefly to consider the issue of the determinacy of rules. Uncertainty arises if the meaning and consequent application of a rule is unclear. We saw in the first chapter that rules are characterized by a degree of indeterminacy, stemming from the inherent indeterminacy of language, and the impossibility of foreseeing all the different future applications of the rule. It was also suggested that this degree of determinacy can be enhanced or reduced by the particular form of words used and rule structure adopted. In particular, words or phrases which may appear relatively indeterminate, such as 'reasonable', 'appropriate', 'fair', may in fact be determinate if the interpretation of such words or phrases is agreed upon by all who read them. So it was suggested

[62] Walker, 'Financial Services: The Principles Initiative', 53.

[63] See, e.g., Morgan, 'The Difference between Rules and Principles'.

[64] The right of action provided to all investors for the breach of any SIB or SRO rule in s. 62 FSA 1986 was amended to make the right available to private investors only, and the Principles were exempted from its scope: s. 62A FSA 1986, inserted by s. 193(1) CA 1989.

that the dimension of clarity / opacity is a subjective one: the ability of the reader to understand what the rule requires is dependent on whether that rule receives a common interpretation in a particular interpretative community.

So the application of rules such as the Principles, which require, for example, 'A firm should take reasonable steps to give a customer it advises, in a comprehensible and timely way, any information needed to enable him to make a balanced and informed decision',[65] may be less indeterminate and more certain than at first appears if the meaning of the terms 'comprehensible, timely, balanced, informed' is one which is shared by all those subject to them. The requirement is clear to that particular community; however those who are outside it might not share that interpretation. This difference of interpretation may not matter; it will do so, though, if those outsiders are to be involved in applying or enforcing that requirement. The community can then no longer rely on its own consensus as to the meaning of the rule being adopted. Certainty would thus be reduced. In order to ensure that certainty remains, those outside the interpretive community must be excluded from applying or enforcing the rules. One of the simplest ways to effect this exclusion is through the rule's status and the sanction attaching to it: to state that breach will give rise to sanctions only imposed by those within the community.[66]

Applying this to the particular context of financial services, by changing the sanction attaching to the rule from one of a civil action in the courts to disciplinary action imposed by the regulators (insiders), this effectively closed the regulatory system, eliminating the courts (outsiders) as potential interpreters of the rules. The closure was complete as far as the Principles are concerned. However, the exclusion of the right of action from those most likely to use it (professional investors), means in practice that the courts, unless called upon to do so in the exercise of their review jurisdiction, will not be involved in the application of the rules. The system is therefore effectively closed off from outside involvement in rule interpretation and application, enabling opaque rules to provide certainty in that particular interpretive community.

[65] Principle 5.

[66] The use of the sanction in this way is thus akin to the use of an ouster clause in excluding the jurisdiction of the courts.

The Core Rules

Whereas the rationales underlying the formation of the Principles were multidimensional, those for the Core Rules were more straightforward. The Core Rules were essentially a means of allowing SIB to set the central elements of the conduct of business rules, which SROs could then elaborate and adapt for their own particular areas. Achieving this aim posed more difficult issues of rule making, however, than the complex motivations for the Principles had posed for their formation. This was partly because there was no clear idea what a Core Rule should actually look like, and with what matters it should deal. If the Principles were to set out in relatively general terms the main principles of regulation, and third tier rules the detail, the Core Rules occupied an undefined middle ground. However, as we have seen, striking the 'right' balance between generality and detail in the Core Rules was of central importance: it was through them that the tensions between SIB and the SROs were to be resolved and the relative roles of the two sets of regulators defined.

The rules are the outcome of protracted negotiations between SIB and the SROs. The New Approach was followed by a bilateral working group of SFA and IMRO, the two SROs most concerned about the state of the initial rules. The Principles were drafted prior to the Core Rules, and the drafting process continued over a period of several months, meetings being chaired by SIB and attended by the legal staff of the all the SROs and SIB and the policy directors of SIB. Approval of the Board of SIB was necessary and was sought on a continuing basis, the Board making final decisions where the meetings had failed to reach a solution. On the basis of these negotiations, in August 1989 SIB produced a draft reworking of the New Approach in the form of Principles and designated rules, which was subject to the statutory consultation process.[67] Two subsequent drafts were produced in October and November 1990,[68] and the rules were published in January 1991.[69]

The hallmark of the drafting process was negotiation an compromise. In the words of one participant: 'decisions were made

[67] SIB, *Proposal.*

[68] SIB, *The Proposed Core Rules,* CP 42, Oct. 1990, and *The Proposed Core Rules: Derogations and other certain points,* CP 47, Nov. 1990.

[69] SIB, *The Core Conduct of Business Rules,* Jan. 1991.

very much on the basis of allowing a compromise here as there are many more issues which need to be dealt with and battles to fight in the future'. This applied to SIB as much as to the SROs. Although SIB was in the legal position of being able to impose its rules on the members of the SROs and controlled the ability for SROs to derogate from the rule, relations between SIB and the SROs were such that negotiation of the Core Rules was essential for the effective, continuing functioning of the regulatory system. Further, the fact that SIB and the SROs have an ongoing relationship in which SIB requires SRO co-operation on other matters such as monitoring, enforcement, and intervention was mentioned as an important factor in this negotiation process; in the words of one official, 'SIB had to consider this relationship as a whole'. Moreover, gaining agreement on the Core Rules was of prime importance given the rationale of the rules was their function as a 'common core', and that their introduction was meant to reduce, not increase, tensions between the two tiers.

The process of drafting was affected by several factors which had a direct impact on the structure of the rules. Politically important was the requirement for speed in their formation and publication, and the requirement of brevity: the overall message of the New Settlement was that the rules should be simple. SIB could not afford long and complex Core Rules. Also important was the requirement for durability: the frequent amendments to both the SIB and SRO rules had increased the uncertainty and complexity of the initial rules, and the New Settlement was a further regulatory change demanding the attention of firms. The Core Rules were meant to lend stability to the system, to provide a common core, a backbone of regulatory requirements. Frequent amendments would operate against the achievement of this aim. The rules also had to be relatively few in number if the message that SIB was 'standing back' from third tier rule making and that the Core Rules set only the 'essential elements' of the regulation was to be effectively conveyed. The initial number of fifty was chosen fairly arbitrarily, and subsequently reduced to forty.

As noted above, there was initially no clear idea in SIB or the SROs what the structure of a Core Rule should be. The structure, status, and substance of the rules were determined essentially by the function of the rules within the rule and regulatory system. They were meant to provide a 'common core' or 'backbone' to the rule system, containing the essential duties, which would apply to all members of the SROs. They were thus meant to provide coherence and central control of regulatory standards, whilst allowing the SROs room to write their own rule books.[70]

Their substance was determined by this statutorily defined status and scope of the rules. The decision as to the rules' substance, what matters the designated rules should deal with, was in part governed by an intuitive sense of what was felt by the drafters to be important, arrived at by induction from the old rule books and the principles in the New Approach rules which had not been used in the ten Principles, and whether the rule applied to all SROs. The more an issue had a single SRO focus, the less was the impetus to include it in the Core Rules. The third tier would be used for the particular application of the rule to the SRO's own section of the financial community.

There were other demands made upon the rules which arose from their position in the overall rule system. The concomitant of the position of the Core Rules as the 'common core', applying directly to SRO members, was that SROs wanted to ensure the Core Rule contained the seeds of the third tier requirements which they wished to include in their own rule books. In the words of one participant in the process: 'each SRO had a difference of emphasis that it thought should be in the Core Rule, but there were no cases where resolution was impossible'. Or as another put it more bluntly, 'there was a great deal of horse-trading going on'. Further, the Core Rules were to be the root of the third tier rules; they therefore had to be capable of incorporation into the third tier rules, unamended, and be structured in such a way that the third tier rules could flow easily from them. There were also inevitable differences between the SROs as to how their third tier rule would build on the Core Rule, differences which SIB felt the Core Rules had to accommodate. One participant commented that it was as if the draftsman was 'drafting in a hall of mirrors'.

Attitudes also differed as to what the drafting exercise should be aiming to achieve: should it simply be a recasting or codification of the old rules, or should it be a deregulatory exercise,

[70] It had been SIB's intention that they should apply also to RPBs; it was the Government's decision that they did not, and their exclusion from the application of the designated rules was described by Large as 'anomalous': A. Large, *Financial Services Regulation: Making the Two Tier System Work* (May 1993), para. 4.15(iv).

changing the substance as well as the structure of the rules? The rules were in fact used as vehicles to embody various policy decisions which had already been made in relation to the regulation of particular investment products,[71] and the categorization of customers was streamlined and the number of duties owed to professional customers reduced. There were also differences as to the standard the Core Rules should be setting: should they set the minimum standard on which SROs could build, or maximum standards? If they were to provide a minimum standard, negotiating agreement was far easier. Those SROs who wanted to impose a higher standard were free to do so in their own rules. A certain amount of self-interest on the part of those involved informed their approach to the issue of maximum or minimum standards. For SIB, for example, minimum standards were more in line with the philosophy of allowing practitioner input into the third tier; it also provided SIB with a defence to charges of overbearing rules and a justification for being very strict on permitting derogations. However, this was not favoured by those who wanted higher standards for their own members, and who wanted to be able to use the shield of the Core Rules to defend their position. Without this they would have to justify to their members why the Core Rule requirement was not sufficient.

The Structure of the Rules

These factors had a direct impact on the structure of the rules. They were to be short and as far as possible capable of application to changing circumstances and new situations without amendment, and to leave the detail to the third tier rules. The rules do not themselves contain lists of factors which must be considered or actions which must be taken. They are imprecise in that they do not indicate the manner in which, for example, disclosures are to be made or the periods at which notification of transactions or portfolio compositions must be given. Indeed, in one instance, conflict of interest, the corresponding Principle is more precise than the Core Rule.[72] Phrases such as 'due despatch' replaced complex definitions of 'business day' and details about the relevant

[71] PEPs and investment trusts, e.g., following the report of a review committee in Mar. 1990, *Regulation of the Marketing of Investment Services and Products*, and the control of appointed representatives: CR 13.

[72] Principle 6 and CR 2.

twenty-four hour period in the rule on confirmations, for example.[73] The rules on customer agreements,[74] contract notes,[75] customer order priority,[76] and timely allocation[77] provide the most striking contrasts with the initial rules, and were themselves made less specific over the successive drafts of the Core Rules. There are however, two distinct features of the Core Rules which illustrate the way the structure of the rule was used to accommodate the range of demands being made on them. These are the provision of derogations and the use of the glossary.

Derogations

The designation of the Core Rules as directly applicable to SRO members had been received by the SROs with a certain amount of hostility. Partly as a trade-off, and partly with the legitimate aim of enabling the necessary practitioner input to take effect, derogations from the Core Rules by the SRO rule books had been provided for in the amendments to the FSA 1986.[78] The statutory amendments made provision for the designated rules to specify the extent to which the rules would apply to a firm, subject to the rules of its SRO, and for the rules to prohibit any modification or waiver in respect of any member.[79]

Derogations were thus an attempt to resolve the tension between the roles of SIB and the SROs and they may be seen as a manifestation of that tension. The twin objectives of having a common core of rules and duties and of facilitating practitioner input into the regulation exerted contradictory pressures. The idea of a common core militated against derogations, as they have the potential to undermine this commonality, yet the demands for practitioner input required that the SROs have the ability to tailor the regulation to suit the market in which their members operate. The primary aim of the Core Rules was to be a harmonizing backbone of regulation, however, and SIB therefore felt that provision of derogations had to be controlled. In addition, SIB stated that part of the adequacy test would be consistency of a rule book with other SRO rules; that consistency might itself be undermined by extensive use of derogations.[80]

[73] CR 19(1). [74] CR 9(2). [75] CR 19. [76] CR 20.
[77] CR 23. [78] S. 47B and s. 63B, inserted by s. 194 CA 1989.
[79] S. 63A(2) and s. 63B, inserted by s. 194 CA 1989. [80] CP 39.

Initially the working rule was adopted that derogations should be conferred for any exception in an SRO rule book that could be traced to the current version of SIB's own rules. In addition, some use of derogations was required by the aim of brevity of the rules, and the desire to keep them at an 'intermediate level of generality'. 'To include . . . within the Core Rules themselves all the various exceptions that will be required in particular sectors . . . would over-complicate them.'[81] Some of the Core Rules contained exceptions within them in that they applied only to private investors or certain types of business. Further exceptions would be necessary with respect to different types of business, and for the sake of brevity and generality, and if SIB was to keep to its line that the New Settlement would hand 'the baton of adaptation and innovation in the third tier'[82] to the SROs, it had to leave the definition of these exceptions to them. Finally, derogations were also used where agreement could not be reached, as a form of compromise.

The form the derogations took altered during the course of drafting, as did their incidence. In the first two drafts where amplification was felt to be necessary, either as to the scope of the obligation or to the manner of complying with it, the Core Rule would state that the firm comply with 'rules made by' or 'requirements of' the firm's regulator.[83] The Core Rules thus in effect expressly delegated the function of defining the content of the rule to the SROs. So, for example, it was provided that:

> Where a firm has a material interest in the subject matter of a possible transaction, or a relationship which gives rise to a conflict of interests in relation to that transaction, it must not advise, or deal in the exercise of discretion, in relation to that transaction *unless it has observed such requirements as may be imposed by its regulator* in order to ensure fair treatment for all its customers.[84]

Amplification was also implicitly indicated by such words as 'adequate', 'relevant' or 'unfairly' or other terms requiring judgement.

[81] SIB, *Proposal*, para. 20.

[82] M. Blair, 'Regulation of the Conduct of Investment Business: SIB's Proposal' (Sept. 1989) *BJIBFL* 398.

[83] These express 'look through' provisions were provided in the rules on inducements, advertisements, risk warnings, stabilization, and client money contained in the Aug. 1989 draft and in CP 42, in draft rules 2 (soft commissions), 9 (off-the-page advertisements), 10 (information on packaged products), 13 (customer agreements), 15 (material interest), 30 (margined transactions), and 33 (reportable transactions).

[84] CP 42, draft rule 15 (emphasis added).

Third tier rules could then provide greater precision, or safe harbours.[85] The use of these express 'look through' provisions, or 'empty carriages' was however criticized on the basis that the rules containing them were not self standing. As one commentator put it, 'they were not so much rules as an indication of something to follow', as on their own the rules provided no indication of what conduct was necessary. Further, the question of *vires* and unlawful sub-delegation of rule making power was raised, in particular by the DTI, which was concerned about the legal ability of SIB to create a rule of that kind. The statutory rule making power had been given to make a rule, not effectively to delegate that power to the SROs. Finally, it was felt that derogations in that form would go against the objective of the endurability of the rules, and of SIB's control over the standards of behaviour required: the rule was effectively subject to any changes in the third tier rules.

These considerations led to the removing of the 'empty carriages'. This led in some instances to a specification of the duty or redefinition of the application of the rule,[86] in others to the inclusion of an implicit 'look through' provision.[87] In the final version, derogations from the rules were flagged by the phrase 'subject to exceptions of the SROs' and appear in only in six instances.[88] SROs could also specifically request derogations, and both IMRO and SFA did so. Some derogations were permitted because of the nature of business being done, the derogations in the case of corporate finance for example, or because they continued exceptions made

[85] SIB, Aug. 1989, paras. 15 and 16.

[86] See changes from CP 42, draft rules 2, 9, 13, and 30. E.g., the rule on off-the-page advertisements became more specific in that a further category of advertisements was identified, and part of the rule narrowed in its application to private investors: CR 5. The empty carriage in relation to customer agreements was replaced by a confinement of the rule to private customers only: CR 14.

[87] See changes from CP 42, draft rules 10 and 15. In relation to information on packaged products the requirement changed from 'written product particulars as prescribed by the firm's regulator' to 'appropriate written product particulars', CR 12(2) and similarly the empty carriage in relation to customer agreements was replaced by the confinement of the rule to private customers only, CR 14.

[88] CR 13: termination of contracts with appointed representatives; CR 16: suitability in relation to non-private customers; CR 18: disclosure of charges and remuneration; CR 19: confirmations and periodic information; CR 25: circumstances dealing ahead of publication should be allowed; CR 32: how customer investments should be safeguarded. There are two other instances of derogation which provide that the SRO may completely disregard the core rule (CR 33, reportable transactions, and CR 39, classes of customer).

in the SRO's previous rule books.[89] The derogations also allow different approaches of the SROs to be reflected in their rules. Differences in the rules of SFA and IMRO are principally ones of rule structure, with IMRO on the whole having more detailed rules, as discussed below. Some of the derogations relate to more fundamental issues, however, as they manifest a different answer to the question of which types of customer should receive which level of protection. They may therefore in practice undermine the common core by going against the regulatory philosophy underlying those rules. The following examples of the different treatment of market counterparties and indirect customers illustrate this point, and indicate the extent, or limit, to which the Core Rules created 'a common core'.

Market Counterparties

Because of the way the Core Rules are crafted, premised on a relationship between a firm and a customer, the narrower the definition of 'customer' the narrower the range of application of the rule. The Core Rule customer definition does not include persons who are market counterparties (MCPs) so the rules which will apply to them are the few of general application which do not mention the word customer.[90] The definition of customer and market counterparties were included very late in the drafting, and the latter are defined in the Core Rules as:

a person dealing with a firm:

> (a) as principal or as agent for an unidentified principal
> (b) in the course of investment business of the same description as that in the course of which the firm acts.[91]

The definition does not create a generic category: it applies on a transaction by transaction basis depending on the status of the

[89] SFA's definition of market counterparty, e.g., considered below.

[90] Those Core Rules applying to MCPs are: CR 5(1–3): issue and approval of advertisements; CR 9(1): fair and clear communication; CR 13: appointed representatives; CR 23: timely allocation; CR 28(1): insider dealing (own account transactions); CR 29: stabilization; CR 31: reportable transactions; CR 33: scope of business; CR 34: compliance; CR 35: complaints; CR 36: chinese walls; CR 38: reliance on others; CR 40: application of CCBRs.

[91] Core Rules, Glossary. Agents acting for identified principals are therefore customers.

person with whom the firm is dealing and the parity of the investment business being conducted.

SFA felt the transaction by transaction approach was impractical for its members, following representations that firms' systems could not be designed to accommodate the provisions, and so the rule was one with which they would find it very difficult to comply. Instead SFA wished to preserve its old generic Market Professional definitions with which its members were familiar and which had enabled them to operate under their own contractual terms with other members. SFA therefore sought a derogation to extend the range of the definition. SFA rule 5-4 provides that in relation to persons dealing in the course of investment business of the same description as that in the course of which the firm acts, that person may be a MCP.[92] SIB was not happy with SFA's provision, but because of the 'standing back' requirements felt it could do no more than require a compromise. SIB therefore insisted that for a person to be a MCP the firm must send to the person a written notice informing it that it is to be treated as a MCP without the benefits of protections afforded to customers, and that person has not notified the firm that it does not wish to be treated as a MCP.[93]

SFA rules further provide that a firm with private customers may permit itself to be treated as a MCP by another firm where it believes on reasonable grounds that those customers will be properly protected under the rules of SFA.[94] However, the Guidance stresses that a firm should take into account customer protections it will lose as a result of such treatment. Where a firm believes that it will be unable to fulfil the duties and obligations owed to its private customers under the rules of SFA, it should not permit itself to be treated as a MCP.[95]

SIB was also reluctant to permit this derogation. Its main concern was that an SFA member would no longer be owed duties by other SFA members which would be owed to it if it were a customer: those relating to execution of orders[96] and those requiring

[92] SFA r. 5-4 also applies to: trading members of investment exchanges for investments/derivatives traded on that exchange; inter-dealer brokers when acting in that capacity; and in relation to debt and money market investments, a country, central bank, international organization of countries and listed money market institutions.

[93] Either generally or in relation to particular kinds of investments.

[94] SFA r. 5-4(4).

[95] SFA r. 5-4 Guidance 3.

[96] Core Rules 19–24.

fair treatment in one form or another.[97] Nor would the other SFA firm owe any duties to the MCP's customers where it might otherwise do so. SIB stressed, therefore, that in forming the reasonable belief about its ability to fulfil all the duties owed to its private customers the firm would have to have regard to the extent to which it was reliant on others for the fulfilment of its obligations to its customers. For example, the timeliness and quality of execution of deals done for it, or when obtaining advice from another member firm what material interests or benefits to that firm may exist that are not disclosed.[98] These concerns were not shared by SFA, who were of the view that other SFA member firms should be sufficiently experienced to realize the potential for soft commission agreements, conflicts, and other potential abuses which were not being disclosed and dictate their own terms of business. In fact under the present Core Rules MCPs are owed more duties than they were under the old system.[99]

Indirect Customers

The notion of indirect customers (IDCs) came from the old TSA rule book and was not contained in the initial SIB rules.[100] The Glossary definition provides that an indirect customer means:

> where a customer is known to be acting as agent, an identified principal who would be a customer if he were dealt with direct.

The definition is wider than the old TSA rule in three respects: it applies to all intermediaries not just those engaged in another profession such as banks and solicitors, to all duties, and there is no mention of being able to limit the application of the duties owed in the contract between the intermediary and the member firm. So where an SFA firm deals with an RPB member (for example)

[97] Core Rules 1–3, 25, 26, 32, and 35.

[98] SIB, *Core Conduct of Business Rules: Commencement for Members of SFA*, CP 55, Dec. 1991, paras. 8–12.

[99] CR 9(1): fair and clear communication and CR 23: timely allocation.

[100] TSA r. 140.01 provided that where a bank or similar institution, or a professional lawyer, accountant or actuary acted as intermediary for a private customer, then certain specified rules would apply in the firm's dealing with the intermediary as if the client were a direct private customer of the firm, including the duties of best execution, know your customer, suitability, material interests, self-dealing and dual agency, and churning. These could all, however, be varied or excluded in the customer documentation with the intermediary: TSA r. 150.1.

who is acting for an identified individual,[101] under the Core Rules the SFA firm had to act as if the RPB's customer is its own, which is of significance principally where that customer is a private customer. The SFA firm therefore had to comply with, for example, the best execution rule where this may otherwise have been disapplied in relation to non-private customers. The definition interacts with that of market counterparty. If an agent is acting for an unidentified principal, then the agent is a market counterparty. If the agent is acting for an identified principal, then the agent is a customer not a MCP, and his or her principal is also a customer of the firm, though there is no contract between them.

SIB's rationale for the concept was that duties should flow through to the principal: the broker and fund manager must comply with the rules relating to private customers when dealing between themselves not for any protections it may provide them, but for the protection of the ultimate investor.[102] IMRO and SFA felt that it should be the firm nearest the customer which should owe the duties (SFA members cannot ensure that the suitability rule, for example, has been complied with by the RPB firm), and both IMRO and SFA amended the Core Rule definition of 'indirect customer'. IMRO provided that a member may treat an agent of the IDC as its customer where the agent is reasonably believed to be an authorized person in respect of the investment services concerned, which would cover other IMRO members.[103] SFA achieved the same effect through its market counterparty definition: SFA member firms are not customers of one another and so indirect customers cannot arise (the agent has to be a customer of the firm for the purposes of the IDC definition).[104] SFA went further and provided that the IDC relationship can be contracted out of in whole or in part by the agent and the firm, again to preserve continuity in substance between their old rule book and the third tier rules. The SROs' approach and concerns thus differed from SIB's, and through the provision of a derogation these differences were allowed to take effect.

[101] i.e., a private customer. What constitutes identification has been the source of some difficulty.

[102] CP 55, para. 15.

[103] Also where the agent does not conduct business in the UK, or the agent has refused to answer enquiries about his principal, IMRO II-2.1(4).

[104] SFA firms have to be reasonably satisfied that they can fulfil the obligations to private customers before accepting market counterparty status.

Glossary

The requirements for brevity and durability of the Core Rules led to extensive reliance being placed by the draftsman on the Glossary. It was anticipated when drafting the rules that various changes would have to be made, and so to ensure that they would be the object of minimum amendment the rules were drafted in such a way that any alterations of scope or application could be made in the Glossary. The Glossary is a drafting technique, described by one senior participant as a 'sleight of hand', which removes the complexity of the rule from its face into an appendix and belies the comparatively simple and imprecise appearance of the Core Rules.

The Core Rules make quite extensive use of what may be termed 'artificial' concepts, or terms which have no commonly understood or particular meaning outside of the rules, to refer to a host of factors and situations which are then defined in the Glossary. The Glossary consequently contains many of the more complex elements of the rules. For example, the rules relating to the retail sector are defined in their application by the phrases 'packaged products' and 'extended group'. These phrases are used in the rules, and then defined in the Glossary. The phrase 'extended group' is defined as 'members of a group of undertakings and the marketing group associates of any of them'. A group of undertakings is defined with reference to the 1986 Act,[105] which itself refers to the Companies Act 1985.[106] This cross-referencing back to a recognized relationship elsewhere in company law replaced the notion of a connected firm which was defined by a complex description of arrangements of relationships between companies.[107]

The Glossary posed a number of advantages for the draftsman, as well as enabling the Core Rules to remain brief and apparently simple. For example, the use of the concept of 'extended group' enabled the manipulation of the idea in a way which produced a more sophisticated result. The Glossary could also be used to

[105] Financial Services Act 1986, Sch. 1, para. 30.

[106] Companies Act 1985, Sch. 4, para. 92.

[107] A further example is the use of the term 'marketing group', which again is defined in the glossary, and facilitates the exception from the 'better than best' rule for investment management which was introduced in the final rule, mirroring the position in TSA's old rule book: CR 17(4). Both definitions also look now more to the substance of the relationship than its form.

correct mistakes made in the drafting of the Core Rule which would otherwise be complicated to rectify. For example, the best execution rule refers to an 'order from a non-private customer'.[108] In the Glossary 'order, in relation to a customer' is defined as an order which causes the firm to act as agent, or a decision by the firm in the exercise of discretion for the customer. The definition arose as a result of a failing in the drafting process. The term 'customer' was not defined until towards the end of the process. When the rules were viewed as a whole it became apparent that the definition of customer meant that the best execution rule applied to all customers, including professionals, a substantial widening of the 1987 requirement and contrary to the deregulatory philosophy which in part underlay the new rules. Inserting the occasions when the rule would have applied would have made it unacceptably long. Here the political demand for brevity informed the decision: the rule had dramatically increased in length by the final draft already.[109] Moreover, altering the definition of 'customer' would have affected other rules where the limitation was not appropriate. So the definition of 'order' was used as the vehicle for the restriction of the application of the rule, limiting its application to where the firm is in a fiduciary relationship with the customer.[110] Without referring to the Glossary this cannot be gleaned from the rule, but for the draftsman the definition could be altered independently from the text of the rule, and the rule is simply (if not, on its face at least, clearly) stated.

The Glossary was also used to provide exceptions or 'safe harbours' to rules, exceptions which are again not apparent on the face of the rule. For example, Core Rule 1 (Inducements) states that a firm must take reasonable steps to ensure that neither it nor any of its agents offers, gives, solicits or accepts an inducement which is likely to conflict significantly with any duties owed by the recipient to customers. 'Inducement' is defined in a negative or residual sense in the Glossary, as not including 'disclosable commission' or 'goods or services which can reasonably be expected to assist in the provision of investment services to customers'

[108] CR 22. [109] See Ch. 6.

[110] The term is also used in CR 20: customer order priority, also applying to own account orders; CR 21: timely execution; and CR 22: best execution in relation to non-private customers. All private customers, fiduciary or otherwise, must receive best execution.

and which are provided under a soft commission agreement: so providing a safe harbour from the rule. The same technique is used in Core Rule 2 (material interest). The rule states that where a firm has a material interest in a transaction for or with a customer which gives rise to a conflict of interest then it may not advise or deal without taking reasonable steps to ensure fair treatment for the customer. The Glossary definition on material interest is again a residual one: not including 'disclosable commission on the transaction', and goods under a soft commission agreement, as above, again creating a safe harbour for disclosable commission payments and soft commission agreements. This is bolstered by paragraph 2 of the Glossary which provides that '[n]either a soft commission agreement nor an arrangement for the payment of disclosable commission' for the purposes of Core Rule 2 is to be taken as creating a conflict of interest in relation to transactions under the arrangement.[111]

The Glossary thus provided a number of advantages for the drafter. Does it add to the comprehensibility of the rules, though? Some argue that it does not. This is partly because words are given definitions which are other than their normal market usage: 'customer', 'order', and 'own account' are some examples. This can make the rules misleading to read, and led to some SROs dealing with the problem typographically, highlighting the terms to indicate to people that the words do not have their ordinary meaning. Others comment that the Glossary may have been a neat legalistic drafting trick, a 'sleight of hand', but has not helped market practitioners in the least. On the contrary, it has made it far more confusing for them, and rendered the rules much less clear.

The Third Tier Rules

The third tier rules are the rules written by the SROs which were meant to flow from the designated or Core Rules, and cover matters relevant to their particular market areas which were not covered in the Core Rule, or covered only in a general manner. They were billed as the opportunity for practitioner input to find its way into the regulation in a way which, it was argued, it had been unable to do under the old equivalency structure. The designation of Core

[111] For a full discussion of the soft commission provisions, see Ch. 6.

Rules obviously limited the scope for practitioner input, but SROs differed in the extent to which they felt the Core Rules limited their ability to draft the rules they want in the way they want. In some areas very little limitation was felt: this may be because developments which had been made in their own initial rule books were carried up into the Core Rules.[112] Another reason may be that the provision of derogations within the rules marked instances where the Core Rules responded to the SROs' need for flexibility in their application,[113] and the requests for extra derogations provide an indication of those areas where constraint was still felt to be too great.[114] Other restrictions appear to have been due more to the style rather than the substance of the Core Rules.[115] SIB was nonetheless closely involved in the formation of the third tier rules to ensure that they conformed to the Core Rules, a degree of involvement which led some to question the extent to which this aspect of the New Settlement was in fact an illusion.[116] Certainly dedesignation of the Core Rules did not prompt wholesale revision of the rules; however the rule books have already consumed a significant amount of regulatory time and further radical changes were unwelcome for both regulator and regulated.

Derogations aside, the third tier rules can be categorized as

[112] e.g., Lautro felt that its categorization of advertisements was adopted by the Core Rules; the same occurred in relation to SFA's approach to the best execution duty. Interviews, May 1992.

[113] The inbuilt derogations, 'subject to the rules of the SRO', which occur in six of the core rules were all used by SFA (though once to extend the application of the rule: the suitability rule is extended to apply to all discretionary customers); IMRO has made use of five.

[114] Specific derogations have been sought by, and granted to, SFA on the definitions of indirect customer and market counterparty, above: SIB, CP 55, Dec. 1991. IMRO requested, but was refused, derogations on disclosure requirements in soft commissions and advertising. The former as the exception would go against the objective of the rule, the latter because a derogation would be contrary to the EC Misleading Advertisements Directive: SIB, *Core Conduct of Business Rules: Commencement for Members of IMRO*, CP 54, Aug. 1991.

[115] IMRO did not amend the text of the Core Rules, but both SFA and Fimbra (even though designation never occurred with respect to Fimbra) felt a need to do this. This was either, in the case of SFA, because amendment facilitated a logical reading of the following third tier rule, or, in the case of Fimbra, because there was a feeling that the language of the Core Rule would not be easily understood by its members. Fimbra's alterations were principally to put the rule into the second rather than the third person: 'you must' rather than 'a firm must', to give a more immediate and direct impact to the rule which Fimbra felt would improve the rule's communication to its members.

[116] See comments by Large, Large Report, para. 1.23.

performing five main functions: detailing, clarifying, expanding, gap-filling, and limiting, including defining the application of the rule. The role of the third tier as detailing the requirements of the Core Rule is that which fits most obviously with the idea of the hierarchy of generality of the Principles, Core Rules, and third tier rules. The third tier rules also expand, or impose more duties on members than required by the Core Rules, and fill gaps in the coverage of the Core Rules. Finally, the third tier rules limit the application of the Core Rules, either by requiring application of only some of the Rules to certain types of business, restricting the application of a particular rule, or providing safe havens or exclusions from the rule, but without using the derogation provisions.[117]

The Role of Guidance

Both IMRO and SFA make a fairly extensive use of Guidance in their rules. Indeed, as saw above, IMRO have simply moved substantial parts of their original rules into form of guidance: flexibility is conferred on detailed rules by changing their status from rules to guidance. The use of guidance is a direct result of the contradictory demands of certainty and flexibility. As one official explained: 'there is a tension in the desires of members—they want vague, general rules like the Principles and detest the detailed rule books, but they also want certainty and detailed information of what is expected of them. Guidance is an attempt to resolve this tension.' Guidance thus indicates what type of conduct will be accepted as compliance, but removes the irritant of prescription.[118]

The status of the guidance is set out in CR 38: a person is taken to act in conformity with a rule to the extent that formal guidance has been issued by SIB or an SRO on compliance with that rule,[119] and relying on those standards, the person believes on reasonable grounds that he is acting in conformity with the rule. IMRO has

[117] This has been done by SFA, e.g., in relation to reliance on others and independence policies: the former permits wider reliance on others than the Core Rule; the latter provides that an independence policy will satisfy the material interest rule requirements: CR 39, SFA r. 5-2; CR 2, SFA r. 5-29.

[118] However, although the status of guidance reduces the level of detailed conduct prescribed by rules, in the realities of day-to-day business operation it is likely that the difference between conduct which is prescribed and that which is recommended is merely semantic.

[119] Defined as written communication intended to have general and continuing effect, Core Rule Glossary.

added that any conduct which differs from that described in such guidance shall not raise or be construed as raising any presumption of a breach of any rule.

Although guidance is used in both rule books, it is of a different nature and used to a different extent. IMRO use guidance on roughly fifty-five occasions, SFA only seventeen.[120] The function of guidance in both rule books is similar. Both SROs use guidance to explain the application of a rule and indicate methods of compliance, for example by indicating what would be considered to be reasonable grounds or reasonable steps, or what information should be given. It is also used to stipulate conditions or standards that *must* be met,[121] limit the application of a rule, to explain the application of a rule, and on occasion clarify doubts as to the meaning of the Core Rule.

Both SROs also issue formal guidance through periodic bulletins. Formal guidance is defined as guidance which is general, written, and intended to have continuing effect. The role of the bulletins is seen as drawing members' attention to a problem the regulators have discovered, or giving notice of the SRO's view on matters which may have been referred to it through enquiries or arisen in the course of the enforcement process. Informal guidance, interpretations given to a particular firm for example over the telephone or in the course of a monitoring visit in relation to a particular matter, are not regarded as binding by the SROs (although the common law position may differ from their conception of the position in this case).[122]

Third Tier Rule Books Compared

SFA and IMRO have taken a notably different approach to the nature of their rule books. SFA have been content not to elaborate

[120] Excluding in both cases guidance which refers to the application of transitional rules.

[121] The Guidance of both rule books can take a more commanding tone: the IMRO Guidance to periodic disclosures stipulates that they *should* include certain information (IMRO II-1.7(4)), e.g., and the contents for policy statements for soft commissions are stipulated in the guidance of both rule books: SFA r. 5-8(3); IMRO II-1.7(3).

[122] See *R* v. *Inland Revenue Commissioners, ex p. MFK Underwriting Agents Ltd* [1990] 1 WLR 1545; for a discussion of the bindingness of representations made by public bodies see P. P. Craig, *Administrative Law* (London, 1994), Ch. 18.

the Core Rules on more occasions than IMRO: SFA have left thirteen Core Rules entirely without third tier elaboration or expansion,[123] and have not included any third tier support for parts of seven Core Rules.[124] They have amended the text of the Core Rule instead of writing a third tier rule in the case of two Core Rules,[125] and in relation to two others have issued short guidance only.[126] The overall size of the SFA rule book has shrunk (a phenomenon enhanced by the judicious reduction to A5 paper, also used by the Stock Exchange Yellow Book and the Code of Takeovers and Mergers): just under fifty rules were deleted in the revision, either because of policy changes, for example in customer categorization or *vis-à-vis* customer agreements, or because the requirement is now covered in a broader Core Rule: for example the timing of disclosure, product bias, and volume overriders. A further twenty-three rules are now mirrored in the Core Rules, and eighteen further rules have been combined into Core Rule requirements.[127] Dealing rules are on the whole less detailed and prescriptive, for example the rules on timely execution, timing of contract notes, and the best execution rule (deletion of definitions of best execution investment and illiquid investment). Rules relating to customer documentation have been relieved by the deletion of model customer agreements from the new rules, and the non-extension of the Core Rule provision that customer agreements need only be

[123] These are (SFA rule number shown in brackets): CR 1: inducements (5-7); CR 4: polarization (5-19); CR 6: issue or approval of advertisements for an overseas person (5-12); CR 7: overseas business for UK private customers (5-13); CR 8: business conducted from an overseas place of business for overseas customers (5-14); CR 15: customers' rights (5-24); CR 20: customer order priority (5-37); CR 21: timely execution (5-40); CR 24: fair allocation (5-42); CR 26: churning and switching (5-43); CR 27: derivatives transactions to be on exchange (5-44); CR 28: insider dealing (5-46); CR 30: off-exchange market makers (5-45).

[124] It has issued no third tier for the following parts of Core Rules: 11(1): information about the firm (5-16); 13(1), (3), & (4): appointed representatives; 18(1): unreasonable charges (5-33(1)); 35(2): co-operation in investigation of complaints (6-3); 36(1), & (3), & (4): chinese walls; 37(1): cessation of authorized business (2-21); 38(3): reliance on others—communication sent to the order of the customer (5-2(3)).

[125] CR 9: fair and clear communications (SFA r. 5-15); CR 36(2): Chinese Walls (established and effective arrangement).

[126] CR 11(2): information about the firm (SFA r. 5-21) and CR 22: best execution (SFA r. 5-39).

[127] Figures derived from an analysis of the changes contained in TSA Board Notice 220, 1.10.90 and further analysis of the changes between the 1990 draft and the 1991 rules.

concluded with private customers (in contrast to the IMRO provisions). Other customer documentation rules mainly repeat the requirements of the TSA 1988 rules, and the provisions as to the contents of contract notes, periodic valuations, advertisements are similar to the TSA 1988 rules.

IMRO has not expanded on the whole of five Core Rules,[128] nor on parts of eight.[129] IMRO has not always followed the change of policy of SIB and SFA: for example it has not followed the policy of using best price as the principal indicator of best execution, but has included its old Commentary into the new rule book in the form of guidance which places more emphasis on the terms of the transaction than SFA's rule.[130] It still requires customer documentation with both private and non-private customers, specifying in full and in rule form the expected contents. It has retained its previous format of different tiers of agreement: the full customer agreement which must be concluded with private investors, with additional contents for discretionary customers, terms of business letters and statements of protection, which replace the occasional customer agreement. Where SFA has included no further expansion of a Core Rule, IMRO has on occasion used detailed guidance, for example in the rules on customer order priority.[131]

IMRO has in fact retained much of its old rule book either in the form of rules or guidance. The rules on timely allocation are taken from the old rule book,[132] and other rules which mirror the requirements of the 1988 Rules include dealing ahead of published research or analysis,[133] periodic information,[134] and contract

[128] These are (IMRO 1991 rule numbers in brackets): CR 7: advertising: overseas business for UK private customers (II-1.8(1)); CR 8: advertising: business conducted from an overseas place of business with overseas customers (II-1.9(1)); CR 15: customer's rights (II-2.5(1)); CR 27: derivatives transactions to be on exchange (II-3.13(1)); CR 28: insider dealing (II-3.14(1)).

[129] These are CR 4.2: polarization status (II-6.1(2)); CR 4.4: polarization: investment managers (II-6.1(2)); CR 16.2: suitability: pooled funds (II-3.1(2)); CR 17.1.b: standards of advice on packaged products: independent intermediaries (II-6.3(2)); CR 17.3: independent intermediaries: best advice (II-6.3(2)); CR 17.5: independent intermediaries not acting as investment managers (II-6.3(2)); CR 17.6: standards of advice: PEPs (II-6.3(2)); CR 40.3: application of Core Conduct of Business rules as to Time (I-3.2(2)).

[130] CR 22; IMRO II-3.8; SFA r. 5-39.

[131] CR 20; IMRO II-3.6(1); SFA r. 5-37.

[132] IMRO II-3.9; IMRO 1988 IV-12.01.

[133] IMRO 1988 IV-11.04 is transposed into IMRO II-3.12.

[134] Contents of the table to IMRO II-4.5(5) taken largely verbatim from IMRO 1988 IV-21.03A.

notes.[135] Elsewhere, provisions of the 1988 Rules have been incorporated into guidance. This is the case, for example, in the rules on fair allocation,[136] churning,[137] and information about the firm.[138] IMRO is also more concerned to detail the meaning of broad terms than SFA: for example IMRO detail the meaning of 'due despatch' in relation to sending contract notes, whereas SFA does not.[139]

The natural consequence of, indeed the rationale for having, different regulators for different market areas is that each may have a slightly different approach to regulation. The trade-off is between tailored regulation and consistency between the rule books. Whilst some substantive differences between the SFA and IMRO rule books do not appear to be based in fundamentally different attitudes to regulation, for example the advertising rules of each, they do adopt differing attitudes concerning the level of protection different customers should be afforded. The differences between their and SIB's treatment of market counterparties and indirect customers has been discussed above. The other principal difference in their treatment of customers relates to discretionary business customers. Generally speaking the TSA/SFA rules provide more protections to discretionary non-private customers than the IMRO rules.

In comparing the nature of the rules in the two rule books, can it be said that SFA has moved further away from detail and prescription of 'how and when' than IMRO? In the Introduction to the final consultative draft of the rules,[140] SFA stated that 'the rules have been revised with the intention of minimising the current detailed prescriptive requirements and introducing a greater element of flexibility into the regulatory structure'. On the face of the rule books, this appears to be the case. Certainly in relation to those rules which apply to non-private customers SFA felt that the removal of the right of action from these customers gave it a much greater freedom to write rules with a less precise and more

[135] The contents of IMRO II-App. 4.4(1) are largely verbatim those of IMRO 1988 IV-18.07 and 18.08.

[136] Guidance to IMRO II-3.10.1 taken from IMRO 1988 IV-12.02.

[137] The guidance to IMRO II-3.11 is the contents of IMRO 1988 IV-8.01.

[138] Guidance to IMRO II-4.2(1) contains contents of IMRO 1988 IV-16.04.

[139] IMRO II-App. 4.4(1), Part II; SFA r. 5-34(1).

[140] SFA Board Notice 2, Part 2 (15 Apr. 1991).

opaque structure, relying on the Principles to act as a safety net to catch actions the rule might not. It is likely, however, that the general prescriptions will be rendered more specific by informal guidance, which is likely to form patterns of expected behaviour and conduct. SFA implicitly indicate this:

> Since the rules are, in general, less prescriptive than their predecessors, it will be important for members to liaise closely with SFA, especially in the early stages, on the practical implications of particular rules. SFA has put in place internal arrangements which, while not bureaucratic, are designed to ensure the maximum level of consistency in interpretations and informal guidance given by staff.[141]

Interpretations of the more general requirements are also likely to be based on the provisions of the old TSA rule book. Precision and complexity, it would seem, are difficult aspects of rules to eliminate.

The Large Report: Changes in the Uses of Rules

The rules introduced as part of the New Settlement, both by SIB and by the SROs, are still in place. Their role as definers of the regulators' relationships has however been replaced by non-rule based mechanisms. In July 1992 Andrew Large was commissioned to report to the Chancellor addressing the question of the reltionship between SIB and the recognized bodies.[142] The report outlined the principle criticisms levelled at the regulatory system by regulatory bodies, firms, and consumers. These indicated a fundamental concern that the structure of financial services regulation, including the rule books, had developed without a sense of overall purpose, that the objectives of the Act were ill-defined, that the regulators had focused too much on rules and not enough on establishing broader objectives, and that SIB's role and purpose were unclear. In particular, SIB was perceived to be a creator of rules, and it was felt this role should be reduced to that of a standard setting body, and that SIB should focus more on the role of supervising the regulatory system as a whole.[143]

141 SFA Briefing 2, at 3 (SFA, Mar. 1992).

142 Large Report.

143 Ibid., para. 1.3.

The report noted that although the New Settlement was 'welcomed as a relief to all concerned', in practice it had worked out differently from the way which had been intended, both because of failures in the regulatory bodies and because SIB had not 'stood back' from third tier rule making to the extent that many had hoped. More fundamentally, SIB's relationship with the recognized bodies was still undefined, and in important respects was contradictory, requiring at once close involvement with those bodies and yet also the maintainenance of a distance and objectivity from them. On the one hand SIB had tried to see the recognized bodies as 'partners in the overall system for investor protection' in terms of both policy and enforcement, and with respect, for example, of EC negotiations and implementation worked closely with them. On the other, SIB had to judge the performance of recognized bodies, take up complaints against them, monitor and supervise them.[144]

Large concluded that SIB needed to act more clearly as the guardian of the public interest in the regulatory system, and so had to be more willing, and better able, to exercise leadership with respect to its workings. Specifically, there needed to be a more explicit commitment to the objective of investor protection and concern with the cost implications of regulation, a much greater transparency about the system, its objectives, standards, performance, and ways of working, a switch in emphasis by SIB from rules and policy to supervision with a greater focus on enforcement and a clear retreat by SIB from direct regulation, a more systematic and active supervisory relationship between SIB and recognized bodies, an emphasis by SIB on setting the standards for recognized bodies and firms, and the devising of performance measures to enable the performance of the system to be evaluated.[145]

In implementing these proposals, Large recommended that SIB should set out a clearer statement of the objectives of the regulatory system, which it did in November 1993, and require each recognized body to do the same. In order to define more clearly its relationship with those bodies, SIB would shift its focus to assessing their performance. To this end it would set standards of regulation and of investor protection which would enable recognized bodies to know what was expected of them, to enable SIB to hold

[144] Ibid., paras. 1.31, 1.37–1.39.

[145] Ibid., para. 1.64.

them to account for their performance, to let firms know what was expected of them, and inform investors and others of what was expected of recognized bodies and firms.[146] By developing standards for the regulation of recognized bodies, SIB aimed 'to put flesh on the bones' of the recognition requirements set out in the Act, by making clear, for example, SIB's view of what constitutes the essential components of 'adequate' and 'effective' arrangements in various operational areas such as admissions, monitoring, investigation, intervention, enforcement, and complaints handling.[147] Standards of investor protection, in contrast, would be directed at the standards to be expected in the delivery of investor protection by firms and in the markets. These would identify the hazards and set out the extent to which the system was intended to eliminate them or reduce their incidence.[148] Both sets of standards, of regulation and investor protection would be accompanied by performance measures, which would attempt to provide an objective basis for assessing compliance with what would still be subjective standards ('integrity', 'suitability'). These would be 'outputs' of the system, 'activity indicators, or concrete events', quantitative assessments in other words, monitoring, for example, patterns of disciplinary activity, the frequency with which firms were visited, complaint-handling times, and with respect to investor protection, lapse rates of insurance policies, incidence of defaults resulting in a loss of investor money, and the incidence of unsuitable advice.[149]

The report thus tried, again, to define SIB's role in the regulatory system, but this time through techniques other than rules, techniques which are more management-orientated, involving statements of aims and objectives, identification of 'action points', the internal management reorganization of SIB, the production of a management and budget plan, and the design and implementation of quantifiable performance targets.[150] There is thus a move away from using rules to achieve this role definition. Indeed their replacement by other techniques is clearly evidenced in the de-designation of the Core Rules in December 1994.[151] In essence,

[146] Ibid., Ch. 3. [147] Ibid., para. 3.10; SIB, *Annual Report 1994–5*, 13–14.
[148] Large Report, para. 3.12. [149] Ibid., paras. 3.15–3.18.
[150] First published in 1995: SIB, *Management Plan and Budget Plan 1996–7*.
[151] Along with the client money rules, with certain exceptions, and the financial supervision rules. In particular, those rules relating to the approval of advertisements

dedesignation is an indication that the Core Rules had achieved the very particular purposes which underlay them. The SROs had adopted them into their rule books, so dedesignation would have little impact on their rules (as indeed it has not). Their function of enabling SIB to identify itself as a central regulator and to set a common core had been achieved; further redefinition of SIB's role as system leader could now be continued through other means, and SIB's focus switched from rule making to enforcement and supervision. The Core Rules would not be revoked and SIB would retain the power to designate rules where an SRO was unwilling to put in place a rule which SIB believed to be necessary to achieve the requisite standard of investor protection. This would be strictly a reserve power, however. SIB would monitor the provisions of the rule books rather through an emphasis on ensuring that the stated standards of investor protection were being met, that SIB was consulted on rule changes, and that the SROs paid attention to the need to ensure coherence between their own rules and those of other SROs.[152]

Correspondingly, SIB's involvement in rule making would occur within this redefined relationship, rather than itself trying to execute that redefinition. SIB would only be involved in rule making and policy making where the recognized body lacked the resources necessary to form policy, where the issue crossed regulatory boundaries,[153] or where 'the importance of a subject for the system as a whole warrants SIB taking the lead, in the interests of securing adequate standards and promoting consistency among front line regulators'.[154]

promoting unregulated collective investment schemes, Chinese Walls, the trust status of client money arrangements remain designated (and their designation with respect to PIA commenced), because they create or allow arrangements which are enabled by statute, and so which the SROs would not be able to implement, namely Chinese Walls (s. 48(2)(h), CR 36) and the client money trust (s. 55(2)(a)), or are adjuncts to the statutory regulation (advertising, s. 76, CR 5(3)). Rules defining client money, the scope of the regulations and provisions as to interest payment also remain designated in order to preserve consistency across the regulators. SIB, *Dedesignation of the Core Conduct of Business Rules, The Client Money Rules and the Financial Supervision Rules*, CP 83, Aug. 1994.

152 Additionally, that the requirements of EC law were met: CP 83, para. 6.

153 Large Report, paras. 6.9–6.10.

154 SIB, *Management and Budget Plan 1996–7*, para. 26.

Conclusion

A range of factors, institutional, political, historical interacted to produce the highly detailed and complex rule books which emerged in 1987; the New Settlement by contrast was a conscious and tactical rule making exercise and the choice of rule type was a significant part of the policy decisions made by financial services regulators. Rules have been used to induce compliance, to affect the degree of control exerted, and to resolve the tension between certainty and flexibility. Underlying this use of rules have been deeper objectives which go beyond the substantive goals that one would expect of investor protection, market efficiency, and international competitiveness. Rules have been used in an attempt to gain legitimacy for the regulation; to gain the acceptance of the regulatory and political community. Rule type has been in a reflexive relationship with the function of the rule making body. It has defined, and been defined by, the position of that agency in the institutional structure. Rules have thus been used as signals, to influence conduct, alter perceptions, and communicate expectations. In concluding this analysis, two principal themes in the use of rules can be identified. The first is the interaction of rules within a regulatory system, the combination of different types of rules and the construction of a tiered rule system; the second is the change in the uses which have been made of rules.

As we have seen, one of the principal criticisms of the initial SIB rule book was its detail and complexity. The rules of the SROs, partly due to the operation of the equivalency requirement, also exhibited similar levels of detail. The level of detail was in part caused by a host of factors to which the regulators, in particular SIB, had to respond, and in part by SIB's own approach. That detailed rules were the best way to control behaviour, as we have seen in the previous section, was the approach taken by most involved in the formation of the initial rules: the DTI insisted on detail to control SIB, SIB did the same in an attempt to control both the regulated and the SROs. Detailed rules were seen to confine and structure the discretion that those subject to the rule had in its interpretation more effectively than any other type. The regulator thus attempted through specificity and precision to control the behaviour of the regulated. Detailed rules are, to an extent, a sign of distrust. In deciding on the structure of rule to adopt, rule makers consider the extent to which they feel they can rely on the person applying the rule to act to further the rule's purpose.

One of the great claims made of the New Settlement and of the redrafting of the rules was that this detail had been reduced. In fact, the amount of detail you see depends on where you look. The vagueness of the Principles does not on the whole indicate indeterminacy of purpose (although there are some exceptions) and they are deliberately drafted requirements. The apparent simplicity of the Core Rules is denied by the Glossary, in which the specification and complexities are contained, and the third tier rule books are still a detailed set of rules, although that of SFA is in particular a rationalization of the pre-New Settlement provisions.

The point about the post-New Settlement rules is not simply whether the level of detail has increased or decreased, however. It is how rules have been used. Significant changes have in fact been made in the uses of rules, both in addressing the relatively technical problem of how best to design a rule system to ameliorate the inherent limitations of rules, and in attempts to achieve goals which are specific to the regulatory system. With respect to the former, the dimensional analysis enables us to see more clearly how rules of different types have been combined within the rule system as a whole. This combination of rule types within the tiered system represents an alternative answer to the pervasive question of how to achieve certainty and flexibility. The initial answer to the problem of certainty was greater precision: to try to specify every possible event in which the rule would apply and cater for it. In the three tier rule system, this attempt was abandoned and instead the aim was to use the Principles as the 'safety net' for future eventualities; to cope with uncertainty through generality. The vaguer, less complex structure of the Principles is not used in isolation, however, but in combination with the dimension of status and sanction, which we have seen has been used to create an interpretive community by 'closing off' the Principles and confer a monopoly of enforcement and application on the regulators, and with the greater specification and complexity of the third tier rules (which now incorporate the Core Rules). Within the third tier rules, status and sanction has also been used in combination with precision, this time to confer flexibility to detailed provisions by transforming them into guidance. Indeed, as we have seen,

IMRO have simply moved substantial parts of their pre-New Settlement rules into the form of guidance without any, or only minimal, changes in their requirements.

The formation of the Principles and the attitude which accompanied them that more general, purposive rules could be more effective techniques of regulation indicates a shift away from detail towards general rules, in one part of the rule system at least. Such a swing from formalistic rules to purposive ones has been identified in other areas of regulation, notably accountancy. There McBarnet and Whelan have identified cycles of formalism, in which there is a shift from detail to generality, but then the trend is reversed and there is a move back again to detail.[155] The pattern observed in financial services regulations differs from this in one important respect: there has never really been a shift away from detail. Detailed rules have remained a central aspect of the rules to which firms are subject; they are simply contained in the third tier rules rather than those of SIB. There has thus been no cycle of formalism as there has never really been a move away from it. Vague or purposive rules have been used not to replace detail but to complement it.

The rhetoric of successive SIB chairmen also suggests greater changes in the attitudes towards rules and the uses to which rules are put, and whilst these uses have been specific to the regulatory system their statements echo the observations made in the first chapter concerning the role of tacit understandings and informed interpretation in the effective use of rules. The role of rules in defining the institutional position of the regulatory bodies has been noted. The case for Principles, Walker argued, also rested on a belief that both regulators and firms could develop a greater maturity of approach to conduct of their business and to the regulatory system. This was expressed in two ways: by the insistence on self-regulation as 'regulation of the self', and through a stress on the reciprocal nature of the relationship between regulator and regulated. The Principles were thus at once an attempt both to confirm the 'self-regulatory' nature of the system and to stimulate the commitment to and understanding of rules that self-regulatory systems are frequently assumed to possess. The regulatory approach

[155] D. McBarnet and C. Whelan, 'The Elusive Spirit of the Law: Formalism and the Struggle for Legal Control' (1991) 54 *MLR* 848.

accompanying the Principles was that regulation was as much the responsibility of the firm as the regulator; that firms should focus on regulating their own internal management and practices, an emphasis which has continued. Further, the relationship between regulator and regulated was expressed in the idea of a 'regulatory contract', a notion adopted by both Walker and his successor Sir Andrew Large.[156] Regulation, both argued, represents a contract between the regulator and regulated in which the regulator agrees not to interfere in the detailed operation of the regulated, but in return expects compliance which goes beyond mere obedience to the letter of the law. In other words, if you, the regulated, act properly then we, the regulators, will not need to be so specific.

The Principles also reflect the interaction of interpretation with the structure of rules. It was suggested in chapter 1 that there exists a strong reciprocal relationship between rule maker and interpreter. The greater the extent to which both understand one another, the more the rule maker can rely on those tacit understandings to inform interpretations of the rule and so the less she needs to resort to precision and specification. This interaction was implicit in the emphasis on 'regulation of the self' and in the regulatory contract, and has been explicitly recognized by Large. Thus in his Report, Large suggested that in the decision as to what mechanism of regulation to use, detailed rule, guidance, principle or code of conduct, the rule maker should consider the quality of training and competence of those involved in understanding and complying with the rules, and their ethical standards. '[T]he more the industry takes on board the challenge of today's consumers in insisting on quality of service, quality of product, and high ethical standards, the less prescriptive the regulator needs to be.'[157]

Finally, the two roles for which rules have been used, at once regulating firms and the market and defining and regulating the relationship between the regulators, have become separated. Both the initial rules and the New Settlement, particularly the Core Rules, in effect represented the use of rules to achieve two distinct purposes: regulation of firms and the market, and regulation of other regulators. So SIB's initial rules were seen to an extent by the DTI as a means of regulating SIB, and by SIB as a means of regulating the SROs. The introduction of the New Settlement,

[156] Large Report, paras. 6.5–6.6. [157] Ibid., para. 6.6.

especially the Core Rules, was an attempt to resolve the tensions between the role of SIB and that of the SROs through the adoption of a particular type of rule. The policy behind the Core Rules was one of simultaneously conferring discretion, through changing the rule structure, and centralization, through changing the application of the rule. In the Large reforms these two purposes have become more clearly separated, and the use of rules to regulate the inter-regulatory relationship has been replaced by a greater emphasis on supervision through standard setting, statements of objectives, and performance targets. Dedesignation is the manifestation of this separation, of the move away from rules as definers of this relationship. Nonetheless, in their use in regulating firms and markets there is a continued emphasis on the importance of tactical and conscious choice in the type of rule used to implement regulatory policy, and of the interaction of rules with other mechanisms, notably training, competence, and high ethical standards, to achieve those aims.

4 Regulating the Retail Sector

Introduction

Making rules when the principal focus of the process is specifically on restructuring rules and questions of the substantive provisions of the regulation are largely settled, as in the New Settlement, inevitably means that issues of rule type will loom large in the rule making decision. The focus of the following two chapters is on rule making in areas where both the policy of the regulation and hence the content of the rule are unformed; one of the consequent questions is thus whether the consideration of rule type is as paramount where substantive policy is being formed as it has been in the case of rule revision and restructuring. The areas of regulation examined differ in their width, although not necessarily their complexity. The regulation of the retail sector has been an area of considerable policy development and rule change, and this chapter examines the principal tenets of its regulation: market structure, commission regulation, disclosure of product information, and the rules on suitability and best advice. The regulation of soft commissions, the subject of the next chapter, is a more contained issue, but the questions which it poses arise in a very different market context, and to an extent receive different solutions.

Three dominant themes are evident in the development of regulation in the retail sector: the impact of the institutional structure on the rule making process, in particular the role conferred by the Act on the OFT to monitor the anti-competitive effects of the rules; the part different bodies' perceptions play in the process, both as to the nature of the problem to be addressed and the means of addressing it, and the extent to which these can change over time; and the impact of the market context on the rule making decisions. The chapter indicates the nature of this context, the regulatory issues to which it gives rise, and outlines in brief the development of regulation in this area before turning to consider in more depth the development of the different aspects of that regulation and the attendant issues of rule formation and rule use.

The Market Context

Defined broadly, the retail market covers all dealings with private investors, including those of banks and building societies, and products such as National Savings certificates and mortgages. Not all of this sector is regulated by the Financial Services Act: National Savings certificates, deposits or mortgages, or interests in occupational pension schemes do not fall within the scope of 'investments' under the Act.[1] The difference in scope between the Act and the range of the financial products and services used by private investors can lead to anomalies. 'Investment business' covers the management of pension schemes, for example, though not the interests in those schemes. So although the trustees of a pension fund may be in breach of the rules, beneficiaries of the fund cannot claim under the statutory compensation scheme.[2] The frequent combination of mortgages with regulated products also leads to complications when loss occurs, as the home income plans affair illustrated,[3] and suggestions have been made that deposits and repayment mortgages should at least receive comparable regulation if not be brought within the FSA remit.[4]

The regulated part of the retail sector thus comprises life assurance, personal pensions, unit trusts, gilt-edged stocks, and equity shares acquired principally through packaged product providers and their agents, insurance and unit trust brokers, independent financial advisers, private portfolio managers, and stockbrokers.[5] With the exception of regulated collective investment schemes the

[1] FSA 1986, Sch. 1.

[2] S. 191. In relation to the Maxwell pensions affair, see Social Security Select Committee, *Report on the Operation of Pension Funds*, 1991/2 HC paper no. 61-I and IMRO, *Submission to the House of Commons Social Security Committee*, Feb. 1992.

[3] Products were designed by life assurance companies and sold by intermediaries which involved advising usually elderly people to remortgage their houses and invest the money. The returns, they were promised, would cover their mortgage payments and provide them with money left over to spend. Many of these collapsed, and although the two aspects of the transaction, mortgages and investment, were inextricably linked in the investor's mind, these are regulated by different rules and there were consequent wrangles over who should provide compensation and in what proportion: by 1995 Investors Compensation Scheme had paid out £30 million to over 2,000 claimants: SIB, *Annual Report 1994/95*.

[4] These were noted by Clucas, but while suggesting that it may be appropriate to consider these issues in the longer term, he did not comment on them further. *Retail Regulation Review: Report of a study by Sir Kenneth Clucas on a new SRO for the Retail Sector* (SIB, Mar. 1992), para. 7.12.

[5] See ibid., para. 1.

regulation does not focus on the product structure, but regulates only the giving of advice and dealing in these products. The regulation separates three types of products for particular regulatory treatment: life policies, units in regulated collective investment schemes, and investment trust savings schemes.

Of these products it is life policies which are most heavily invested in by private investors, mainly through mortgage related endowment policies. The number of products on the market is enormous, as banks and building societies have developed their own products alongside those of the life and unit trust companies. The structure of the products varies. Unit trusts are the most transparent as the price of the units is linked to the underlying fund and details are published in the daily broadsheet newspapers. The investor may therefore track the performance of the investment. Life policies have been increasingly used for investment purposes and are more opaque. On most types of policy the investor may not know how much the investment will be worth, and in the most frequently purchased type (with profits policies) the amount which is returned is at the discretion of the life company.

The distribution of these products is usually through the direct sales forces of the life offices, banks or building societies or their agents, or independent advisers. The market for investment advice has become increasingly competitive over the last ten years due to the deregulation of banks and building societies,[6] and competition for distribution outlets is severe. With the exception of one building society, all the major high street banks and building societies act as agents of a life office as well as sell their own products.[7] All sellers are paid commission by the product provider. Due to the opacity of the products and the difficulties investors have in distinguishing products on the ground of quality, competition between product providers is centred on distribution, which is seen by companies as the key to market share. Product providers thus compete on the level of commission paid for a sale, and commission levels vary between companies and between the products of one company.

[6] The removal of controls on bank lending in 1980 (the Corset) enabled banks to enter the mortgage market, and the 1986 Building Societies Act enabled the Societies to compete effectively with banks in offering personal banking services, offer insurance and investment advice and to recapture the mortgage market by enabling them to go to the money markets to raise capital.

[7] The exception is the Bradford and Bingley Building Society.

Average commission levels have risen significantly in the post-FSA era and in 1993 for endowment policies were 124 per cent of the original stipulated levels for independent advisers and 144 per cent for tied agents.[8]

Regulatory Issues

Three aspects of the retail market raise particular regulatory issues: the nature of products on offer; the nature of the retail market, including its remuneration structure; and the nature of the investor. The products are highly complex and their quality is difficult to assess. Inter-product comparison is difficult both due to this complexity, and particularly because the ultimate return on the investment is based on the future performance of the funds. The investor is therefore having to make a judgement on the investment skill of the producer or service provider. The investor may be able to assess this skill quite quickly, for example if he or she has a contract with a discretionary fund manager which provides him or her with frequent reports as to the value of the funds, and allows him or her to terminate the contract with no penalties. In relation to long-term investment vehicles, however, the investor has to wait ten or twenty years before he or she will know what his or her ultimate return will be. Even then the investor may not be able to recognize the quality of return and assess whether another product would have been better. Experience of a product is therefore not sufficient to inform a consumer: the investor cannot tell whether or not his or her investment 'works' or has been a 'good buy'.[9] Further, performance can vary widely between and within the different product types, and funds managed by the same institution can vary widely in their performance.[10] Problems in assessing quality have two implications. First, the familiar 'market for lemons' argument: that as a consumer cannot assess quality, competition between producers occurs on other attributes, for example, price. This may lead to a general depression of quality in the market as the bad, but lower priced, products, drive out those which are of better quality but

[8] *Fair Trading and Life Assurance Savings Products* (OFT, Mar. 1993), para. 2.9. Commission payments were set by Lautro until 1 Jan. 1990; see below.

[9] In economic terms, the goods are thus credence goods.

[10] For examples see J. Mitchell, *Savings and Investments* (London, 1992), 24.

more expensive.[11] Second, reliance on the intermediary increases; unable to assess quality for him or herself, the investor relies on intermediaries to provide both accurate information and assessment of the product.

The problems of product opacity and the associated reliance of the investor on the intermediary is not alleviated by the market structure. Products are sold through intermediaries who are remunerated by the product company on a commission basis. The market is highly competitive, but competition focuses on distribution of products. Product companies compete principally by securing distribution outlets and on the level of commission paid to the intermediary rather than on the quality of the product sold. Two particular problems arise: the confusion as to who the intermediary is acting for, and commission driven selling. The pre-FSA era was characterized by intense commission wars between product companies, and a lack of clarity as to who the intermediary was acting for. Independent intermediaries existed, but they could in practice be selling the products of only a small number of companies. Some companies had their own direct sales forces, but the majority sold their products through agents who were tied to one company but whose contracts allowed them to sell the products of other companies in certain circumstances. The greatest confusion was caused by this 'middle ground': those agents who were tied to two or three companies, but gave the impression that they were independent brokers.[12] Not only did these practices give rise to considerable confusion for the customer on the position and interests of the intermediary, this 'quasi-independence' also raised a legal issue: under the principles of agency law the intermediary could not on the one hand claim to be acting for the customer as his/her agent, whilst on the other accepting benefits such as payment of office

[11] G. Akerlof, 'The Market for "Lemons": Qualitative Uncertainty and the Market Mechanism' (1970) 84 *Quarterly Journal of Economics* 488. See J. Stiglitz and A. Weiss, 'Credit Rationing in Markets with Imperfect Information', (1981) 71 *American Economic Review* 393 for an application of the model to financial markets.

[12] The forms of the 'tie' varied: e.g., a life office might give an interest free loan to a firm of intermediaries, on condition that the life office or group received a certain volume of business from that company. Or the life office might, on similar conditions, acquire a substantial interest in the ownership of the intermediary firm. Or the amount of commission received on an individual transaction would increase markedly with the increase in volume of total business the intermediary gave the office.

expenses, volume related bonuses, and the like without disclosing this to the customer.

Finally, the investor is usually ill-equipped to navigate these competitive waters. For most individuals their involvement with the financial services market is through the indirect investment packages of these institutions; over the last thirty years individual investors have invested increasingly in these types of investment products, rather than directly in shares.[13] However, investors who purchase these retail products are usually unsophisticated with a low level of understanding of the financial products they are buying. In 1991 research commissioned by SIB and Lautro found that consumers had a low level of confidence in understanding insurance and 'most consumers regard insurance with little interest and little curiosity and therefore are not inclined to spend much time in "shopping around" or even in improving their knowledge of what products are available',[14] a finding confirmed by a survey by the Office of Fair Trading.[15] When asked how competent they felt in their general financial affairs, however, eighty-nine per cent of consumers claimed they were confident about handling their own finances. The OFT report concluded '[t]his dissonant combination of confidence and lack of sophistication suggests that consumers are especially vulnerable on savings and investment issues'.[16]

The combination of a complex and opaque product, an ignorant and unsophisticated consumer, and a competitive market whose focus is sales and control of distribution rather than product quality is a recipe for poor quality products being sold to consumers who lack the skills and knowledge to make rational choices. The consequent regulatory concerns are imperfect market operation and a poor deal for consumers. Exactly how poor a deal is illustrated by the recent disclosure of widespread misselling of personal pensions, where the level of compensation which firms are being required to pay out is currently estimated to be between £1–4 billion. Misselling can have wider implications, however: investment serves

[13] In 1963, 54% of shares listed on the Stock Exchange were held by individuals. In 1990 individuals held only 18–20%, with institutions holding approximately 65–70%: H. McRae and F. Cairncross, *Capital City* (London, 1992), 107–8.

[14] *Review of Retail Regulation: Consumer Research by Taylor Nelson Financial*, SIB Disclosures Research Report, Jan. 1992, commissioned by SIB and Lautro, 6–7.

[15] *Savings and Investments, Consumer Issues: An Occasional Paper to the OFT by J. Mitchell and H. Weisner* (OFT, June 1992).

[16] Ibid., 15.

the economic function of capital provision; it also enables people to protect themselves financially, in old age for example, and so serves the social function of relieving the State from a financial burden that might otherwise fall on it in the way of welfare provisions. This argument is one which the life and pensions industry play on, and which has been recognized by successive Governments.[17] That people should be encouraged to invest in life insurance, pension provision, and other investment vehicles is a theme which runs through the regulation, and which is of increasing concern as political views shift towards private provision of welfare and pensions.[18]

The Development of Regulation

Prior to 1986 there was no regulation of the conduct of intermediaries selling life assurance or unit trust products, nor was there any regulation of the number of companies' products an intermediary could sell. In the mid-1970s the practices of the intermediaries and salesmen had been the subject of Government attention. A consultative paper highlighted four areas of concern: the absence of rules on financial resources and handling clients' money, inadequate training, the extent to which agents were controlled by the companies they worked for, and the lack of clear distinction between insurance brokers, who held themselves out as offering disinterested advice to their clients, and intermediaries who acted as agents representing one or more companies.[19] The introduction of the Insurance Brokers Registration Act 1977 was an attempt to address these issues and distinguish brokers and salesmen in the consumer's mind by allowing only registered brokers to call themselves 'insurance brokers'. A Government proposal to require an agent to be either tied or independent was not pursued.[20]

When Gower was conducting his review, the concerns which the Labour Government had felt were still alive.[21] He rejected the individual registration of agents on the pragmatic basis that they were a large and fluctuating body which made registration

[17] See, e.g., DoT, *Insurance Intermediaries*, Cmnd. 6715 (London, 1977), para 3.

[18] It may also mean that the regulator is placed in a position of a conflict of objectives, if not interest, if it is implicitly or explicitly charged with stimulating investment in these products, yet imposing regulation which through its provisions may discourage such investment.

[19] Cmnd. 6715.

[20] Ibid.

[21] See L. C. B. Gower, *Review of Investor Protection: Discussion Document* (London, 1982) and *Review of Investor Protection, Report, Part I*, Cmnd. 9125 (London, 1984).

extremely difficult,[22] recommending instead that the company to which they were tied be made fully responsible for their activities, even where the salesman sold the product of another company.[23] The IBRA 1977 had proved to be too easy to avoid (intermediaries could avoid regulation simply by not calling themselves 'brokers') and he recommended that this loophole be plugged and that all agents, selling insurance or not, be subject to a licensing scheme. Following the commission wars of the early 1980s and the collapse of the industry-imposed Register of Life Assurance Commissions (ROLAC), Gower also recommended that the Government intervene to control commissions of both tied agents and intermediaries, believing that the experience of voluntary agreements had shown that the interests of investors could not be protected in any other way.[24]

The FSA regulators have addressed these issues using a range of regulatory techniques: imposing a particular market structure for the distribution of products, imposing price controls through regulating commission levels, regulating the conduct of sellers and product providers, and prescribing disclosure requirements. The initial regulation was formed by the Marketing of Investments Board Organising Committee (MIBOC), which subsequently merged with SIB. MIBOC's proposals were strongly influenced by the prevailing market practices and perceived failings of the pre-1986 regulation. The regulation proposed by MIBOC comprised four main elements. First, a requirement that intermediaries sell either the products of one company or the products of all (polarization); in turn, independent intermediaries required authorization under the Act, but tied agents did not need authorization as they could be appointed representatives of product companies, who under the Act would be responsible for their actions.[25] Second, polarization would be supported by a control on the level of commissions which could be paid to independent intermediaries by the product companies, which would ensure that independent intermediaries were not tempted to recommend one company's products over another.

[22] Gower, *Report, Part I*, para. 8.50. This had also been proposed by the Labour Government in 1977, but rejected by the trade associations on the grounds of practicability and cost: Cmnd. 6715, paras. 14–15.

[23] Ibid., para. 8.35. This proposal had also been made by the Government in 1977, which had further tentatively suggested that an agent should be permitted to sell the products of only one company: Cmnd. 6715, para. 15.

[24] Gower, *Report, Part I*, para. 8.40.

[25] S. 44.

This control of commission levels was seen as an essential part of the polarization regime. SIB had been prohibited by the Act from introducing such controls, so it was necessary for an SRO to institute and monitor this maximum commissions agreement (MCA). Third, the regulation required that both tied and independent intermediaries recommended only investments which were suitable for the investor, and as a further buttress to polarization the regulators imposed a 'best advice rule': the product recommended had to be the product which would best meet the customer's needs out of either that company's range of products, or of products generally available on the market. Finally, the initial regulation proided that the investor should be given information on surrender values, charges, and illustrations (the 'product particulars'), although it did not provide that expenses on one type of life assurance product, with profits policies,[26] should be disclosed.

Rule making and rule revision has been continual in this area. A number of the initial provisions were assessed by the Director General of Fair Trading to be anti-competitive, and the Secretary of State required SIB to amend some of its rules, notably to abolish the maximum commissions agreement and improve significantly on the disclosures made in the product particulars. A review of the rules was announced in December 1988, the results of which were implemented in January 1990. Some of these provisions were again judged to be anti-competitive by the DGFT, principally the failure to disclose information on product charges and expenses prior to sale, and failure of independent intermediaries to disclose the amount of their commission prior to sale. The Secretary of State again required SIB to revise its rules, and the Retail Regulation Review commenced in April 1991.[27] The DGFT again judged some of the provisions to be anti-competitive, notably the continuing failure to require independent intermediaries to disclose the amount of their commissions prior to sale, and in July 1993 the Chancellor required SIB to further amend its rules, this time going further

[26] With profits policies are life assurance products which promise to pay the holder a stipulated sum, with an expectation that bonuses will also be paid at the discretion of the life office annually (reversionary bonus) and/or on death or maturity of the policy (terminal bonuses).

[27] SIB, *Retail Regulation: Issues for Review*, Apr. 1991; SIB, *Polarisation*, DP 2, Sept. 1991; SIB, *Disclosure*, DP 3, Oct. 1991; SIB, *Disclosure, Polarisation and Standards of Advice*, CP 60, Mar. 1992; SIB, *Disclosure and Standards of Advice, A Policy Statement*, May 1992.

than the DGFT's recommendations.[28] The debate so far has involved three SIB chairmen, two DGFTs,[29] two government departments, and several government ministers.[30]

Rule Making in the Retail Sector: Tensions, Influences, and Constraints

The chapter examines rule making in the four main areas of retail regulation: the regulation of the structure of the distribution channels (polarization), commission regulation, disclosure requirements, and finally the attempt to raise the quality of service received through the requirement to recommend only products which are suitable for the investor. Three principal themes characterize the rule making process in the retail sector. First, the impact of the competition review by the OFT provided for in the FSA. As we have seen, the FSA regulation is exempted from normal competition law, and instead the OFT is under a duty to review the rules for their anti-competitive effect and to advise the Secretary of State, now the Chancellor. The only instance in which the Government can intervene in the rules of SIB is with respect to anti-competitive provisions; if he or she judges the rules to be significantly anti-competitive, and that such rules are not merited by investor protection concerns, the Chancellor can direct SIB to alter its rules.[31] Rule making has in this area been continually prompted by directions from the Government following adverse reports from the DGFT, a phenomenon which is almost unique to this area of financial services regulation; other areas of SIB's rules have not been affected either at all, or at least not to the same extent. Differences between SIB and the DGFT may to an extent be ascribed to the over-sympathetic ear which the regulators initially bent towards industry. Subsequently, however, there have been very real differences between the two bodies as to the perceptions of what regulation has in fact created, what its impact is likely to be, and towards the intelligence and awareness of consumers themselves, differences which have meant that although the ultimate goals may be shared, the means by which they should be attained has been fundamentally disputed.

[28] Directions under ss. 120(4) and 121(3) of the Financial Services Act 1993, July 1993 (hereafter 'Treasury Direction'), reprinted in SIB, CP 77, App. B.

[29] Sir Gordon Borrie, and from 1992 Sir Bryan Carsberg.

[30] Responsibility for financial services regulation was given to the Treasury in Nov. 1992.

[31] Ss. 119–122.

The second theme which characterizes rule making in this area is the shift in the regulators' own approach. Since the formation of the initial rules by MIBOC and some differences with Lautro on particular issues, the policy and rule making process has been largely SIB-led; the IFA regulator, Fimbra, has played almost no role in initiating regulation; Lautro has played a slightly larger role, but on the whole the process has been dominated by SIB. The recently formed PIA may subsequently take more initiative, but the rule process examined here largely predates its formation. SIB's own approach to regulation has moved away, albeit slowly, from MIBOC's close relationship with the industry towards a more independent position. Reliance on actuarial reports and concern for technical accuracy, for example, once dominant, is now balanced against, and even outweighed by, concern for comprehensibility of information and reliance on market research into consumer understanding. Rather than providing an example of regulatory 'capture', the formation of retail regulation can almost be characterized as a process of 'regulatory escape'.

The third theme is the role played by the nature of the market, the nature of the products sold, and the nature of the consumer in moulding the concerns involved in rule formation. The problem of consumer ignorance and ease with which consumers can be misled has preoccupied the regulators to an increasing degree. In forming rules, the fact that those rules are attempting to regulate the conduct of thousands of salespersons operating in an environment which is difficult to monitor, and trying to ensure that they accurately assess and fairly respond to the investment needs of millions of individual investors, has had an impact on the type of rule used and there has been an increasing awareness on the part of the regulator of the implications of using different rule types. Ultimately, however, regulation of the retail sector shows in stark form the limits of rules: the regulation is aiming to raise standards; rules, however, cannot dictate quality of individual behaviour.

Structuring the Market: Polarization

Described by SIB as 'a regulatory fissure cutting deep across the market landscape',[32] polarization is the hallmark of the regulatory

[32] DP 2, para. 19.

regime. It structures the distribution networks of certain specified retail products, namely life assurance contracts,[33] unit trusts, investment trusts, and PEPs whose plan investments include these products, requiring intermediaries to sell either the products of one company, a tied agent, or to sell the products of all companies, an independent intermediary or financial adviser (IFA).

Polarization and the maximum commissions agreement (MCA) which accompanied it were a direct response to the market situation which existed in the mid-1980s. As we have seen, both statutory and self-regulatory responses to this situation had been spectacularly unsuccessful. The Investment Brokers Registration Act 1977 had been easily avoided and had patently failed to achieve its objective. Successive attempts to maintain a voluntary agreement on maximum commission levels had collapsed and the industry had engaged in severe commission wars.

The aim of polarization was to remove the confusion over the status of the person who was selling the products by making the intermediary unambiguously either independent or tied. Previously, intermediaries, although appearing to be independent, had in fact been tied to product companies in a variety of ways, for example through loans given on condition of receipt of a certain level of business; commissions which rose with the volume of business generated; or through the product provider having a stake in the ownership of the intermediary. Whilst many (if not all) of these practices could have been, and were, addressed by prohibitions on volume overriders,[34] benefits in kind,[35] and differential pricing,[36] it was felt that given the character of the life assurance product 'the customer has a particular need to know to whom he can turn for genuinely independent advice and on whose behalf the salesman is acting'.[37] Conduct regulation and disclosure alone were felt to be necessary but not sufficient; a more draconian regulatory

[33] As covered by Sch. 1, para. 10 of the Act.

[34] Commission levels which are conditional on a specified amount of business being given in the future.

[35] Giving services or other benefits instead of commission.

[36] Allowing some distribution outlets to sell the same product at a lower price. Initially prohibited, the Treasury directed that differential pricing be allowed within the tied distribution channel for life assurance products, following assessment by the DGFT that the rule was significantly anti-competitive: Treasury Direction, 22 July 1993; SIB, *Life Assurance: Disclosure of Commissions and Other Matters*, CP 77 (Feb. 1994), paras. 6–9.

[37] SIB and MIBOC, *Life Assurance, Unit Trusts and the Investor*, Apr. 1986, para. 7.

technique was required: imposing a particular market structure on the distribution of retail products.

There was no necessary logic which required representatives to be tied to only one company. However, MIBOC decided that the 'purist approach'[38] of single company tying should be adopted for two reasons. The first was to ensure complete clarity as to the intermediary's status. Against the background of an existing chaotic market-place and with no experience of regulation or compliance departments, it was felt that single company representation was the safest way of avoiding a 'halo effect', or the impression that the intermediary is authorized by the product company for all his actions, the product company's name giving credence to the intermediary's actions. The second was to maintain a balance between independents and non-independents. Independents were for the first time to be made subject to requirements of best advice and their independence was in effect to be ensured by compliance with a Maximum Commissions Agreement, which would limit their income, on pain of explicit commission disclosure.[39] MIBOC argued that the privilege of exemption from these requirements should go only to those who had accepted the limitation of their business of selling the products of only one company.[40]

The Impact of Polarization: Unforeseen Developments and Unintended Consequences

Polarization and its accompanying regulatory support, the MCA, were reactive measures directed at the market situation which existed at the time; however the market has developed under the polarization regulation in a manner which was unforeseen and unintended by the regulators. The principal sources of advice and sales, the banks and building societies, have not remained independent but have tied to product companies. As these institutions are the first places the majority of consumers go for advice and more significantly for their mortgages, which are frequently sold in combination with a life assurance product (endowment mortgages), there was, and is, a concern amongst the regulators that consumer choice was being curtailed.

[38] SIB and MIBOC, *Life Assurance and Unit Trusts: Independent Intermediaries, Tied Agents and Company Representatives*, Dec. 1985, para. 24. [39] See below.
[40] Dec. 1985, para. 75.

This development has had a significant impact on the regulatory debates, particularly in relation to commission disclosure (discussed below), and prompted the review of the polarization regime by SIB in 1991. SIB was concerned about the consequences of these developments for the widespread availability of independent advice and the constraints polarization posed on the development of production / distribution relationships, and so in an issues paper asked if the rules should be altered in any respect in the light of these developments.[41] In the subsequent discussion paper, proposals to dilute the polarization requirements were considered which echoed those considered by MIBOC when it was forming the initial polarization rules. These focused on whether the division between IFAs and tied agents should be altered in three respects. Firstly, whether an agent should be able to tie to more than one company, a 'multi-tie'.[42] 'Multi-ties' were advocated particularly strongly by some of the banks and building societies; and indeed Halifax Building Society attempted to resurrect the issue in 1993 by indicating that it would only join the Personal Investment Authority if multi-tying were allowed.[43] A variety of forms of tie have been suggested: the agent could be tied principally to one company but in certain circumstances sell the products of others (paramount tie), could sell different products of different companies (segmented tie) or sell all products of a range of companies (overlapping ties).[44] All had been prevalent modes of business practice prior to 1985. Secondly, whether an intermediary should be allowed to sell certain products of other companies to supplement the product range of the company to which it was tied, 'badging'.[45] Finally, whether the range of products to which polarization applied should be reduced.

These proposals were rejected both in 1985 and again in 1991–2. The arguments at both times were wide-ranging, but can be distilled into two principal elements: concern not to jeopardize the polarization regime itself, and concern at the implications of the proposal for the effective operation of associated elements of the regulation. With respect to the aims underlying polarization, SIB was concerned that multi-tying, and to an extent badging, could undermine the purpose of the polarization regime by reducing the

[41] Apr. 1991, para. 7.
[42] Dec. 1985, paras. 24–35; Apr. 1986, paras. 24–38; DP 2, paras. 45–51.
[43] *FT*, 28 Mar. 1993. [44] DP 2, para. 47.
[45] Dec. 1985, paras. 36–45; Apr. 1986, paras. 33–8; and DP 2, paras. 41–4.

clarity of status between types of intermediary and confusing the lines of responsibility between the product company and the tied agent.[46] It was also unclear how either multi-tying or badging would operate in the context of the requirement that the product recommended had to be the product which would best meet the customer's needs out of either that company's range of products, or of products generally available on the market, the 'best advice' rule.[47] What criteria he or she should use when advising an investor, and indeed how the intermediary should choose to which companies and for which products to tie.[48]

SIB also considered, but rejected, restricting the products to which polarization applied by excluding unit trust products from the rule.[49] This proposal was supported by the unit trust industry, but not supported by the life companies who were consistent in their view that there should be no further dilution of the polarization requirements and argued that the characteristics of products were not relevant. The rationale behind the proposals was that it was the particular nature of life products, their complexity, opacity, and illiquidity, and their commission driven distribution which gave rise to the need for such an emphasis on the status and independence of the seller. Unit trusts and investment trust savings schemes (ITSSs) do not share these product characteristics and SIB considered whether they should be treated more as equities.[50] It also considered the difficulties to which the definition of polarized products could lead when categorizing new products, which could stifle product innovation.[51] However, although SIB recognized that polarization was directed at life products and greater consumer choice could result from its limitation to these, it was swayed by the consideration that as unit trusts and ITSSs are sold alongside life products, the confusion over the status of the seller which could arise posed too great a risk to the polarization regime. An investor would be unlikely to appreciate that an adviser who could sell the products of all unit trust companies could sell the products of only one life company.[52] Again, clarity of intermediary status was the dominant force behind maintaining the 'purity' of the polarization regime.

[46] July 1986, paras. 35–8; CP 60, para. 49. [47] Ibid. [48] DP 2, para. 42.
[49] Ibid., paras. 52–4. [50] Ibid., para. 52. [51] Ibid., para. 53.
[52] CP 60, paras. 45–9.

Competition, Consumer Choice, and Consumer Confusion

In rejecting proposals to modify the polarization regime, considerations of competition and consumer choice have been outweighed by a concern to maintain two aspects of polarization: clear lines of responsibility between life companies and their agents, and maintaining clarity of status of the intermediary. The reason for the need to maintain this clarity lies in the nature of the products being sold, and the nature of the investor. SIB has thus placed a strong emphasis on the importance of status disclosure to supplement the structural regulation: the point of polarization is missed, after all, if the investor does not know or understand who is advising him or her. We saw above that the concern not to contaminate or undermine polarization by obscuring the status of the adviser has informed the debates on multi-tying and badging, as it has on status disclosure. All considerations of wider consumer choice or reducing barriers to entry into the market have been outweighed by the concern that nothing should confuse the investor as to who was advising him or her. The concern was not just that the adviser be independent or tied, but that the investor be absolutely clear what the status of the adviser was.

Relaxations in the polarization rule have been made, however, in two cases: investment managers of discretionary portfolios, and the ability of financial conglomerates to have both tied and independent companies within one group (dual status distribution). In the first case, the opportunity for confusion was felt not to arise (as the consumer is not purchasing the product directly from the manager).[53] In the second, the principle of clarity of status has been itself outweighed by another principle: the availability of independent advice.

Under the rules, financial conglomerates are permitted to comprise companies acting as tied agents and subsidiaries which act as IFAs, and maintain a 'conduit' between the two so that the tied company may advise the investor to go to that IFA subsidiary. These rules were a source of dispute between SIB and Lautro when the initial rule books were being written. The provision is used principally by the banks and building societies, which have separate

[53] The exclusion for managers of investment portfolios was incorporated into the Core Rules: CR 4(4).

subsidiaries to which their branch staff can advise investors to go if the company to which the bank is tied has no suitable product. The banks and building societies strongly lobbied for the provision; it would enable them to have a presence in both sectors of the market. Partly for this reason, they sought direct regulation from SIB, whose rules permitted dual status distribution. The life offices, who were members of Lautro and already feeling the competition from the bank and building society sector, were not in favour of dual status distribution because of the competitive advantage it would provide to the latter. Lautro's initial rules consequently imposed far greater restrictions on the circumstances when customers could be referred to the independent branch. Following criticism of the DGFT that Lautro's rules distorted and restricted competition to a significant extent,[54] 'and would tend to leave . . . customers bereft of advice in a field where to act without advice is to leap in the dark',[55] the Secretary of State required Lautro to bring its rules in line with SIB's.

The maintenance of dual status distribution was reconsidered in the Retail Review and the status disclosure provisions were tightened, requiring disclosure on the premises and on mortgage advertisements. Concern over consumer confusion, paramount in the debates on multi-ties and badging, has thus been outweighed by a greater concern for consumer choice and the availability of independent advice. Given the prominence of banks and building societies as distribution outlets for products and the frequency with which investors will go to them for advice, SIB was swayed by the argument that if banks and building societies could not direct customers to independent advisers then the customer would be less well served and there would be a substantial reduction in the availability of independent advice,[56] a view shared by the OFT and the Consumers' Association.[57]

SIB has maintained that given the complexity of the products and the sophistication of the investment decision the consumer needs the benefit of independent advice. The belief that the independent sector is inherently beneficial to the market and to the consumer, and a consequent concern that it be at least maintained if not promoted, was dominant in the structuring of the initial

[54] OFT, *Life Assurance and Unit Trust Regulatory Organisation*, Mar. 1988, paras. 1.12 and 4.39.

[55] Ibid., para. 1.13.

[56] DP 3, para. 38.

[57] Consumers' Association response to DP 2.

regime and the limitation of the company representative to *one* product company. The threat to the integrity of independent advice posed by the dual status of financial conglomerates has been felt to be less than the reduction in independent advice which SIB and the OFT have felt would result from its prohibition. These concerns have also informed the debate on the next issue, commission regulation, but as debates on this issue show, shared objectives do not necessarily lead to agreement on a rule's formation.

Regulation of Commissions

Gower's Report had been written against a background of a voluntary commissions agreement which had failed to work as companies broke away from it in the battle to gain distribution outlets.[58] He concluded that some control over the level of commissions was desirable, and that given the failures of voluntary agreements some form of statutory backing was necessary, a proposal supported by the life offices.[59] Just as it had rejected the appeals of the main life assurance trade associations for a statutory system after the failure of an industry-imposed agreement in 1982, the Government rejected statutory control on the grounds that it would amount to price-fixing. It explicitly prohibited SIB from making rules setting maximum amounts of commission levels, the only statutory provision on SIB's legislative powers which prohibits it from making a rule on a particular issue.[60] However, it suggested in the White Paper that commission levels of independent intermediaries could be regulated by a voluntary agreement.[61]

Both Gower and MIBOC[62] felt that mere disclosure of commission would not be a solution to the problem of commission driven sales as without information on other rates or other products, or the same products between different IFAs, the consumer could not evaluate the information. Greater restriction on the amounts of commission which could be paid were necessary. MIBOC therefore followed the White Paper, which had been partly drawn up

[58] The Register of Life Assurance Commissions (ROLAC) Agreement.

[59] Gower, *Report, Part I*, paras. 8.42–8.43, Recommendation 46.

[60] S. 48(3).

[61] DTI, *Financial Services in the United Kingdom: A New Framework for Investor Protection*, Cmnd. 9432 (London, 1985), paras. 10.10–10.11.

[62] Apr. 1986, para. 58.

by a group of advisers on the life assurance industry and proposed that given the statutory restriction on SIB, an agreement on commission levels be drawn up and enforced by an SRO, Lautro. The task of setting up and monitoring the MCA was in fact the main reason for Lautro's existence; its members were already automatically authorized under the Act and so it was unique among the SROs in not being formed to enable firms to conduct investment business. As with the MCA's predecessor, the agreement only applied to the commissions paid to independent intermediaries, payments to tied agents were exempt. Those companies who joined the agreement were constrained in the amount of commission which they could pay IFAs, and through the rules of their SRO, Fimbra, IFAs were obliged not to accept a greater level of commission from those companies.

In order to ensure the MCA greater longevity than its predecessors, as a bait to ensure companies adhered to it the MCA was accompanied by 'soft disclosure', i.e., disclosure that the commission level was in accordance with levels set by Lautro.[63] Those companies which did not join the MCA, and the IFAs selling that company's product, had to give hard disclosure, i.e., disclosure of the amount of commission paid, at the point of sale. Firms directly authorized by SIB therefore had to give hard disclosure. In addition, the Lautro rules required that the MCA had to apply to the whole of a financial conglomerate, not just part. So corporate groups which comprised both tied and independent subsidiaries had to apply the agreement across both IFAs and tied agents.[64]

The MCA was seen by MIBOC as the second pillar of the polarization regulation, the division of the distribution outlets being the first. The structural regulation, Gower felt, could only be effective if supported by price regulation to ensure that commission driven selling by IFAs did not lead to company bias (selling the products of one company on the basis of commission paid) and the return of the 'middle ground'. The nature of the products sold, particularly life products, and the reliance the investor placed on the adviser were again the two rationales which drove the rule formation process. The MCA would ensure the effectiveness of the independent pole and prevent the undermining of polarization.

[63] Parts 4 and 5 of the Lautro Rules 1988. The proposal had also been in the White Paper.

[64] Lautro Rules 1988, r. 4.8(2).

The decision to have an MCA occurred amidst a fierce debate, however, between those who saw the agreement as a means of protecting the consumer from biased advice and avoiding escalating commission costs, and those who saw it as little more than a cartel arrangement through which those companies with large market share and established reputations could protect themselves from smaller, newer companies. These companies, unable to attract the intermediaries' attention through past performance figures or well-known names, would be prevented from using higher commission levels as a way of entering the market and securing distribution. Prior attempts by the industry to agree commission levels amongst themselves had spectacularly collapsed, and the MCA was seen by many as an ideal opportunity to ensure enforcement of commission levels via a statute-backed regulatory system. The MCA and its accompanying regime of soft disclosure was thus described in some quarters as 'a cosy agreement between the insurance companies and the regulators'.[65]

In fact the MCA followed its predecessors to an early grave, but one dug this time not by the life companies but by the DGFT. In his report on Lautro in 1988 the DGFT stated that the combined effect of the MCA and soft disclosure restricted and distorted competition to a significant extent and was in danger of falling foul of EC requirements on competition and price control.[66] They should be replaced by a wide promulgation of the standard rates of commissions coupled with disclosure of the amount of commission prior to sale.[67]

As a consequence of the OFT report and difficulties with EC competition law, the Secretary of State, Lord Young, advised SIB and Lautro that Lautro's recognition as an SRO should not be granted until a date was set for the removal of the MCA and soft disclosure rules. The date for the abolition of the MCA was set at 1 January 1990. In December 1988 SIB produced a consultative document on what should replace the MCA. In fact it became clear that an interim regime would have to be introduced between May and December 1989 as the differences between the commission levels paid to IFAs and those paid to tied agents were becoming so great that many firms were leaving the independent

[65] *FT*, Leader 31 May 1989.
[66] Mar. 1988, paras. 3.21–3.30.
[67] Ibid., para. 3.31.

sector to become tied. Some reports put tied agents' commissions as much as seventy per cent higher than MCA levels. SIB and Lautro therefore required that IFAs paid in excess of the MCA rates should disclose at the point of sale the fact that they were receiving commission, and that details of the amount would be forthcoming from the product company. These rules formed the basis for the rules introduced in December 1989, which provided that after the point of sale details of commission would be sent to the investor, expressed as a percentage of premium.[68] These were again rejected by the DGFT in his report in April 1990 as restricting and distorting competition to a significant extent.[69] In its Retail Review SIB remained fast to its position that soft disclosure was adequate. The OFT predictably rejected the provisions,[70] and in July 1993 the Chancellor directed SIB to amend its proposals to require hard disclosure for IFAs.

Identifying Consequences and Predicting Developments

The differences between the FSA regulators and the OFT on the question of commission disclosure have arisen from their contrasting answers to two key questions: what has regulation created, and what would be the effect of further regulation? Would automatic cash disclosure of commission without any similar disclosure by company representatives lead to the demise of the independent sector, or would it lead to a better service for the consumer in the form of lower commission levels? The FSA regulators believe that upfront commission disclosure would result in consumers being discouraged from seeking independent advice and going to tied agents in the illusion that the advice they received there was free, leading to a significant erosion in the independent sector. The OFT believes that this is not the case. Each has commissioned

[68] Introduced following consultation papers, SIB, *Life Assurance and Unit Trust Disclosure*, CP 23, *Life Assurance and Unit Trust Disclosure*, May 1989, CP 27 Parts 1 and 2, Aug. 1989, and SIB, *Life Assurance and Unit Trust Disclosure: Outstanding Matters*, CP 30, Nov. 1989.

[69] OFT, *Disclosure of Information about Life Insurance Products and Commissions paid to IFAs*, Apr. 1990, paras. 4.3–4.12.

[70] OFT, *The Marketing and Sale of Investment-Linked Insurance Products, The Rules of the Securities and Investments Board and the Life Assurance and Unit Trust Regulatory Organisation*, Mar. 1993.

its own research on the matter, but neither has been conclusive.[71] Further, whilst support of the independent sector has been the objective of both, the OFT subsequently amended its view slightly, arguing, with the Consumers' Association, that the regulators should not become involved in supporting the independent sector: 'the size and health of this market must depend, once the conditions for proper competition are in place, on the demand for independent advice; there is no other objectively correct measure of what its size and turnover should be'.[72] The issue still remains, however, of what these conditions are.

The arguments have over time focused on four issues. Initially the issue arose as to whether cash disclosure was technically feasible. SIB argued that it was not, the DGFT argued that it was, and that anyway this was not sufficient ground for avoiding point of sale disclosure.[73] The second argument centres on the necessity of the information. SIB argued that information on commission levels was 'interesting and important rather than vital', and that if disclosed at the point of sale the investor would attach undue importance to it.[74] The DGFT argued that the information was vital as it affects competition between IFAs,[75] and should therefore be disclosed as early as possible in the sales process. He argued further that the objection of undue importance 'has never been a respectable argument' as the IFA should be capable of putting the information in context.[76]

The third argument centred around different perceptions of what the commission payment is. SIB argued that there was no reason in principle to distinguish between the disclosure of commissions for tied agents and IFAs as both are paid by the product company. IFA commission is not a price paid by the client for independent advice, but the price paid by the product company for the introduction of business to it, and reflects the value to that

[71] SIB, Retail Regulation Review, *Consumer Research by Taylor Nelson Financial*, Mar. 1992, 30–1; OFT, *Independent Financial Advisers and the Impact of Commission Disclosure by London Economics Ltd*, Oct. 1992. A Consumers' Association survey of 209 IFAs found only 4% would definitely go tied if commission had to be disclosed at the point of sale. The main reasons for tying were the regulatory costs involved in being independent: *FT*, 17 Apr. 1989.

[72] Mar. 1993, para. 5.27.

[73] Mar. 1988, para. 3.24; Apr. 1990, para. 4.7.

[74] CP 60, para. 40.

[75] Apr. 1990, paras. 4.3 and 4.6; Mar. 1993, para. 5.22.

[76] Mar. 1988, para. 3.26; Apr. 1990, para. 4.10.

company of the business received rather than the value of advice given to the client.[77] The OFT agreed, but argued that as the commission is ultimately paid for by the investor, disclosure should come from the IFA to indicate the nature of the relationships between the IFA and the investor and the IFA and the company.[78] Points about agency law have also been introduced, by SIB as an argument in favour of commission disclosure,[79] and by the OFT as an argument for hard disclosure.[80] The Law Commission has concluded that agency and fiduciary law do not require hard disclosure provided the amount of commission is normal,[81] but this conclusion has not figured in the arguments of either.

The OFT's views on this and the fourth point, the impact on the independent sector of hard disclosure, are largely informed by its perception of the market. Although not articulated in its previous reports, the OFT has now explicitly taken the view that the polarization rules have created two markets, the retail market and the advice market. The IFAs compete in the advice market, and the IFAs and tied agents compete in the retail market.[82] IFAs and tied agents can thus be treated differently. It is worth noting at this stage that the OFT has never advocated that the remuneration of tied agents should be disclosed,[83] a point to which we will return below. SIB and Lautro argue that there is only one market: that for advice. IFAs and tied agents should thus be subject to similar regulatory provisions. It is this perception which has led SIB to the fourth argument, that treating IFAs and tied agent remuneration disclosure differently creates a risk of distribution bias.[84] Investors would consider that advice and products from a tied agent was 'free', and so buy a product through them. The OFT has argued that IFAs would be able to counter the effect disclosure might have on the investor's perceptions by indicating 'the secrecy of arrangements' when buying through tied agents,[85] a view which SIB described as 'naïve'.[86]

The Treasury direction took a different approach. It required

[77] DP 3, para. 43. [78] Apr. 1990, para. 4.11; Mar. 1993, paras. 5.24–5.25.

[79] Dec. 1988, para. 18. [80] Mar. 1993, para. 5.26.

[81] Law Commission, *Fiduciary Duties and Regulatory Rules: A Consultation Paper*, CP No. 124 (HMSO, London, 1992), para. 3.4.20.

[82] Mar. 1993, paras. 2.4 and 5.29.

[83] See Apr. 1990, para. 4.8 and Mar. 1993, para. 5.32.

[84] DP 3, para. 37, CP 60, para. 43.

[85] Mar. 1988, para. 3.29, and Apr. 1990, para. 4.10. [86] CP 60, para. 40.

hard disclosure of IFA commission, but went further than either SIB or the DGFT had done in requiring that all selling life products should be required to disclose the remuneration received in relation to the sale.[87] This policy had previously been consistently rejected by both SIB and the OFT. The DGFT reckoned that disclosure of remuneration across the board was feasible, but that the costs would probably outweigh the benefits and it would be difficult to devise a means of measuring and comparing the remuneration of tied agents and IFAs.[88] He also introduced a new argument against the disclosure in his March 1993 report: hard disclosure of remuneration by all intermediaries would blur the effectiveness of status disclosure and partially recreate a single market for product distribution.[89] In contrast, SIB maintained that disclosure was neither desirable nor feasible. It argued strongly that commission was simply one element of overall costs, and so did not require separate disclosure; moreover that the total costs, rather than simply the commission, were more important. Further, it argued that it would be almost impossible to form rules which would make sense or could not be avoided. Some tied agents may not themselves receive commission: bank and building society staff do not receive separate payments for products sold. The form of remuneration will also come not just in the form of commission but other benefits: payments of overheads, computer systems, cars, and bonus payments. Calculating the proportion of these which was attributable to each sale would be very difficult, but focusing only on commission would enable the rules to be easily avoided as product companies could pay very low commissions, but give remuneration in other forms.[90]

The Treasury direction followed SIB's argument that both sectors, tied and IFA, should be subject to equivalent rules, but in requiring disclosure clearly rejected the arguments of both the DGFT and SIB as to desirability and feasibility. SIB's concerns as to the avoidance strategies which firms might employ to reduce the amount of commission disclosed have led it to adopt additional requirements as to monitoring and reporting. Firms would have to get advice from either an actuary or auditor as to whether the figure disclosed represented a true and fair view of the commission equivalent disclosed, and report to the regulator if it was

[87] Treasury Direction, para. 4. [88] Mar. 1993, paras. 5.31–5.32.
[89] Ibid., para. 5.32. [90] Dec. 1988, paras. 48–50; CP 23, para. 21.

not stating reasons why, to report commission figures to the regulator to facilitate monitoring of levels, and to spot check customers to ensure that they received the prescribed disclosures.[91]

Disclosure of Product Information

There were two possible approaches to the regulation of the product which the intermediary sold. The first, put forward by many insurers at the time of the FSA, was that SIB would sanction the companies, policies, agents, and commissions; the investor's only decision would be to choose a policy. This was rejected, however, as too restrictive. The second was the market-orientated approach: the investor was to be told everything about the product. In the political and economic climate of the 1980s, this was the only acceptable manner of government intervention: enabling a person to make his or her own choice, and letting the market operate as free as possible from restrictions. As much information as possible should therefore be disclosed to the customer.[92] The rationale for regulation was to be found in the incidence of market failure: the role of regulation was to repair these and enable the market to operate properly. The remedy: the investor was to be equipped with the tools to make 'an informed decision'.[93]

There are two broad approaches which the regulators could have adopted: specifying in extreme detail all the information to be given and the time at which it was to be given, and simply requiring the product company or adviser to provide the investor with 'sufficient information' to make an informed investment decision. In line with the tenor of the initial rule books, detailed prescription was the course initially adopted; this was quickly replaced by the less precise requirement to give 'sufficient information'. This has in turn been replaced by a prescriptive regime. The debates on product information have had three main themes: the pendulum swing between prescription and purposive rules; anti-avoidance and creative compliance concerns; and a tension between concerns for technical accuracy of the information and its comprehensibility.

[91] CP 77, paras. 35–7.
[92] See the White Paper, para. 3.2.
[93] FSA 1986, Sch. 8, para. 7.

Rule making in this area has also been dominated by differences between the FSA regulators and the OFT. The constant changes in the regulation have been mainly prompted by a series of reports from the OFT concluding that the rules significantly distort or restrict competition. It is largely through OFT prompting that the FSA regulators have moved away from industry positions. Following the trend in the debates on commission disclosure, differences between the two were initially due to an over-sympathetic attitude on the part of the regulators towards industry. In the more recent review, however, differences appear to lie now in the perceptions of the two, both as to the nature of the investor and the nature of the market, perceptions which again have only emerged slowly over the course of the rules' formation. It has become apparent that the OFT has a slightly different conception of the investor than the FSA regulators. The OFT tends to see the investor as a rational being who will be capable of seeking out information and using that which he or she is given; the FSA regulators see the investor as a rather less sophisticated consumer. These differences in perceptions lead to differences in prescriptions for what the regulation should provide. The FSA regulators, particularly since their research into consumer understanding, are now more concerned than they ever have been to ensure that the information is comprehensible to the investor, and due to that research have a more focused view of what the nature of that information has to be. The result has been a change from the detailed and complex information which was given before, to a much more simplified version of point of sale disclosure.

By contrast, the OFT began to move in a different direction, preferring more information to be given even though SIB has finally produced a disclosure regime more or less in line with what have been the OFT's requirements since 1987. In 1993 the DGFT also assessed the product disclosure rules under the Fair Trading Act 1973 for the first time.[94] The DGFT recommended a client and product specific disclosure statement should be given to the investor before he or she had taken the policy. In addition to the information already given, the disclosure should contain itemized charges and the company's policy on the allocation of their investment

[94] OFT, *Fair Trading and Life Insurance Savings Products*, Mar. 1993. The report is written under the Fair Trading Act 1973, s. 2 using powers under s. 125(4).

earnings. It should show how the projected returns to consumers would accrue by accumulating premiums paid, less expenses incurred, at particular rates of investment return. It should also show surrender values up until the end of the policy, and provide information on persistency rates: how long a policy of this type is kept for before it is surrendered. SIB's view is that the investor would be swamped by this volume of information, and that given the unsophistication of the investor and the consequent dangers of information overload, the proposals do not distinguish sharply enough between information which is essential, and that which is interesting.

Prescription or Generality?

In regulating disclosure, the regulators have recognized the dual responsibility of both the intermediary and the product provider to provide that information. Exactly who should provide what information, and when, has been a constant issue. To what extent the regulator should prescribe what information should be given and the way in which it is expressed has also been in issue, and the regulators have indicated an increasing awareness of the implications of different rule types. On the whole, the area is marked by a tendency to prescribe in detail every last item of information to be disclosed, including for example the basis for calculating charges or illustrations of future benefits, which is in marked contrast to the rules on all other forms of customer agreements, the detail of which SIB and SFA[95] have substantially reduced, even in relation to private customers.

The initial rules provided for the information on surrender values, charges, and illustrations (the 'product particulars') to be given to the investor both by the intermediary at the point of recommendation, or if advice was given by an IFA, immediately after, and to be provided by the product company on effecting the transaction. In December 1988, when reviewing the regime, the SIB Board accepted the arguments of the life offices and the view of Lautro that this involved too much duplication, and did not adequately recognize the extent to which detailed information on product particulars would be in the hands not of the person making

[95] If not IMRO: see Ch. 3.

the recommendation but of the life office or unit trust manager.[96] The resulting rules consequently made no provision for this information to be provided in written form at the point of sale. It would instead be sent by the product company prior to the ending of the cancellation period. The rule simply provided that the adviser should provide the investor with 'sufficient information' to make an informed investment decision.[97]

The reasons SIB gave were both principled and pragmatic. To require the objective of an 'informed investment decision' to be achieved by the provision of specific pieces of written information was, in SIB's view, 'impracticable' given the complexity of the information and the variety of selling situations, which, given the cold-calling rules, could include telephone calls. Further, SIB argued that:

> a prescriptive approach by it as to how the onus on the adviser is to be discharged in each and every case would be inappropriate and less effective, in regulatory terms, than requiring the adviser to ensure that the information he provides, and the form in which he provides it, meets the needs of the particular investor with whom he is dealing.[98]

Perceptions of the effectiveness of detailed rules and of the appropriate role of the regulator thus led to the revised requirement that only 'sufficient information' be given.

The decision was trenchantly criticized by the DGFT who stated that disclosure of expenses after the point of sale restricted and distorted competition to a significant extent.[99] The purpose of the cancellation period was to enable the investor to reconsider his decision, not to compare the merits of one life assurance product with another, information on which he or she would not have in any case.[100] A subsequent DTI report concluded that the rules did not automatically provide the investor with all the information he needed at an early stage to make an informed investment decision.

The DGFT's report prompted a review of the regulation. The consequent retail review accepted the concern that the disclosure arrangements were 'still failing to highlight the essential points and were instead contributing to "information overload"'.[101] It proposed

[96] Dec. 1988, para. 86.
[97] Financial Services (Conduct of Business) Rules 1990, r. 5.12A.
[98] CP 23, para. 12.
[99] Apr. 1990, paras. 4.13–4.16, and 4.19.
[100] Ibid., para. 4.16.
[101] SIB, Apr. 1991, para. 7.

substantial changes to both the presentation of the information and the timing of its provision, which represented a policy change on the nature of the information to be given and for greater precision in the rules. The result was that the timing of the information provision remained the same, but the rules indicated with far more precision what information was to be given. The rules now distinguish between three tiers of information. The information to be given at point of sale, known as the key features document, is short, its format and the information which it is to contain are prescribed by the regulators in a pro forma document, with the aim that it must aid comprehension and product comparison by the investor, and relate only to that product being advised upon.[102] The second tier, 'important information' is to contain more details on product particulars, ultimately in a client specific form. The third tier, 'useful information' is to comprise full details of the total range of funds available under unit linked contract, the with profits guide and the scheme particulars in the case of a collective investment scheme: to be available to investors and others on request and signposted in the key features. The audience for the latter is not just the ordinary investor, but those who can filter the information for that person's use: advisers, financial journalists, and the regulators feel it can therefore usefully be more technical as it will be interpreted by others.

In considering the implementation of the Treasury direction on commission disclosure, SIB showed an awareness of the type of rule which it felt would be most effective. It rejected the approach of devising an exhaustive list of services and assistance, for example, which an intermediary could be permitted to receive from a product company on the basis that 'such a list would probably result in the use of creative terminology to ensure that items were not covered by the list and therefore to be disregarded in the calculations'.[103] The rules on commission disclosure were deliberately comparatively short and backed by guidance. Detailed rules, SIB argued, would simply create loopholes and could not possibly anticipate all future situations; whereas guidance would enable unusual situations to be catered for without requiring either a rule breach or

[102] It requires information on the nature of financial commitment, a description of benefits payable and whether guaranteed, an indication of the risks, the consequences of early surrender, an indication of charges and expenses, and signposting to more detailed information to follow.

[103] CP 77, para. 31.

rule amendments.[104] In this way more responsibility could be placed on practitioners to meet the rule requirements in order to provide information in a way which is clear, fair, and not misleading.[105] Mindful of previous experience, SIB however indicated that it would keep the position under review. In terms which echo that of the trust relationship emphasized by SIB in the New Settlement rule formation, SIB stated: 'if it proves that there is any widespread abuse by the industry of its freedom to formulate its own description of the commission disclosure then the need for prescribed wording should be reconsidered'.[106]

Accuracy and Comprehensibility

The issue of disclosure of information concerning the product sold to the consumer has been one of the most technically complex and debate has occurred at a very detailed level involving such arcane matters as the costing structures of different types of policy and becoming embroiled in actuarial debates over the most accurate method of reflecting these complicated structures. The question concerns not just what information should be disclosed, but how it should be expressed. The balance between information which is accurate and comprehensive and that which is comprehensible has been one which the regulators have found hard to strike, however. The tenor of the debate has changed considerably since the inception of the regulation. The charge of regulatory capture, or regulation in industry's interests, is in this particular area hard to dispute, at least with respect to the early stages of the regulation's development. However, SIB has shown increasing independence from industry, prompted in no small part by the reviews of the DGFT.

The level of technical complexity has posed both SIB and consumer representatives with a great deal of difficulty. As with every other area of the regulation the majority of respondents to cosultations are the market participants, here the life companies and their actuaries, and it has been an area where the consumer bodies, lacking the technical expertise, have been at a disadvantage as a detailed knowledge of the area is required before they can effectively participate in the process. The regulators are thus faced with the

[104] Ibid., para. 32. [105] Ibid. [106] Ibid., para. 27.

problem of how to evaluate responses which may be simply industry lobbying. Experiments to include more representatives than the Consumers' Association, who have invested a considerable amount of resources in reviewing the FSA rules, have failed due to this complexity. In this area, the regulators have had actively to seek alternative sources of information, and rule formation in this area is now characterized by a high degree of reliance on market research on consumer understanding of information disclosed.

The issue of complexity, accuracy, and comprehensibility has been most evident in the issue of disclosure of costs and charges associated with the product. The debate, as with most of the issues relating to information about the product, centres on life products. Most life assurance products fall into one of three types: without profits, with profits, and unit linked.[107] The charging structure of each varies. Briefly, the charges on unit linked products are separately identifiable to each policy holder, and by reducing the amount of money invested will affect the ultimate return. In relation to without profits policies, the return is fixed, so the amount of charges or expenses will not surprise the investor by reducing the amount he or she expects to receive. Disclosure of charges on the latter policies has therefore never been required. In the case of with profits policies, which are the majority of policies sold, the life office pays a fixed benefit, plus a share of profits which is at the discretion of the office. Expenses are not allocated to a particular policy. All premiums received on without profits as well as with profits policies, together with investment income, realized capital gains, and other income are pooled in the company's life assurance fund, from which expenses and claims are met; expenses relating to a particular policy are not deducted from that policy's premiums.

The arguments of the life offices have been that only accurate information should be given, otherwise the investor will be misled.

[107] A *with profits policy* is a life assurance product which promises to pay the holder a stipulated sum, with an expectation that bonuses will also be paid at the discretion of the life office annually (reversionary bonus) and/or on death or maturity of the policy (terminal bonuses); a *without profits policy* is a life assurance product which promises to pay the holder a stipulated sum on death or maturity; a *unit linked policy* is a life assurance product in which a specified number of units in a specified unit trust are attributed to the policy. The sum paid out will reflect the value of the units at that time.

The concern of the life offices for technical accuracy is illustrated in one respondent's reply to the retail review:

> The use of cash expressions (14p in the £ in the SIB example) [to express the effect of charges] will lead some investors to believe that this represents actual cash deductions to meet expenses. They are most unlikely to understand that the figure is derived from accumulating premiums at interest net of expenses or charges to a projected date and comparing the result with the corresponding accumulation, totally hypothetical, without expenses or charges.[108]

The concern for accuracy dominated the early phases of the regulation. MIBOC saw the lack of methodology to calculate expenses and the complexities involved in giving accurate information as reason not to provide disclosure at all. It accepted industry arguments that disclosure was technically infeasible, the information could not be given accurately and consistently and so should not be given at all as simplifications would be misleading, and that the information would not be understood and anyway was unnecessary.[109] It further argued that it did not consider it would be 'appropriate' for it to seek to impose 'a detailed system of classification and allocation of expenses that would be necessary to produce the required result'.[110]

SIB, though pressured by the OFT and ministers[111] to require some form of disclosure, were persuaded by this view. An advisory committee of representatives from SIB, Lautro, Fimbra, the ABI, actuaries, and the Consumers' Association expressed a strong concern that the information should be accurate, should not mislead or display a 'spurious sense of accuracy' and should not be open to manipulation by companies.[112] This informed SIB's decision to express the effect of charges as the 'reduction in yield' of the

[108] Response to the Retail Regulation Review 1990–1.

[109] SIB and MIBOC, *Product Disclosure: Illustrations, Surrender Values and Past Performance*, July 1986, paras. 21–6, and *Life Assurance Companies, Disclosure of Expenses and Charges*, Dec. 1986.

[110] Ibid., para. 26.

[111] MIBOC's decision was made as the Financial Services Bill was going through Parliament and increased concern that the new regulatory structure would simply enable industry to cast regulation in its own interest. This failure to provide for disclosure of expenses on life policies was strongly criticized in Parliament, and followed assurances from the Minister for Corporate and Consumer Affairs that a policy statement would be sought on the issue: 1985/6 HC Standing Committee E, cc. 409–24.

[112] See the summary of the report in CP 27.

investment (RIY), but without a further disclosure explaining this figure to the investor.[113] Reliance instead was to be on journalists and financial advisers using the with-profits guide to inform the investor about the product.

Following further criticism by the DGFT that the information was not meaningful to the investor and did not enable comparison either of products or of the charges associated with buying from a tied agent or an IFA,[114] SIB and Lautro decided to commission consumer research on the issue to discover what the consumer could and could not understand. The research found that there was a relatively low awareness of the cost of fund management and confirmed that RIY was ill understood by a large majority.[115] So although charges and expenses were being disclosed, the form of that disclosure in practice disguised to the investor the effect of different levels of charges and expenses over the period of compound growth.

[113] SIB initially rejected RIY as it felt it would not be understood by investors, and that investors in fact wanted to know how much of their money was being invested. It therefore favoured an alternative method of disclosure, reduction in premium. Despite its initial misgivings, however, SIB was swayed by the life offices' and actuaries' arguments that RIY disclosure was more accurate, emphasized the long-term nature of the investment, enabled greater comparison between life assurance and competing products (bank and building society accounts), and that the short-term impact of charges was shown in the disclosure of surrender values: CP 23, paras. 42–4.

[114] The DGFT criticized RIY disclosure for charges and expenses as anti-competitive on the grounds that although a 'most useful' form of disclosure it would not be meaningful to the investor. Further, as disclosure of costs was made in terms of reduction in yield and IFA's commission disclosure as reduction in premium, the two could not be compared and IFAs could not put their commission in the context of overall expenses. He also criticized the fact that the cost of the risk and investment elements were not distinguished, so preventing comparison with other investment products, but would keep this under review: Apr. 1990, paras. 4.15 and 4.17.

[115] SIB, *Consumer Research by Taylor Nelson Financial, Jan. 1992*, May 1992. Some interpreted the figures to be the amount that would actually be paid to them, many misinterpreted the figures as indicating that a 10 year policy was cheaper than a 25 year one. These findings are supported by a 1990 Gallup survey which found that consumers could not understand the absolute figures, nor the significance of what appeared to be small differences between them. The survey found that 65% of consumers thought a 2% RIY sounded 'reasonable' to 'very low'. However, on a £1,000 annual premium on a 25 year term pension plan, a 2% RIY reduces the value of the fund by over £26 in every £100 otherwise payable. A 1% difference in RIY can affect the final payment on such a policy by over £12 in every £100 otherwise payable. See further Business Performance Group, *Disclosure in the Retail Financial Products Market*, (LSE, 1991), 13.

Various ways of expressing charges were suggested in the Review, each criticized on the basis of its lack of accuracy. Showing charges in the form of a reduction in maturity proceeds, for example, was criticized on the basis that it made it appear as if deductions were only made at maturity; reduction in premium on the grounds that expenses are not deducted from the premiums before investment but from the pooled life fund, that it did not reflect the changing incidence of costs over the term of the policy, and would give an illusion of accuracy by setting premiums which are known against expenses which are not.[116] The industry was also concerned that some methods of disclosure would be suitable for some types of products, not others. For example, reduction in benefit (effect of charges and expenses is to reduce benefit by *n*p in £) was felt to be satisfactory for investment contracts but not term assurance life cover contracts where the cover was shown with mortality risk and the amount is guaranteed at the end, and it was argued that reduction in premium was not suitable for the long term nature of the investment, as it gave no indication of the effect on eventual benefits and was not suitable for lump sum investments.

In formulating rules on disclosure of costs, surrender values, illustrations and commissions, SIB has relied increasingly on market research to test the effectiveness of its proposed disclosure requirements. SIB first used market research to test the form of costs disclosure which should be adopted (RIY, projected cash values, reduction in premium in cash terms).[117] Following the changes consequent on the Treasury's directions it commissioned two companies to carry out market research on the disclosure vehicle which should be adopted;[118] following these it produced a revised version of the form of disclosures and warnings, which again was subjected to

[116] Responses to the Retail Review 1990–1.

[117] Lautro preferred the form of disclosure which its consumer research indicated had been found to be a highly attractive method of presentation: disclosure of costs over the full term of the policy based on projected cash values; disclosures would be product and client specific but based on a standard assumed investment return; SIB however felt that the investor would take the conjectural figures as guarantees of what would be paid, that further statements as to the effect of inflation would be necessary, and that it would magnify small differences in assumptions. DP 3, paras. 22–3 and CP 60 paras. 21–33. In the end SIB decided to supplement RIY with a reduction in premium in cash terms, a proposal which has been approved by the DGFT: Mar. 1993, paras. 4.20–4.22.

[118] 'Life assurance disclosure—reports on market research conducted in 1993', available from SIB.

further research to check that the disclosures do improve customer understanding.[119] So in the battle between accuracy and comprehensibility, that of comprehensibility is now winning. Measures of effectiveness of the regulation have been identified clearly to be whether or not the rules actually result in improving the understanding of the customer as to the product he or she is buying. This has now become the key test of the rules.

Avoidance and Manipulation

There has also been a very strong concern on the part of the regulators, particularly SIB, that the disclosures required should not be capable of being manipulated by the product companies for their own ends or give rise to spurious competition. The low level of investor knowledge of the investment products being sold exacerbates the problem; consumer surveys conducted by SIB and Lautro indicated that the consumer can only understand a very limited amount of information; there is a danger that giving only some information on products will either mislead the consumer or that the information disclosed will be manipulated by the product company and by the intermediary in the selling process. Moreover, there is a danger that the scope of the rules may be drawn in such a manner that companies will exploit the provisions and compete on disclosed matters, altering those aspects of their product which are not covered by the rules. A study for SIB, for example, found that companies who had a poor ratio of surrender values to maturity values, which is not required to be disclosed, had actually inflated their maturity values so as to be included in the top ten companies of several financial press rankings by maturity values, although the penalties for surrender remained high right up until the end of the policy.[120]

These concerns have been dominant in decisions concerning the disclosure of surrender values (what the policy is worth if it is surrendered before completion of its term) and illustrations of future value of the policy. Again, SIB has been in dispute with the OFT. Again, the objective is shared: that the investor should receive

[119] CP 77, para. 82.

[120] '1992 With Profits Survey', *Money Marketing*, cited in OFT, *Fair Trading*, paras. 3.15–3.16.

as much information as he or she needs to make an informed decision. Again, however, the disagreement is as to what means can achieve these ends; more particularly, what information the investor can understand, and what information would be misinterpreted or would otherwise mislead.

The issue centres in essence on illustrations of future benefits. One of the problems of the pre-FSA (and to an extent post-FSA) era was the extreme use of projections for competitive purposes. SIB and MIBOC have shared the concern that projections are of a subjective and conjectural nature which makes it 'inappropriate' for them to be used as a basis for selection between product companies.[121] Further, they may easily be manipulated, with companies competing for business on the basis of escalating and unrealistic projections of future performance, projections which may be taken by the investor to be actual statements of how much he or she will receive. However, despite these dangers, both SIB and MIBOC felt that the investor should have some indication of futher prospects and so projections should not be prohibited.[122] Moreover as salesmen or IFAs will give them regardless, it was thought better to control them than leave them to the 'back of the envelope' calculations of the seller.

The solution arrived at was to permit illustrations but to prescribe the basis of their calculation, requiring them to be given on the basis of two prescribed rates of investment return, and be accompanied by an indication of the effect of inflation.[123] The costs of the product are deducted from the illustration, but these are also prescribed by the regulators. The subsequent debate has been whether these costs should be those of the office, particularly now the company is required to disclose these in the same document (see above), or whether they should be the standardized costs. Although SIB stated in its discussion paper that it favoured moving to an 'own charges' basis, in the final consultative paper it rejected this idea, again arguing that the charges are too open to manipulation, would be misleading as they represent current not future costs and create an impression that current differences would determine future performance, and that undue weight could be put on them by the investor in making the decision.[124]

[121] SIB, CPs 30 and 60.
[122] Apr. 1986, para. 51.
[123] July 1986, paras. 6–21.
[124] CP 60, para. 39.

The OFT for the first time ruled this basis of calculation to be anti-competitive in March 1993.[125] It shares SIB's concern at the marketing use companies may make of illustrations, which it feels is a justification for illustrations being on the basis of standardized assumptions. However, with Fimbra, the DGFT is opposed to using standardized charges. He stated that they prevent the investor from assessing the effects of the life office's level of costs, and competition between firms will then be limited to premiums. Companies with low premiums would be at a competitive advantage, but could simply raise their charges. Further, charges rarely change significantly over the life of a policy, particularly due to the practice of front end loading. Finally, the combination of own charges for expenses and standard charges for illustrations could be confusing. The DGFT's view has prevailed, and in July 1993 the Treasury directed SIB to provide disclosure of costs on an 'own charges' basis.[126]

The conflicting views on illustrations led to a further difference with respect to surrender values. The charging structure of most products is such that the majority of charges are taken out of the first few years' premiums, a practice known as 'front end loading'. The consequence is that if the policy is surrendered in the first few years the investor is likely to receive less than he or she has paid in premiums. Disclosure of surrender values has always been required under the regulation, but it has not always been clear. The Retail Review, in this as in other aspects of the Key Features document, used consumer research to inform policy on disclosure. This led the regulators to emphasize that withdrawal even after five years could be disadvantageous and SIB's proposed rules provide that surrender values should be shown for the first five years of the policy, but no longer.

These rules did not receive the approval of the DGFT, who stated that preventing disclosures of surrender values in the later years of a policy masks the differences which may exist between policies and so limits the investor's ability to make an informed decision. He concluded that the rules were likely to restrict and distort competition to a significant extent.[127] In addition, a report commissioned by SIB recommended that surrender values should be given for

[125] Mar. 1993, paras. 4.31–4.43. [126] Treasury Direction, para. 2.
[127] OFT, Mar. 1993, paras. 4.25–4.27.

the full term of the policy.[128] However, these proposals clash with SIB's policy on illustrations. A requirement to have surrender values shown to the end of the policy would institutionalize the provision of illustrations in a manner of which SIB was not favour, as it felt it would place too much emphasis on conjectural amounts which should not be used for competition, and which the investor may take to be guaranteed sums and use them to base his or her investment decision. Nonetheless, the Treasury directed SIB to alter its rules to provide surrender values beyond the initial five years. Still concerned that investors would interpret the table of cash surrender values as guarantees of what they would receive, SIB commissioned further research into the interpretation that investors put on the figures disclosed. In addition it took the unusual step of seeking views from the Insurance Ombudsman on how it would view a complaint from an investor who alleged that he had been led into believing that the figures quoted represented guaranteed sums. Both lines of inquiry indicated that further and clearer warnings as to the speculative nature of the figures were necessary.[129]

The Limits of Rules: Suitability and Best Advice

SIB's retail review predated discovery of the pensions misselling, and with hindsight the preoccupation with the precise formulation of the rules seem to be a case of fiddling while Rome burns.[130] All investment advisers are under a duty not to make a recommendation to a private customer[131] unless the recommendation is suitable for him or her, having regard to the facts disclosed by the customer and others of which the firm is, or should reasonably be, aware.[132] Under Principle 4 a firm is under a duty to seek any information from its advisory or discretionary customers about their circumstances and objectives 'which might reasonably be expected

[128] T. Miller, *Curbing the Sale of Unsuitable Products, A Report to the SIB*, SIB, May 1993.

[129] CP 77, paras. 14–15.

[130] This may be a little harsh: a study commissioned by SIB into the scale of non-compliance with the rules in advising on pension transfers found that the level of compliance did improve following the issuance of guidance on compliance with the rules in the case of pension transfers, rising from a level of 5% to 20%. Report by KMPG Peat Marwick, Jan. 1994.

[131] And discretionary portfolio managers in relation to all customers (SIB and SFA) or private customers (IMRO). SIB CR 16.

[132] CR 16.1.

to be relevant in enabling it to fulfil its responsibilities to them'. Intermediaries advising on polarized products are also under further rules governing the standard of advice which must be given. The 'best advice' rule is an application to the retail sector of the best execution principle.[133] It requires the intermediary to inform itself on the products which it can sell (tied agent) or are generally available on the market 'and on which it can advise' (IFA), and not to sell a product if there is another generally available product which would better meet the customer's needs.[134] IFAs which are part of a financial conglomerate which also markets its own products are under a more stringent requirement: under the 'better than best' rule they must not recommend one of the products of the group if there is another product on the market which would meet the investor's needs as well as the group's product.[135]

SIB has stressed the importance of these rules, describing the suitability rule as 'a direct statement of one of the basic aims of investor protection—that if an investor puts his trust in the judgement of an investor firm . . . that firm should vindicate his trust by tailoring its advice to his needs . . .'.[136] However the suitability and accompanying best advice rules indicate two of the problems which rules and rule makers face. Firstly, particularly in relation to the best advice rule, there is a question of whether the rules are requiring something which is impossible to achieve. Secondly, the conduct required by these rules is not mechanical, such as that required by reporting requirements or even precise disclosure rules. It requires the exercise of judgement on the part of the adviser. Rules cannot create informed judgement where none exists, however. As the analysis in chapter 1 suggests, rules rely for their operation on the judgement of those subject to them; where that judgement is lacking the rule itself cannot provide it. The rule can perhaps provide guidelines and leave less to the discretion of the addressee, but it cannot do more.

Non-compliance with the suitability and best advice rules is one of the largest problems which the regulators have to face, and the

[133] CR 22. See MIBOC, Dec. 1985, paras. 15–17. [134] CR 17.

[135] The 'better than best' rule was assessed to be anti-competitive by the DGFT when he reviewed SIB's rules: Mar. 1987, para. 3.49. However, the Secretary of State did not require any changes in the rules and although the Review included proposals to drop the requirement, SIB feared that subsidiaries may come under too great a degree of pressure to recommend the products of group companies and the requirement remains, despite objections by the bank and building society trade associations: CP 60, para. 50 and CR 17(5). [136] Mar. 1990, para. 3.3.

investors suffer. SIB expressed its dissatisfaction with practitioner performance in the area of suitable advice, as evidenced by complaints from investors, internal company information, and its own research, in the Retail Review. Its research indicated that one-third of policies sold in 1990 were surrendered within the first two years. The highest surrender rates were in unit linked life assurances (endowment policies), an average of 37.1 per cent, and in sales from company representatives (32.5 per cent).[137] Though SIB accepted that there were shortcomings with the methodology used to collate the figures, it maintained that 'the message is clear': unsuitable policies were being sold to investors.[138]

Evidence from other research reinforces this view.[139] The most prevalent area of non-compliance was initially seen to be the recommendation of endowment policies when straight repayment mortgages would be more suitable, and the experience of the home income plans is one of the most striking examples of non-compliance with the requirements.[140] Other sectors of the retail market also criticize the life assurance companies' behaviour in this context, although research finds the High Street banks to be equally guilty. The Unit Trust Association described the life assurance companies' sales abuses in unusually harsh terms and criticized the commission structure which it argued foisted unsuitable products on an unsophisticated public.[141] Resignations of membership by five large life companies caused it to revise its submission to reflect these companies' views,[142] but the incident indicated the depth of feeling and resentment of the commercial success, and

[137] The survey was of 61 life companies, calculating termination rates using information about premiums rather than policy values. The survey found that in unit linked life assurance the termination rates within the first two years were 37.2% for direct sales, 40.1% for company representatives, 30.3% for IFAs; for non-linked life assurance the rates were 24.7% for direct sales, 24.8% for company representatives, and 22.1% for IFAs.

[138] Colette Bowe, Retail Division Policy Director, letter to the *FT*, 30 Jan. 1992. Ms Bowe is currently chief executive of PIA.

[139] See research conducted by the Consumers' Association, published in *Which?*, Feb. 1992 and May 1993.

[140] Life assurance companies made products which entailed the taking out of a second mortgage to raise money for investment. Customers, predominantly retired people, were told that the investment would cover the second mortgage, and give them some money left over which they could spend as they wished. Many of the investments failed to raise sufficient amounts to meet the repayments, leading to repossession orders on the homes.

[141] Initial response to DP 2.

[142] Prudential, Legal and General, Guardian Royal Exchange, Scottish Provident, and Allied Dunbar resigned in Dec. 1992, cutting the UTA's revenues by 10%.

political lobbying power, of the life companies. The widespread misselling of pensions, and the extent to which that misselling was found to be endemic in the system, from the largest life companies to the smallest advisers, is an even greater indication of the extent to which the requirements of suitability and best advice have been simply flouted. A report commissioned by SIB in January 1994 found that in advising on pension transfers only nine per cent of firms investigated had substantially complied with the principal conduct of business rules, including those of know your customer, suitability, and best advice.[143]

Dictating Quality?

Altering the structure of the suitability and best advice rules was considered in the retail review (which predated the discovery of the pensions misselling) as a means by which compliance with these rules could be achieved. Both the suitability and best advice rules have been the subject of considerable confusion as to their scope and meaning, particularly as to two issues. First, did the suitability rule require that only the most suitable product be recommended, or was it sufficient simply to recommend a product which was suitable (though not perhaps the most suitable), and further, did it prohibit advising on products which were unsuitable? Second, to comply with the 'best advice' rule, what range of products did IFAs have to survey?

With respect to the suitability rule, SIB was concerned that the general statement of the duty, with greater room for its interpretation, was insufficiently indicating the nature of conduct required. SIB therefore considered amending the rule to make it clear that recommendation of an unsuitable product was prohibited.[144] It ultimately concluded that simply restating the duty would not improve the situation: any elaboration of the requirement should be made

[143] Report by KMPG Peat Marwick, Jan. 1994. The study examined the extent of compliance with regulator's requirements in all instances of lump sum pension transfers for the period Jan. 1991–June 1993. The study covered a representative sample of firms from Lautro, Fimbra, and IMRO. 735 client files were reviewed by officers of SROs and the results monitored by KMPG. The report found that in four out of five cases the adviser made a recommendation on the basis of insufficient information about the customer's position.

[144] SIB, *Regulation of the Conduct of Investment Business: A Proposal*, Aug. 1989, Annex C, Draft Designated Rules, r. 8; Review Committee Report, Mar. 1990, para. 3.7; DP 2, para. 26.

specific to particular types of business, rather than formulated in the 'abstract'. In line with the New Settlement rule structure and philosophy, the SROs should detail the rule in the third tier to set out what would be reasonable grounds for a recommendation or factors to be taken into account in giving advice.[145] This was an attempt to use more detailed rules to improve compliance and control in the face not of creative compliance but inadequate compliance.

Specifying further the standard of conduct required was also considered with respect to the best advice rules. SIB expressed concern that the widely differing interpretations meant practitioners could not understand their responsibilities to their clients in this area, producing an 'uncertainty and lack of clarity in a vital area of investor protection' which in the interests of investors could not be allowed to continue.[146] Criticism has also focused on the phrase 'best advice'. The 'best advice' rule does not in fact contain the phrase, requiring that the adviser only recommend a product if it is not aware of another which would 'better meet [the customer's] needs'. The label, however, has been criticized on the grounds that it is inaccurate and thus misleading, implying that one product above all others could be identified as the 'best buy', whereas in fact several products could qualify, especially given the uncertainties of future performance.[147] Many suggested that the label 'best advice' had become simply a marketing device which had been so exploited by companies in their selling that it should be decently buried.

Two concerns dominated consideration of the best advice rule: the impact of the rule on the development of the market, and whether 'best advice' is in fact a feasible or desirable requirement. The scope of enquiry independent advisers must make as to products available on the market has the potential to impact on the development of specialist or niche players. If a market wide survey is required, it may effectively act as a barrier to such operators; however, allowing a limited survey may legitimize incompetence, sanctioning failures to explore the market fully. On the other

[145] The Law Society in particular, however, remain concerned that it does not sufficiently indicate that non-FSA products should be included when making the suitability assessment: response by the Law Society to SIB's CP 60, May 1992.

[146] DP 2, para. 28.

[147] Views taken from responses to the Retail Review 1990–1 provided to the author.

hand, requiring a full survey may not only impact on particular market players, it may simply be an infeasible requirement. The concern here is essentially to maintain the reputation of the regulation. The tension is between the Scylla of setting the requirement so high that compliance is infeasible, or at least excessively costly, which would itself bring the regulation into disrepute, and the Charybdis of lowering the requirement so that it becomes meaningless. The same tension led SIB to maintain the 'best advice' label, despite its extensive use as a marketing device, on the basis that either subsuming the rule into the suitability requirement or altering its label or wording to 'good advice' would signal a dilution of the obligation that the regulation could ill afford.

Monitoring Quality

Rules cannot dictate quality. Nor, in this area at least, can the consumer be relied upon to insist upon or monitor quality of advice. In an attempt to assist monitoring, both by the investor and by regulators, and also to try to structure the behaviour of the adviser, SIB focused instead on 'proxies' for good judgement: visible, quantifiable, and so monitorable requirements that could (but not necessarily would) lead to improved quality. It proposed first that customers should be required to sign the statement containing the information about them given to the adviser (the 'fact find'), which should apply wherever Principle 4 applied. Second, the customer must be provided with written reasons for the recommendation given. The scope of the latter requirement is confined to long-term products;[148] the amendment is directed principally at life assurance products, in line with most of the rules in this area, but SIB is unsure whether its scope should be confined to these.

The giving of written reasons was proposed by the Consumers' Association,[149] and the aim of the amendments is to provide a discipline which would encourage 'wholehearted compliance' with the rule, as well as foster a 'spirit of personal responsibility on the part of investors'.[150] SIB hoped to improve compliance by requiring some form of visible conduct which could be monitored, and which might also influence the behaviour of the adviser. The trade-

[148] CP 60, paras. 70–6.
[149] Consumers' Association response to SIB, Apr. 1991.
[150] CP 60, para. 75.

off is thus between qualitative rules which aim to ensure a high standard of quality of conduct, but full compliance with which is difficult, if not impossible, to monitor, and what may be termed quantitative and precise rules which in an attempt to aid monitoring and so improve compliance focus on visible and easily measurable proxies of quality. The danger of course is that such rules will prompt a mechanistic compliance with no overall improvement in quality.

Conclusion

The development of regulation in the retail sector has followed a repeating pattern: the FSA regulators produce rules, which are declared uncompetitive by the DGFT, and the Secretary of State (now Chancellor) then directs the regulators to alter the rules in particular respects. This institutional structure has meant that differences in perceptions between the different bodies which are involved in rule formation have thus played a significant role in the regulation's development. Other themes can also be identified: the impact of the nature of the market, products, and consumer in shaping both perceptions and regulation, the role played by interest groups in shaping, and in certain cases determining the regulation, and changes in the regulator's own approach to policy and rule formation. Further, there have been concerns that developments in one area of regulation should not undermine key principles in others; that regulation should pre-empt, or at least not encourage anti-avoidance and creative compliance; and attempts to address the unanticipated consequences of regulation, and the limits of rules.

The most striking aspect of the regulation's development has been the impact of the institutional structure, the involvement of the OFT in the competition review of the FSA regulators' rules. This has led to the reversal of key policies, notably the abolition of the MCA (the administration of which had been the main rationale behind Lautro's formation), the initial prohibition against dual status distribution in Lautro's rules, and requiring hard disclosure of commission payments to IFAs; the Chancellor has himself gone further with respect to the latter, extending hard disclosure to tied agents.

The debate between the OFT and the FSA regulators has turned in essence on their different perceptions of the nature of the market, the nature of the problem, the nature of the consequences of any action, and the acceptability of those consequences. Thus with respect to commission disclosure, for example, there were initial differences over its technical feasibility, and continuing disputes over its necessity for the consumer, as to the exact nature of the commission payment, and so the regulatory need for its disclosure, for example to ensure parity between the tied and independent sectors, over the strategic question of the consequences of hard disclosure on the IFA sector, and on the desirability of those consequences.

These perceptions are themselves shaped by the competitive structure of the market, the opacity of the products being sold, and the unsophisticated nature of the consumer. The initial form of the regulation, the polarization of the distribution channels into the independent and tied sectors, the tying of agents to only one product provider, and the MCA, was itself a reaction to the market structure which prevailed in the late 1970s and early 1980s. The market has taken a form under this regulation which however was unforeseen and unintended, with the majority of major high street banks and building societies forsaking independent status and becoming tied to one product provider. In the face of these developments, the regulators have found tensions between the policy of maintaining the clarity of the status of the adviser, and in encouraging the provision of independent advice. There have thus been trade-offs between promoting competition, ensuring consumer choice, and avoiding consumer confusion as to the status of the person advising him or her.

The combination of opaque products, a competitive selling environment, and consumers who are largely ignorant of the characteristics and quality of the products being sold has been an intractable problem. It is also one which illustrates the nature of the relationship between the particular regulatory technique adopted and the nature of the market in which it is operating. Three regulatory techniques dominate: structural regulation (which structures the market: polarization), conduct regulation (the best advice and suitability rules), and disclosure. Disclosure is usually seen as the least interventionist; however it is particularly susceptible to the skill and ability of the person receiving the information, and correspondingly vulnerable to manipulation by those imparting it. The aim of disclosure is to enable the consumer to act in an informed and rational manner; it can succeed only if the information provided is accurate and not misleading, and if the consumer can understand it. Initially, the emphasis was on accuracy, at the expense of comprehensibility. Changes in regulatory approach and most significantly in the sources of information on which regulators rely in forming rules (the increased reliance on testing consumer understanding of different disclosure statements), have led to a far greater emphasis on comprehensibility, even if this may mean a small loss of accuracy.

Concern at the ability of product providers and advisers to manipulate the information disclosed, or to adopt other avoidance techniques, has involved compromise between different regulatory policies, for example between not wanting to encourage reliance on illustrations of future value but recognizing the importance of disclosing surrender values, which themselves require illustrations of future values. It has also led to a highly prescriptive disclosure regime, in which every aspect of disclosure is regulated, including the format in which the information is provided. Here still, however, the problem remains that given the limited ability of the consumer to understand and digest information, only a limited amount of information can be disclosed. Information is thus not provided on significant aspects of the products. However, the likelihood is that companies will simply alter the product's characteristics so as to ensure that it performs favourably on those indices which are disclosed, and not on those which are not. Attempts to address this avoidance strategy have thus focused on providing different types of information to different end users; basic information to consumers, more complex information to advisers. Disclosure to the latter is then backed by the rules on best advice and suitability; however, the problem still remains that the regulator cannot through specification hope to ensure that all aspects of a product are covered. Under-inclusion in the initial rule, accompanied by product innovation and development, will ensure that creative compliance remains a feature of the regulation.

Creative compliance has prompted the consideration of rule use, in particular of the use of different types of rules. Whereas detailed prescription is the dominant feature of the disclosure regime for product information, other considerations have affected the formation of rules for the disclosure of commissions. Thus

SIB rejected rules which specified what services and assistance an intermediary could be permitted to receive from a product company without incurring the obligation to disclose on the basis that it would simply be avoided. Less specific rules were thus adopted, backed by detailed guidance.

A similar combination of rule types has been adopted with respect to the suitability rule, although the problem here is not so much creative compliance as inadequate compliance. The regulatory technique used here is that of conduct regulation, aiming to ensure a higher standard of advice and service to the consumer. However, given the infinite variety of consumers' financial circumstances and needs, it is impossible to state comprehensively what advice would be suitable in each situation. A vague rule has to be used if chronic under- or over-inclusion is to be avoided. However, this does not express what the regulator considers should be the precise level of conduct required in any case. Compliance is also difficult to monitor on a widespread scale. The attempt has been made, therefore, to back up this qualititative technique and the vague rule structure in which it is expressed by rules which are more specific and require behaviour which may easily be monitored: the fact find and the 'reason why' letter. In focusing on proxies of quality, however, the rule may fail to raise actual levels of quality. Moreover, it does not address the question of what reasons should provide the basis of the advice, what, in short, suitable advice amounts to. Rules cannot address this issue; rules such as the suitability and best advice rule require an informed reading which they themselves cannot provide.

5 Rules and Regulatory Technique

Introduction

The regulation of soft commission agreements between fund managers and brokers is a more contained issue than that of retail regulation. The questions to which it gives rise, however, are just as complex. In particular, the issue highlights the difficulties in interpreting and balancing the objectives of the regulation, and indicates that when it is not clear which course of action will serve which objective then the decision is significantly affected by the regulator's own perceptions of the appropriate role of regulation, and by concerns to protect existing regulatory provisions which are threatened by developing market practices. Regulators are not left to make these decisions in splendid isolation, however: different constituencies make competing (and voluble) demands, and the ability of regulation to structure the market means that rules become weapons in the competitive battle for market share. Moreover, the focus of the rule making process shifts in response to new events and market developments, and regulators are further constrained by the institutional and legal context in which the regulation operates. In addition, the subject matter of the rule has a particular impact: it is a financial arrangement between two sets of market participants, fund managers and brokers; both the nature of the arrangement being regulated and the incentives to avoid regulation mean that concerns of creative compliance loom large, and problems of identifying exactly what the rule should encompass and what it should not are significant. Different techniques of regulation have therefore been tried, in association with different rule types; ultimately, however, a combination of factors: market structure, institutional differences, and the regulator's perceptions, has resulted in a rule which may not in fact achieve its aim.

The Nature of Soft Commission Agreements

Soft commission agreements are arrangements between fund managers and brokers whereby in return for an agreed amount of commission business from the fund manager, the broker will pay for services which the manager has received from third parties (for example Reuters' screens). The broker and manager agree the multiple, the ratio of commission to the value of services supplied. So for a multiple of 1.5, for example, for every £1.50 in commission paid by the manager to the broker, the manager receives £1 in services. The broker pays for the services out of commission received on each trade and retains the balance. Multiples vary with the volume of business, the markets in which transactions are being executed, and the manner in which the service invoices are paid.

Soft commissions crossed the Atlantic from the US and entered the UK market whilst the old Stock Exchange minimum commission rules were operative. Unable to compete on the basis of commission levels, brokers began to compete on the basis of services that would be provided to investors and fund managers in return for business. As the volume of business declined rapidly following the stock market crash of October 1987,[1] brokers competed fiercely for business. Because of the advantages soft commissions offer brokers and managers (see below), brokers continued to offer them after the abolition of minimum commissions in the competition for market share, and increased the proportion of commission income used to pay for the services. Not only brokers but market makers had arrangements with fund managers whereby managers agreed to provide a stipulated volume of turnover in return for services, usually computer hardware. These were termed 'soft for net' arrangements as managers would deal with the market maker on a 'net' or no commission basis.

Soft commissions differ from traditional arrangements in which the fund manager pays the broker a commission, in return for which the broker provides a total servicing of the fund manager's accounts: execution, custodianship of the securities, and research, all of which are provided in-house, and none of which are separately priced. An amount of business is not agreed, and the manager cannot choose, or price, the services he receives in return, which are provided by the broker. The two principal differences between the two types of arrangement are thus that, firstly, under

[1] In 1988 securities houses made a collective loss of approximately £500 million on dealings in British equities and by September 1990 daily turnover in British shares on the Stock Exchange was £630 million, a third less than the previous year and nearly half of the pre-crash levels. See *The Economist*, 8 July 1989 and 27 Feb. 1990.

a soft commission (or 'softing') agreement the manager and broker agree an amount of business to be given to the broker to cover the payment for services received by the manager. Secondly, the broker does not provide the service, he pays for its provision by a third party. Moreover, the manager can choose and price the services he receives, simply sending the invoices to the broker to be paid. The most common services are Reuters screens (which provide on-line stock price quotations), performance measurement, custodian services, and independent research.

Soft commissions provide both brokers and fund managers with a number of advantages. The fund manager can choose which service he or she requires and can have these paid for out of commissions without having to charge the investor directly. This enables managers to keep their fees to the client lower than if the services were paid for directly by the manager. The broker in return is assured a certain amount of business. The customer may also benefit if the services provided assist the fund manager in providing an investment service, though it is likely that all accounts will benefit, not just those in which trades are executed as part of the soft commission arrangement.

Two principal types of stockbroking firms use soft commission agreements: specialist houses that only supply third party services, and integrated houses that use softing alongside their traditional arrangements. The extent of soft commission business was estimated to be approximately 13 per cent of total commissions paid by the institutions in 1990, up from 5 per cent from the year before,[2] though others put the figure at 20 per cent.[3] Over 80 per cent of unit trust or investment companies' fund managers, nearly 70 per cent of investment advisers, and 40 per cent of the insurance companies used soft commissions in 1990, and typically managers had

[2] 'Soft Commissions', Winter 1991, *SEQ* with *Quality of Markets Review*, 27 from a survey by Greenwich Associates.

[3] Suggestions put to SIB and cited in SIB, *Soft Commissions in the Securities Markets*, CP 29, Oct. 1989. There has recently been a move away from soft commission business, particularly in the US, to 'directed commission' business. In this latter arrangement, the fund manager's client asks the fund manager for part of the commission to go to the broker, and the broker in return pays the client's management fees or fees for investment consultancy. Moves away from soft commission business are also occurring in the UK: in Jan. 1995 Mercury Asset Management announced that it would no longer deal under soft commission arrangements, a move which it stated reflected a growing resistance to SCAs in UK pension funds. See further Butterworth's *Financial Services Law and Practice*, Bulletin 68.

softing arrangements with three brokers.[4] The figure was still much lower than the US, where in 1990 soft commission business accounted for 35 per cent of all commission business.[5]

Regulatory Concerns

Soft commissions raise a number of concerns for regulators. These relate primarily to the question of conflicts of interest, particularly the probity of the fund manager and misuse of customer's funds, and to issues of market distortion and competition. Soft commission agreements, as we have seen, have two essential elements, an agreed amount of commission business and the provision of services chosen by the fund manager by a third party. The agreement to provide a set amount of business raises concerns that the agreements also have the potential to distort market structure and competition as the fund manager could be effectively tied to the broker, and brokers may compete on terms other than price and execution. It also raises significant issues of conflicts of interest. For example, there is a danger that a fund manager will feel constrained to deal through the broker even when the broker is not executing the transaction at the best price, and that the fund manager will be tempted to 'churn' the accounts (deal excessively) in order to generate the required commission levels, both involving breaches of the conduct of business rules.

The payment of the commission itself also raises potential conflicts of interest. For example, the payment of commission by the manager to the broker raises the issue of whether the manager is in fact receiving benefits or inducements which are paid for from commission taken out of the customer's account, but from which the account does not benefit, either at all, or in proportion to the amount of services generated through it. The practice thus raises the question of whether the manager is taking secret profits under fiduciary law,[6] or whether the customer is receiving, in SIB's terms, 'value for money'.[7] Alternatively, or in addition, the manager may overcharge the customer by failing to deduct from the

[4] 'Soft Commissions'. [5] Ibid.

[6] See the Law Commission, *Fiduciary Duties and Regulatory Rules*, CP No. 24, (HMSO, 1992), Ch. 3, and *Fiduciary Duties and Regulatory Rules*, Cmnd. 3049 (Dec. 1995). [7] CP 29, para. 10.

management fee services paid for out of the brokerage commissions, for which the customer is also charged. The customer thus pays twice for the same service.

The customer may suffer further if the manager fails to negotiate the lowest commission rates available, and chooses the broker not on the basis of the execution but on the nature of the ancillary services provided. One of the principal concerns is the threat posed to best execution (the duty to ascertain the best price available on the market and deal at a price no less advantageous). The manager may not have the incentive to demand best execution, and the broker may accept a worse execution to subsidize the cost of providing the services.

The practice of 'soft for net' agreements between fund managers and market makers poses even greater problems for competition and standards of conduct as fund managers are then entering agreements with market makers to provide an agreed volume of turnover in return for services. The managers deal with the market maker on a 'net' or no commission basis. The issue of best execution is enhanced as the manager is simply accepting that market maker's prices, whereas at least when dealing through a broker the broker has the capacity to 'shop around' for the best deal. In addition, there exists the danger that market makers, in the absence of commission payments, will widen their spread (the difference between their buy and sell prices) to subsidize the provision of softed services, threatening best execution further. This also has an effect on market liquidity (the ability to buy and sell large blocks of shares without moving prices) as the wider the spread, the greater the price movements on the sale and purchase of large blocks of shares.

Soft commission agreements with brokers of integrated houses raise similar issues. The fund manager has an agreement with a broker of an integrated house; the broker then puts the deal through its market making arm. The fund manager is thus effectively tied to the market maker by the actions of the broker. The temptation exists for the market making arm to widen the spread on the deal, so that the manager gets a less advantageous price and the house's increased profit on the sale subsidizes the payment of services by the firm for the manager.

Soft commissions thus raise significant regulatory concerns of conflicts of interest, probity, inducements, secret profits, malign competition, market distortion, best execution, and 'value for money' for the customer. However, they also offer some attractions. The agreements provide price transparency as the services are separately priced. Because managers can choose services from third parties they also encourage independent service providers and research analysts and introduce competition between them. Traditional arrangements, on the other hand, provide no choice of services, no impetus for competition in service provision as all services are provided in-house, and no price transparency as there is no breakdown of the costs of the services for which the commission was paying. Furthermore, although under traditional arrangements there is no agreement that a certain amount of business would be sent the broker's way, there is usually an understanding that a certain amount of business would be generated.[8]

Finally, different sectors of the market had much to gain, and lose, from regulation on soft commissions. Soft commissions favoured smaller fund managers who could receive a large part of their overheads, particularly information services, through soft commission agreements, without having to raise their fees to clients. They could also select the services they needed, without having to pay for the full servicing provided by the integrated houses. As these services were often bought in from third parties, soft commission arrangements also favoured independent research firms, whose research would be bought in by the broking firm who would then provide it to the manager. Soft commission business had indeed been initially concentrated with three broking firms (houses) which provided only softing services. However the larger integrated houses, concerned at the threat of loss of business to specialist houses and attracted by the guaranteed order flow which softing provided, started to offer their own soft commission deals at multiples well below industry average, and with which the smaller houses said they could not compete. The smaller broking houses accused the integrated firms of using other activities of the firm to subsidize these multiples, particularly through using their market maker arms to widen their spreads on softed deals. Decisions about how to regulate one small part of this complicated market would therefore inevitably involve the regulators in turf fights for competitive advantage between the different market participants.

[8] Ibid., para. 25.

Regulatory Options

There is a range of possible approaches which could be adopted to address these concerns, both of regulatory technique and of rule type, which can be ranked in order of their intervention in the market. First, an outright ban of soft commissions could be imposed. In eliminating soft commissions, it would hope to eliminate the concerns which they raise. However, it would be highly interventionist, and would also confer competitive advantage on a particular set of market participants, namely the integrated houses. Moving down the interventionist scale, the regulators could impose a form of price regulation by limiting the multiples at which the soft commission agreements are set. This could be embodied either in a 'bright line' rule which set a limit, for example of 1.5, or a more opaque rule which required the level to be 'reasonable', which would confer more discretion on both regulator and regulated.

Regulating multiples would address the concern that there should be no cross subsidies between market making and broking arms in integrated houses. It would not however meet the other concerns soft commissions raise, particularly the issue of conflicts of interest between the manager and client. To meet this question, regulators could require that the services provided under the soft commission agreement should benefit clients. However, compliance with a simple exhortation would be difficult to monitor and enforce; the regulator could alternatively set out what services it considers would benefit clients, and / or require proof that the services provided did in fact benefit clients generally, or individually.

Alternatively, or in addition, the onus could be placed on the client to decide whether or not she wanted to engage a manager who would be involved in soft commission agreements. Regulation would simply require disclosure of the fact that soft commission agreements would be entered into, leaving it to the client to make the choice. Disclosure provisions could either be general, simply requiring, for example, a statement that soft commission arrangements would be entered into, or more specific, stipulating the percentage of business softed, the multiple levels, and services received. Further, in order to promote competition between softing and traditional arrangements, regulators could also require greater transparency in the latter by insisting that services be separately priced to the fund manager, and either disclosed or not to the customer, depending again on whom the onus for monitoring the agreements between managers and brokers was to be placed. Finally, and least interventionist of all, the regulators could simply do nothing: allow soft commissions and rely on other rules relating to best execution and churning, for example, to ensure that agreements between managers and brokers were not to the client's detriment.

In all but the last option, what constitutes a soft commission agreement has of course to be defined. Problems of under- and over-inclusiveness thus arise. However, it is important to note that the implications of designing a rule which is, for example, over-inclusive depend on the regulatory strategy or technique which is then adopted. If an outright ban is imposed, then the consequences of an over-inclusive rule are greater than if a disclosure provision is imposed. Similarly with concerns of creative compliance: there may indeed be more incentive for creative compliance in the case of a ban than in the case of disclosure.

The Development of Regulation

Soft commissions were permitted under the initial rules, but their regulation was widely seen as ineffective. Following the approach of US regulation[9] and the London Stock Exchange rules,[10] the 1987 SIB Rules permitted the supply of 'services and benefits the nature of which is such that their provision will improve the performance of the recipient firm in providing services to its customers'.[11] IMRO similarly required that the services must be designed to improve the fund manager's services to its customers;[12] TSA simply required that the firm must reasonably believe that

[9] Soft commissions were permitted by US regulation in 1975 when the Securities and Exchange Act 1934 was amended to allow fund managers to direct business to brokers other than the cheapest broker without breaching their fiduciary duties under certain circumstances, specifying the services which could be provided: s. 28(e) SEA.

[10] The rules had not specified services, but had instead required that they should be intended to improve the ability of the recipient to make investment decisions or evaluate the performance of his or her investments: Stock Exchange Rules, r. 310.

[11] SIB 1987 r. 5.09.

[12] IMRO 1988 IV-6.01.

they would.[13] Under SIB and IMRO rules either best execution has to be given, or disclosure had to be made which set out the 'specified particulars' of the arrangement and stated that the services were dependent on business being placed with the provider.[14] The aim of disclosure was 'to ensure that clients had sufficient information to enable them to judge whether they were getting value for money'.[15] Disclosure was only required by TSA's rules if the agreement operated against the best interests of the customer.

The impetus to reconsider the regulation of soft commissions came in mid-1988 from market participants, principally the integrated houses who operated under traditional arrangements, who called on SIB to examine the issue. SIB stated that it would not act unless someone indicated that the rules were being broken, or otherwise set out reasons for concern.[16] In late 1988 a group of full-service stockbroking firms called on SIB to ban the practice completely.[17] They argued that in practice the rules did not require a level of disclosure sufficient to achieve SIB's objectives. Firstly, the nature of services which could be provided was too broadly defined and a wide range of interpretations as to what constituted legitimate services existed, with the result that services were being provided which were marginal to the fund manager's performance and which the manager would not otherwise purchase. Secondly, they argued that the exceptions to the disclosure requirements were widely used and specific disclosure was rarely being made under either the IMRO or TSA rules.[18]

SIB agreed to consider the issue, and in its February 1989 discussion paper SIB reported that most respondents felt that the rules were giving insufficient guidance, and that disclosure was 'woefully inadequate'.[19] These weaknesses in the rules, it was felt, were contributing to the potential for abuse. For example, respondents suggested that broker dealers were widening their spreads on 'softed' deals[20] so that their net revenue from the manager remained the same, some managers were closing accounts with those brokers who did not offer a softed service, and, to reward brokers

[13] TSA r. 280. [14] SIB 1987 r. 5.09; IMRO 1988, IV-6.02.

[15] CP 29, para. 11. [16] *The Economist*, 9 July 1988.

[17] *FT*, 7 Mar. 1989.

[18] SIB, *Soft Commission Arrangements in the Securities Markets: A Discussion Paper*, Feb. 1989, para. 13. [19] Ibid., para. 23.

[20] i.e., those conducted under a soft commission agreement.

for the provision of soft services, some fund managers were placing the brokers' new issues in their clients' accounts.

In its first policy documents SIB considered banning soft commissions, setting multiples, limiting the proportion of business that could be softed. All these were rejected, for reasons which are considered below, and SIB decided to continue, with some attempt at improvement, its initial policy of disclosure plus benefit to the client. In considering the regulatory options available to it, SIB was influenced by several factors: the question of enforceability and effectiveness, the impact of regulation on different participants within the market, and the implications of the regulation adopted on London's international competitiveness, one of the perceived objectives of the regulation. It was also constrained in its decision by external legal rules, notably EC provisions, and by the OFT, which as we have seen occupies an important position within the institutional structure, assessing the rules for their anti-competitive effect. Finally, its decisions were affected by SIB's own perceptions of the role regulation was meant to play in the market.

The idea of banning soft commissions, floated in its first discussion paper in February 1989, was quickly rejected on grounds of enforcement and effectiveness, of London's competitiveness, and of the appropriateness of regulation being used to structure the market.[21] In relation to enforcement, it was argued that a ban would be impossible to enforce for two reasons. First, the internationalization of the securities business would make it very difficult to enforce a ban imposed by one national regulator in isolation.[22] Second, unless a ban was coupled with a requirement that integrated houses itemize and separately price services they provided under the traditional agreements it would be difficult to judge whether soft commission arrangements were being entered into or not.[23] SIB accepted this, and showed no inclination to want to impose such transparency on integrated houses, although did not at this stage indicate why.

Internationalization also prompted a further concern: that a ban could simply force business to those jurisdictions which permitted

[21] CP 29.

[22] SIB, *Soft Commissions in the Securities Markets: Soft for Net*, CP 46, Nov. 1992, para. 2.

[23] Ibid., para. 18.

softing, for example the US, thus adversely affecting London's international competitive position.[24] However, it was principally considerations of the appropriate role for regulation in the market which motivated the decision not to ban. As we have seen, soft commission agreements were used largely by specialist houses, smaller fund managers, and employed, *inter alia*, the services of independent researchers. Traditional brokers and integrated houses, who provided all services in-house, were those who were feeling the competition of these smaller bodies. SIB accepted the argument that a ban would favour in-house service providers and hinder the ability of independent researchers to market their services on a commission basis, 'vital for small fund managers and those competing in an international arena'.[25] Traditional brokers, it stated, were 'not entitled to a particular market share in perpetuity'.[26] Its response to the argument that softing arrangements could distort management fee structures was simply that traditional services could have the same effect.[27] In sum, although soft commissions could themselves distort the market by tying a manager to a broker, SIB felt that 'on balance, the threat was not so great as to justify the interference in the market which would be caused by a ban, partial or total'.[28]

In fact, SIB did consider as an alternative that SROs could set limits on the amount of business which could be softed. This would have been a precise 'bright line' rule, and a figure of twenty-five per cent was suggested.[29] It was dropped on similar grounds as the ban, however, after opposition that it would artificially reserve a large sector of the market to traditional brokers, would discriminate against those in fixed commission markets, and against specialist houses and independent researchers.[30] Moreover, the use of a precise requirement in this way, it was argued, would be in danger of defeating the purpose of the regulation and of opening opportunities for evasion. First, the level set could have the effect of increasing the amount of soft business done as it would be interpreted as the norm; pressure could be placed on fund managers to increase their softing business to that level. Second, it could be easily avoided as firms could do all their business on

[24] CP 29, para. 21. [25] CP 46, para. 2. [26] Ibid., para. 15.
[27] CP 29, para. 18. [28] Ibid. [29] CP 29, Supplementary.
[30] SIB, *Soft Commission Arrangements in the Securities Markets, Policy Statement*, July 1990, paras. 13–14, and see below.

one market on a soft basis and on another on a traditional basis, again going against the purpose of the rule. Finally it was rejected on the basis that the rule would in fact be unworkable and unenforceable. Commission was paid in advance, whereas the total amount of commission business fluctuated. It would therefore be difficult to assess what value of commission would be twenty-five per cent of an undefined total.[31]

Still playing with the idea of imposing precise controls on the conduct of the business, SIB proposed that SROs could set guidance on the levels of multiples which should be paid.[32] This was directly aimed at trying to ensure that integrated houses did not subsidize softing through their market making arm. However, SIB was constrained from adopting this approach by two different elements: the legal context, and the OFT. SIB was advised that guidance on multiples would effectively amount to price control, and as with the limits on business SIB was advised that it would be contrary to EC provisions. With respect to both the issue of multiples and that of setting levels of permitted softed business, the attitude of the OFT was also influential. The OFT considered that the broking industry was not sufficiently responsive to the needs of investors and fund managers and wished to see greater unbundling and price transparency and disaggregation of service provision. It therefore favoured soft commissions for the competition they provided in the market, and considered that banning them would prevent the disaggregation and unbundling which it wished to see from the traditional houses. Similarly it was opposed to a limit on the amount of business which could be softed as it would guarantee a percentage of the market to traditionals and again hamper unbundling.

So, SIB decided that it would simply improve on its existing approach of defining soft commission agreements and permitted softed services more clearly and relying on disclosure. In line with its approach in other areas, SIB stated that it saw disclosure as 'a necessary and vital part of an investor protection regime'[33] and emphasized that investors themselves had to take responsibility for monitoring soft commission arrangements. Noting that the situation was 'unusual' as disclosure was being made to mainly professional clients, it stressed that the duty of disclosure had to be

[31] Ibid. [32] CP 29, Supplementary. [33] Feb. 1989, para. 28.

balanced by a duty on these clients to use and monitor the information to satisfy themselves that the services were legitimate.[34]

The 1987 rule had been criticized as too general, both in its policy and in its structure, and neither SIB nor the SRO rules had contained any details of permitted softing services.[35] In drafting the new rule, SIB was strongly influenced by the provisions of the US Securities and Exchange Act, section 28(e), and the Ontario Securities Commission, rule 1.9, which it included in its October 1989 discussion paper as possible models to adopt. Section 28(e) provided that research and brokerage services could be provided, indicating that this would comprise the furnishing of advice, analyses, and reports and the effecting of securities transactions and performance of incidental functions. The Ontario Securities Commission rule 1.9 provided for a similar type of services, defined as 'order execution' and 'investment decision making', and it was this model which SIB proposed to adopt.[36]

SIB was in favour of such a generic definition feeling that 'it would be broad enough to embrace new product developments without amendment. It would also put the onus on the fund manager to demonstrate a positive link between the services and benefits.'[37] The rule could cope with the heterogeneity of the subject-matter, and a purposive approach would be injected. However, SIB feared that such a definition would be too broadly interpreted and that 'any service could conceivably be covered if the fund manager were ingenious enough'.[38] Moreover 'SIB and the SROs might be called upon continually to provide interpretations for particular services.'[39] So SIB proposed that the third tier rule structure could be used to include an exemplary list of services in the guidance of the SROs which could be updated from time to time.[40]

[34] CP 29, paras. 36 and 52. [35] See above. [36] CP 29, para. 33.
[37] CP 29, para. 32. [38] Ibid. [39] Ibid.
[40] Ibid. The requirement that services which benefited a particular client should be identified was dropped as impractical, and as a consequence the Law Commission provisionally concluded that the rules do not satisfy agency law: *Fiduciary Duties and Regulatory Rules,* CP No. 124, paras. 3.4.26–3.4.29. However, following *Kelly* v. *Cooper* [1993] AC 205 (PC) and *Clark Boyce* v. *Mouat* [1994] 1 AC 428 (PC) the Commission concluded in its final report that the court would follow *Jones* v. *Canavan* [1972] 2 NSWLR 236 and hold a trade custom which permits a fiduciary to act in a situation of conflict to be reasonable if it incorporates adequate protection for the customer's interests, and on this basis the soft commission rule would satisfy fiduciary law: Law Commission, *Fiduciary Duties and Regulatory Rules,* No. 236, paras. 7.6–7.7.

In the question of rule structure, therefore, two factors were significant. First, the decision that any detailed specification should have the status of guidance provides an example of the use of the dimensions of rules to attempt to balance certainty with flexibility. The detail is given, but problems of over- and under-inclusiveness are mitigated by the lack of sanction for breach of the rule. Secondly, the particular context of the New Settlement rule system impacted on the rule's structure. The soft commissions rule was being drafted in parallel with the other Core Rules, and its structure changed as the role and structure of the Core Rules developed.[41] Initially, the proposed Core Rule contained the type of services,[42] then these were omitted and an 'empty carriage' derogation inserted instead,[43] and finally the rule stated the purpose of the rule: that the services had to be used for the provision of investment services to the customers.[44] The generic definitions of the types of services were moved to the third tier rules, and the SFA rule contains guidance on particular services which are and are not permitted.[45]

Changing Focus

It was developments in market practice which raised new concerns and prompted SIB to move beyond reliance on disclosure and permitted services, and indeed to alter its perception of how precise the soft commission rule should be. Emerging practices revealed that 'the rule structure is not sufficiently specific, and

[41] See Ch. 3. [42] CP 29. [43] July 1990. [44] CP 46 and CR 3.

[45] SFA r. 5-8; IMRO II-1.7. The Core Rule also provides only that 'adequate prior and periodic disclosure is made': CR 3e. The IMRO and SFA rules contain disclosure provisions which are substantially the same, and provide that a firm must disclose its policy towards soft agreements at the outset of the relationship, and give periodic disclosure containing a statement detailing the percentage of total commission paid under a soft commission agreement, the summary and the value of goods and services received, a list of brokers with whom the firm has such agreements, and a statement as to the firm's policy on soft commissions: IMRO II-1.7; SFA r. 5-8(4) (although only the policy statement need be disclosed to beneficiaries of funds under the firm's management, and a private customer (unless a small business investor) need only receive a policy statement and estimated percentage of softed business; the other information to be made available on request: SFA r. 5-8(4)(c)).

does not enable regulators readily to detect breaches'.[46] Integrated houses, concerned at the competition for business coming from specialist softing houses and attracted by the guaranteed order flow which softing provided, were already beginning to offer softing services. In summer 1990, during the course of the rule formation process, one major house, S. G. Warburgs, started to offer multiples of 1.2, well below the industry average and with which the specialist houses said they could not compete. It obtained a ruling from SIB that it was not infringing the rules, as long as brokers explicitly accepted the obligation to secure best execution. The ruling was denounced by independent houses as going against the spirit of the rules.[47] Prompted by this practice and a large number of requests from fund managers and brokers for clarification, and the regulators' own concerns about the threats posed to best execution, the regulators began to consider how the draft soft commissions rule should be tightened to address this practice, and the main concerns of the rule formation process then became directed at the integrated houses.

In November 1990, SIB issued a consultative paper to consider whether the practices amounted to soft for net agreements.[48] In this issue, considerations of investor protection and regulatory interference in the market met head on. The low multiples, SIB concluded, must be being subsidized by market makers widening their spreads on the softed deals.[49] However, imposing a ban on soft commission agreements with brokers in integrated houses would be a far greater intrusion into market structures and operations than banning soft for net arrangements with market makers. It would require integrated houses to establish separate broker subsidiaries to handle all softed business. One house had already adopted this course in 1989 (Barclays de Zoete Wedd, which established Thamesway), and the SEC had just imposed such a ban in the US. However, SIB was wary of prescribing such a restructuring as it could threaten the integration between brokers and market makers which had been at the heart of the Stock Exchange's deregulation in 1986. Hence it decided that:

[46] CP 46, para. 6.
[47] See reports in the *FT*, 31 July 1990, 2 Aug. 1990, and 16 Aug. 1990.
[48] CP 46. [49] Ibid., para. 7.

> [w]hile not ruling out this approach in the longer term, SIB is reluctant to accept that questions concerning the fulfilment of obligations owed to investors by brokers, dealers and fund managers should be resolved by adaptation of corporate structures in response to regulatory fiat. SIB would much prefer responsibilities to be clearly agreed amongst market participants and for the core rules to *reflect* that agreement. SIB believes that in the context of an evolving UK securities market and a fund management industry of ever increasing sophistication this would be the most desirable outcome of the present debate.[50]

Faced with diverging options for meeting regulatory objectives, therefore, the regulators' own sense of what they could justifiably do or not do determined the action that they took. SIB's attitude was that if the market evolved into a structure of separate broker subsidiaries, that was one matter; however it was not the regulators' role to require it. The role of regulation, in other words, was not to structure but to shape and influence.

This self-defined and self-imposed constraint led to a policy to restrict the ban to soft for net agreements only, and an attempt to address the question of cross subsidy through a means other than requiring separate broker subsidiaries. The solution adopted in the rule, however, is arguably ineffective. The rule provides that:

> A firm which deals for a customer on an advisory basis or in the exercise of discretion may not so deal through a broker pursuant to a soft commission agreement unless: . . .
>
> (d) in transactions in which the broker acts as principal, he is not remunerated by spread alone;[51]

The provision that remuneration must not be only through the spread means that remuneration which includes commission will not be caught by the rule, however, making avoidance an easy matter. The rule is also difficult to monitor in the area at which it is in part addressed: integrated houses. The integrated house is acting in a dual capacity in such cases, receiving both commission and profits from the spread and so can avoid the ban, as the apportionment of commission and spread to a transaction is largely in the hands of the house. Integrated firms may pass business through the market making arm yet make most of the money on the spread while still satisfying the best execution requirements.

[50] Ibid., para. 14 (emphasis added).

[51] CR 3(d).

Cross subsidies, which the rule aimed to prevent, are thus very difficult to detect.

So whilst considerations of enforceability and effectiveness would have required separate softing subsidiaries to be created, self-defined and self-imposed constraints on what it considered to be an appropriate level of intervention pulled away from pursuing this course. SFA have addressed the issue and attempted to block this loophole through guidance which provides that the provision is not complied with unless the majority of the remuneration is in the form of commission.[52] Furthermore, it requires that the broker should set its multiple at a level which it can demonstrate would generate sufficient commission income from softing transactions to cover the cost of the services provided, dealing and settling the transaction, and specialized softing administration.[53] There are still concerns, however, because of the difficulty of monitoring the apportionment of commission and spread, over whether the limit on remuneration from spreads can be monitored.[54]

Developing Regulatory Techniques

If it did not feel it could require separate broker subsidiaries, SIB did feel that the practices of the integrated houses had to be subjected to greater regulation than mere requirements to disclose. Setting multiples and levels of business had already been rejected. The approach it adopted instead was to identify one of the participants in the arrangement who it judged to be in the best position to monitor the arrangement, the fund manager. The rule imposed three duties on fund managers: establishing with the broker that the latter had to provide best execution, making a professional judgement on the terms and conditions of the agreement to ensure that the multiple, rate, and other relevant factors were consistent with best execution, and assessing their own skills and resources and the leverage which they could exert in the market-place, and on the basis of this judgement determining with which type of broker they could enter into soft commission agreements:

> If [the manager] concludes that he is able to monitor and enforce compliance by a broker with the best execution obligation on a trade by trade

[52] SFA r. 5-8(1) Guidance 5. [53] SFA r. 5-8(1) Guidance 6.
[54] See, e.g., 'Soft Commissions'.

basis, he can enter into a soft commission agreement under the proposed rule with any broker who satisfies the conditions [pertaining to best execution]. If not, he can only select a soft commission broker on the basis of the latter's demonstrating independence of action within the market place. This is unlikely to be fulfilled in circumstances where the broker deals exclusively with one market maker.[55]

The aim was to achieve the same effect as a rule which effectively imposed a structural requirement prohibiting integrated houses from undertaking softed business, but through conduct requirements on managers to ensure that best execution would in fact be given. The danger at which the rule was directed was market makers widening the spread. Hence the rule focused on best execution, and on one aspect of it, price.[56] The rule requires fund manages to ensure that 'the broker's terms of business and methods [of operation] . . . do not involve any potential for comparative price disadvantage'.[57]

This responsibility was fiercely opposed by fund managers and resisted by their regulator, IMRO. Fund managers argued that ensuring compliance with the rule would be impossible for smaller fund managers particularly, who would be incapable of assessing the business operations of a large integrated house and would be forced to deal through the specialist houses. The strictness of the obligations, they argued, favoured larger managers.[58] IMRO was firmly against the provision on three grounds. Firstly, it was not happy with the idea that its members had to monitor SFA members and supervise their compliance with the soft commission rule. Secondly, it argued that the rule is impractical, and in practice unenforceable as compliance requires the manager to investigate the internal costing structure of the integrated house. Finally, it saw the provision to be unnecessary. If the broker has agreed to provide best execution, and is bound by SFA rules to do so, then, IMRO argued, IMRO members can accept that the broker will comply with the requirements and further monitoring is not necessary. IMRO thus rejected that 'internal monitor' approach suggested by SIB, that market participants should be used to enforce the rules, not just the regulators. Its attitude that compliance with the rule is impractical has influenced the structure of its rule: it has not provided any guidance on compliance with the provision.

[55] CP 46, para. 11. [56] See below. [57] CR 3c. [58] See below.

This is in contrast to SFA, who have adopted the policy of the consultative papers and provide that a manager will comply if it can monitor the individual transaction and is satisfied that the broker has complied with its best execution obligation, or that there is no need for the manager to disclose at the time of giving the order to the broker that the commission is to be allocated to the manager's softing account.[59] If neither of these can be satisfied, then the firm should select a broker 'on his ability to demonstrate independence of action in the market place. This is unlikely to be fulfilled in circumstances where the broker deals exclusively with one market maker.'[60]

The Interaction of Rules: Soft Commissions and Best Execution

The fund manager is thus effectively co-opted into the process of monitoring and enforcement of the soft commissions rule. The benchmark against which compliance with the soft commissions rule is to be tested is whether or not best execution is provided. Concern is thus to maintain the principle of best execution, which is the central plank of the dealing rules, and indeed to reinforce it. The soft commission rule in fact imposes a more onerous requirement than the best execution rule itself, as non-private customers may not waive the requirement,[61] and the onus for ensuring compliance with the rule is placed firmly on the fund manager, whereas the best execution rule allows the fund manager to delegate this duty and rely on another to provide best execution.[62]

The interaction of the two rules is a key part of the regulation of soft commissions; however the focus and development of the two rules differed, with the result that there is not a perfect fit between them. The rules are addressed at slightly different issues, the best execution rule at providing protections for investors against

[59] SFA r. 5-8(1), Guidance 3.

[60] SFA r. 5-8(1), Guidance 4. The rule will in practice rarely apply, however. This is because this branch of the rule applies to fund managers, the majority of whom are regulated by IMRO and so subject to its rules. These rules, as we have noted, contain no similar provisions. So although neither rule removes the difficulties of interpreting the Core Rule provision, the majority of fund managers are not subject to the more helpful guidance of SFA's rule.

[61] See amendments to CR 22 in SFA r. 5-38 and IMRO II-3.8.

[62] CR 22(3).

brokers dealing as principal at less advantageous prices than those available generally and at providing protections against wider risks of counterparty unreliability, and this part of the soft commission rule at ensuring that integrated houses did not subsidize their softing services through widening the spread. This in part explains the difference between them. The soft commission rule focuses on price; it differs in this respect from the definition of best execution, which has two elements, price and terms.[63] The best execution rule provides that a firm must take reasonable care to ascertain the best price available on that market for transactions in the size and kind concerned, and deal at a price no less advantageous, but this requirement is waived if dealing at that price would not be in the interests of the customer.[64]

The two parts to the best execution rule reflect the two different approaches to best execution taken by SIB and IMRO on the one part, and TSA (subsequently SFA) on the other, which in turn stemmed from their slightly different historical bases. SIB and IMRO rules had followed the tenor of the Council for the Securities Industry's Draft Code by requiring that the terms of the transaction must be the best apparently available.[65] TSA's rule followed the Stock Exchange's draft rule, which focused on the transaction price, which could be ascertained from the price quoted by market makers on the Stock Exchange Automatic Quotation system (SEAQ) at the time of the transaction.[66] In the pre-New Settlement rule books these two approaches simply existed in parallel; the New Settlement meant that they had somehow to be combined. The best execution rule was too central to the regulation of dealing to be left to SROs to form, and as members of IMRO and SFA are on opposite sides of the contracts, it crosses regulatory boundaries. Such differences of approach in one of the key rules could

[63] The initial drafts of the rule were in fact less explicit on this point, and required the fund manager to ensure that the terms of business offered by the broker were compatible with the satisfaction of its best execution duty: CP 46, draft core rule.

[64] CR 22(4). The rule does not apply to life policies or units in collective investment schemes, CR 22(5).

[65] SIB 1987 r. 5.4, IMRO 1988 IV-3. CSI Draft Code of Conduct on the Management of Conflicts of Interest, paras. 7–9, printed in CSI, *Annual Report 1985*, Annex B.

[66] TSA r. 450. Stock Exchange, *Conflicts of Interest and their Regulation: Discussion Document*, paras. 3.1 and 3.3.2, printed in 1984 *SEQ* 18.

not therefore continue and they somehow had to be merged in the Core Rule. In the drafting process of the best execution rule, as in that of the soft commission rule, each SRO sought to protect its own approach, and members. In the words of one participant, 'the best execution rule was an example where the SFA saw the issue through the eyes of their broking community and had their own corner to fight, whereas fund managers took a different view. The length of the rule is explained by this severe difference of opinion.'[67] As in the case of the soft commissions rule, differences between different market sectors, manifested in a difference between their regulatory bodies, became embodied in the rule. However, different preoccupations meant that the disputes which surrounded the best execution rule were not carried into the soft commission rule.

Both the soft commission and the best execution rules also raise a perhaps more fundamental issue concerning the relationship between rules, regulatory technique, and enforcement. In best execution, part of the issue in the question of price and / or terms was how to at once ensure high standards of protection and facilitate monitoring. SFA wanted the primary focus of the best execution rule to be on price as it could then monitor compliance by comparing the prices of transactions with those prevailing on the market at the time. If the focus was on the terms of the transaction then it argued that monitoring would be impeded as the inspectors would have to examine the type of transaction, reliability of the counterparty, and so on. In contrast, inspectors have a database of prices, and if the transaction price is worse than those quoted at the time then the firm has to justify why it dealt at the worse price, and only then does the inspector have to examine the terms. In forming the best execution rule, therefore, SFA pressed for price to be the principal determinant, and the Core Rule was amended to provide this. IMRO's concerns came from the management rather than the broking perspective: it was concerned that risks were posed to investors which went beyond price, and included the reliability of the counterparty and likely length of settlement, both of which can cause investors loss,[68] hence it wanted the emphasis of the

[67] Interview, May 1992.

[68] See further J. Franks and C. Mayer, *Risk, Regulation and Investor Protection* (Oxford, 1991).

rule to recognize that whilst price was important it was only one factor which should be taken into account. Whilst this was not incorporated into the soft commission Core Rule, in its third tier rules IMRO continued the emphasis on the terms of the transaction, simply placing the provisions of the old rule in guidance.[69]

Both best execution and soft commissions raised the problem of how to ensure both high standards of conduct and facilitate monitoring and enforcement: the answer was to rely on a proxy for quality of conduct, price. But not only is best execution difficult to monitor, the concept itself is difficult to define generally and in advance. What is 'best' execution for any trade of a particular size at any time is dependent on a number of factors including the liquidity of the stock and the size of the transaction. When transactions are done outside the standard sizes or in illiquid markets the 'best' price is difficult to assess. Given the number of trades executed every day, detailed investigation of each is impossible; instead the regulators simply compare the transaction price with those quoted on screen at the time of the transaction. However, in concentrating on quoted prices for monitoring purposes, the rule is allowing execution at prices which the market would normally regard as disadvantageous. Execution is usually at prices better than those quoted on screen: one independent broker reckoned that over seventy per cent of its trade is done 'inside the yellow strip', i.e., at better than quoted prices. Execution may thus be done at levels which are lower than those prevailing in the market, but which comply with the regulations, unless customers demand otherwise. This leaves open the possibility of the market maker making greater profits on some deals simply by executing them at the quoted price, which may then be used to subsidize other services. A rule based approach to this issue is difficult: the rule already states that the broker has to search for and ascertain the best price available, but for monitoring purposes using quoted prices as indicators is the most practical approach. Rules which impose qualitative requirements involving the exercise of judgement necessarily rely on the quality of judgement of others for their implementation; they are hard to monitor, however, for if compliance is to be assessed properly, each decision has to be examined. This is simply not possible in the context in which the rules operate.

[69] IMRO II-3.8. See Ch. 3.

Compliance has to be assessed instead through the use of proxies for quality which are easily monitorable. However, these may in turn establish a lower standard than the qualitative or purposive rule may at its highest demand.

Finally, these issues, of the difficulty of monitoring the limit on remuneration from spreads, of whether 'best' execution is a meaningful concept, raised the further question of whether regulators can ever be sure that best execution is being provided in an integrated house. This issue was recognized by the regulators at the time, but because the implications of the suggestion were so fundamental to the whole structure of the City institutions, it was one which they chose not to address. Self-restraint was thus exercised in accordance with an assessment of what level of regulation it would be justifiable, and acceptable to impose.

Conclusion

The process of forming the rules on soft commission agreements was incremental, raising a wide range of factors and considerations with the result that the rule itself is directed at many different actors and problems. Soft commissions came onto the regulatory agenda because of concerns of widespread abuse in terms of the services being provided. The initial focus was thus on defining the legitimate services and on providing disclosure. Then changes in market practice (offering low multiples) prompted a change in concerns, this time to best execution and integrated houses. The focus of rule making switched and the rule was altered to address these issues. Finally, further market developments (the increased amount of soft commission business done with integrated houses) prompted SIB to readdress the rule, this time to see if it was effective. SIB asked fund managers whether they were managing to comply with the rule: the answer was in the affirmative, and so no rule change was proposed.

In forming the rule the rule makers were strongly affected by their assessment of what the rule should aim to achieve, and what means it should use. The regulatory concerns related to the potential for breaches of other rules, principally churning and best execution, whether the investor was receiving value for money, and the effect of the practices on competition. The answers to these issues were not clear cut and the objectives of market efficiency and investor protection did not provide clear guidance. Soft commissions could either improve or hinder the value investors received from the services; they could improve competitiveness through price transparency and encouraging disaggregation of services, but impede it by tying managers to brokers and encouraging brokers to compete on terms other than commission levels. Traditional arrangements were not themselves ideal: they disguised prices, and may not themselves aid the manager's performance, although the scope for abuse on this count was less than in soft commission arrangeents. The potential for regulation to affect the competitive conditions in the market meant that support or criticism of soft commissions by the regulated could amount to little more than appeals to protect, or develop, their market position. Indeed, many argue that through regulating soft commissions the regulators have in fact provided a practice which was widely abused with legitimacy, and the publications of one specialist house, for example, state that regulation has been 'a key factor in the development of a soft commission industry'.[70]

The regulators' perceptions of the appropriate role of regulation and what they felt they could require thus had a significant influence on their rule making decisions. There were certain approaches the regulators felt they could not adopt. These mainly concerned the imposition of structural and price regulation. Price regulation was quickly dropped due to its potential to contravene EU law. Structural regulation, which would structure the market in a particular way, was rejected in the form both of a ban on soft commissions and of limiting the amount of business which could be softed on the basis that such action by the regulator would effectively ensure one part of the market a competitive advantage over the other. As this would not be the result of imposing a ban on soft for net, and because of the greater concerns soft for net raised, a ban was felt to be justified in that case.

Structural regulation was also rejected in relation to soft commission agreements with integrated houses. Here the considerations were not simply that regulation could affect the competitive structure of the market, but that the regulation would be requiring

[70] Publications of Thamesway Ltd.

firms to adopt a particular corporate structure. The regulators already felt inhibited from requiring traditional houses to unbundle or separately price their services as it was felt this would require too great a change in customary business practices, and SIB stated it could not be imposed in the short term.[71] Requiring integrated houses, the results of the huge restructuring the City had undergone only a few years previously, to form separate subsidiaries for softed business SIB felt to be too fundamental a change to impose and thus to be an approach it could not take, at least until the rules had time to operate.

Conduct regulation was imposed instead as a far less intrusive form of regulation, and combined with the co-option of one sector of the regulated to monitor the other. The structure of these rules is more general as the aim was to use the judgement and assessment of fund managers to achieve the rule's purpose of ensuring best execution. Conduct regulation, combined with the different rule structure enabled SIB to avoid the difficulties of setting multiples, limits on business, and effectively imposing structural requirements on the market, and to avoid the implications these had for the role of the regulator. The problems of definition of limits and line drawing did not have to be addressed by the regulator or dealt with in the rule: they were delegated to the fund manager. The objectives in setting these multiples and limits would still be achieved, but the judgement would not be made in advance by the regulator, rather on an individualized basis by the fund manager. However, as we have seen, although a less intrusive form of regulation, the vagueness of the rule on this point and IMRO's view that it adds nothing to the best execution rule, and so does not require further elaboration in guidance, means that the rule may be ineffective.

The emphasis of the rules on the conduct of participants and the monitoring of one by the other, including the duties on trustees, follows the philosophy behind the Principles: that compliance is for each individual firm, and goes further in involving all who are party to investment agreements in monitoring others. The aim was to achieve this wider involvement through disclosure, in the hope that those party to the agreements and their own customers

[71] July 1990, para. 5.

would use this information to make their own assessments as to the desirability of the arrangement. It was hoped given the increased sophistication of investors in this section of the market, in comparison with the retail sector, that greater reliance could be placed on investors and managers to protect themselves using that information. Monitoring may be difficult, however, and there are quesions as to whether trustees, for example, who are the clients of fund managers, can monitor the agreements sufficiently, even if given detailed disclosure, as they may not understand the information. As in retail regulation, then, the issue again illustrates that rules on disclosure are only as good as the comprehension the receiver has of the information given.[72]

The problem of monitoring both by parties to the agreement and by regulators was readdressed by SIB following an increase in the amount of soft commission business being conducted by integrated houses. In December 1991 it issued a further policy statement asking managers to state how they were complying with Core Rule 3c.[73] Managers' replies included such measures as ensuring that they had a range of counterparties with whom they had agreements, calculating the amount of guaranteed business in accordance with what could be provided on best execution grounds, not using specialized softing desks in integrated houses, only concluding soft commission agreements with integrated houses with whom they have a large amount of business, and giving no prior disclosure of whether a transaction is soft or not. Although recognizing that many of these measures may only be possible for larger houses, SIB, in agreement with SFA and IMRO, concluded that on the basis of this there was 'insufficient evidence to justify a change in the Core Rule on the grounds of investor protection'.[74]

Finally the institutional structure and SIB's own policies on the development of the rule system affected the formation of the rule. SIB was constrained in the detail it could include in the Core Rule by the overall structure which the Core Rules were required to have for wider political reasons, viz. brevity, stability, and the need for the Core Rules to operate at an 'intermediate level of generality'.[75] This did provide certain drafting benefits, however, as the

[72] See Ch. 4.

[73] SIB, *Soft Commissions: Recent Developments*, CP 56 and Policy Statement, Dec. 1991.

[74] SIB, Press Release, 3 Apr. 1992.

[75] See Ch. 3.

Core Rule could contain general statements which could be combined with detailed third tier rules, as illustrated in chapter 3. So in relation to the definition of services which could be softed a purposive statement was combined with more detailed requirements in an attempt to provide certainty whilst avoiding possibilities of 'creative compliance'.

However, the division of responsibility for rule drafting between SIB and the SROs meant that their differing approaches could affect whether and how the more general provisions of the Core Rule were in fact supplemented in the third tier. IMRO's reservations about the rule, particularly concerning its practicability, meant that unlike SFA it has not given any guidance on the policy behind the part of the rule which imposes monitoring duties on fund managers and has not chosen to adopt a listing of services as SFA has done. IMRO's reluctance about the rule was further indicated when it sought a derogation from the requirement to make disclosures to professional customers. This was refused by SIB on the grounds that it would be contrary to the purpose of the rule;[76] however SIB felt that it could not press IMRO to adopt a rule akin to SFA's due to the political requirement of 'standing back'. The functional organization of the regulators also means that whilst SFA's elaboration of the rule and duties of fund managers may be more in line with the policy documents which led up to the rule, as few fund managers are SFA members this part of SFA's rule will in fact rarely apply.

The formation of the soft commissions rule, then, was characterized by a complex interaction of different views, demands, and perceptions, of reactions to market developments, of the institutional and legal context, of the impact of other regulatory policy decisions and rules, of concerns to minimize the scope for creative compliance and avoidance of the rule, and to avoid unwanted consequences which the rule may have. The process further indicates the nature of the trade-offs involved in rule formation, the association of rule structure with the substance of the rule, and in particular the problems to which the vague, relatively opaque structure of a qualitative and judgemental rule can give rise in the context of monitoring compliance and the attempts to address this by

[76] SIB, *Core Conduct of Business Rules, Commencement for Members of IMRO*, CP 54, Aug. 1991, para. 9.

widening the responsibility for ensuring compliance to other participants in the regulated activity. Finally, it illustrates the 'ripple effect' of rules, the ways in which a change in rule can have effects which reverberate beyond the particular activity being focused on and the impact that both the potential and realization of this effect has on the rule making decision.

6 Making Rules

Examining the rule making of financial services regulators provides an insightful study into the uses which have been made of rules both to address their inherent limitations and to further particular regulatory strategies. Resources have been devoted specifically to the question of rule type, and awareness of some of the implications of using rules in different ways has been articulated to varying degrees. The rule making process has however involved both the strategic and non-strategic use of rules. The process has been structured and buffeted by institutional pressures, political and interest group demands, changes in market practices: the range of factors which are often associated with policy making and decision making in organizations and bureaucracies. The process also has its own internal dynamic: regulation itself creates new interests, has unanticipated consequences and unforeseen effects which have to be addressed, and regulators have their own, changing, views of what and how they should regulate.

This final chapter will explore the uses which have been made of rules in financial services regulation and the nature of the limitations and trade-offs involved in rule formation which they indicate. It will also seek to understand in greater depth the nature of the rule making decision. The rule making process is in part a policy process; it is also a particular form of organizational or bureaucratic decision making (and if conducted within a system of powers conferred by the legislature, a particular use of discretionary power). It differs from other types of bureaucratic decision, however, in particular the individualized decision making, or the decision of how to apply rules in a particular instance, which has been the main focus of studies of discretionary decision making.[1] It is also more than a policy making process. Rules are instruments

[1] See particularly K. Hawkins (ed.), *The Uses of Discretion* (Oxford, 1992), id., 'Discretion in Making Legal Decisions' (1986) 43 *Washington and Lee LR* 1161, and id., *Environment and Enforcement* (Oxford, 1984); D. J. Galligan, *Discretionary Powers* (1986); R. Baldwin and K. Hawkins, 'Discretionary Justice, Davis Reconsidered' [1984] *Public Law* 570; G. M. Richardson et al., *Policing Pollution: A Study of Regulation and Enforcement* (Oxford, 1983); B. M. Hutter, *The Reasonable Arm of the Law* (Oxford, 1988).

for both expressing and implementing that policy; they have been aptly described as the '"skin" of a living policy'.[2] Rules are a technique of regulation in themselves. They have distinctive properties which form both their limitations and potential as instruments of regulation.

In order to understand rule making, it is thus suggested, we have to understand the nature of policy making, the nature of decision making, and the nature of rules, their implications and their possible uses. In so doing, it is important to separate the strategic use of rules from the fact that in forming rules regulators are affected by a wide range of factors. Factors both external and internal to the process shape and affect the strategy adopted but they do not mean that strategy is not possible. A strategic use of rules does require as a precondition, however, a sophistication and awareness of the nature of rules on the part of the rule maker and the legal powers to form rules of a wide range of types. Without the former, a strategic use of rules is impossible; without the latter, it is restricted.

The chapter first examines the different uses made of rules before turning to explore in greater depth the nature of the rule making process. It identifies four principal themes in the use of rules: the changing ways in which the tension between certainty and flexibility has been addressed; the various attempts made to use rule type to distribute discretion; the attempts made to address the problems of uncertainty, honest perplexity, and creative compliance through the development of interpretive communities; and finally the interaction between the use of rules and the characterization of the system as one of self-regulation and the manner in which rules have been used to define the roles of the regulators within that system.

In turning to consider the nature of the rule making process, the chapter argues for an approach to rule making which is contextual, stressing the significance of the market and political context, the institutional and legal structure, and of the dynamics of the system itself, its history, the norms and perceptions of the regulators and their awareness of the potential uses of rules, and the stage that the system is at in its own evolution. These factors interact,

[2] C. S. Diver, 'Regulatory Precision', in K. Hawkins and J. Thomas, *Making Regulatory Policy* (Pittsburgh, 1989), 199.

shaping both each other and the rule making decision. The rule making process is characterized by a high degree of causal complexity, involving the interaction and confluence of these different factors. The influence of some may be constant and structural, others ephemeral; some may act as catalysts, reacting with another to exert a particular type of influence or pressure at a particular time; some may always dominate, others only at particular points. Although the analysis offered here of rule use and rule making is context dependent, it is suggested that certain aspects of that analysis may be generalizable to other regulatory systems. Four are identified: the significance of the design of the regulatory system; the importance of the market context; the circumstances in which interpretive communities may develop; and the relevance of the system's own evolution for the use that can be made of rules.

Using Rules

Rule making has been a continuous activity for the regulators since the regulation's inception. In the process of rule formation and re-formation, four dominant themes in the use of rules can be identified: first, the changing ways in which the tension between certainty and flexibility have been addressed; secondly, the different attempts made to use rule type to distribute discretion and exert control within the rule system; thirdly, the attempts made to develop interpretive communities and so to address the problems of uncertainty, honest perplexity, and creative compliance; and fourthly the use made of rules to reinforce the 'self-regulatory' characterization of the system and to define the roles of regulators within that system. Rules have thus been used both to address the inherent limitations of rules indicated in chapter 1, particularly the problems of flexibility, certainty, and interpretation, and to achieve broader regulatory goals.

In the uses made of rules, different answers have been provided to perennial questions, in particular that of how to achieve both certainty and flexibility. The need to address the tension between certainty and flexibility has been pressing: certainty is lauded as a value in its own right, with its overtones of the 'rule of law' values of open, general, stable, and prospective rules which enable an individual to plan his or her life.[3] Flexibility is emphasized as one of the hallmarks of a sophisticated regulatory regime, and as the means by which to ensure innovation is not stifled and international competitiveness not impeded. Initially, the emphasis of the regulation was on certainty and its achievement was seen to be through precise, specific rules. Whilst that emphasis has remained and, as we have seen, detailed rules are not absent from the rule system as a whole, flexibility has been achieved in two ways: through the change in the status of many detailed rules to guidance, and through the use of the Principles, vague rules of disciplinary status only, as 'safety nets', catching what may otherwise slip through the inevitable and unforeseen loopholes which can be the product of specific rules.

The use of rule type in a deliberate attempt to confer discretion or decisional jurisdiction within the rule system and to exert control has been clearly evident. The conscious and strategic use of terms which are vague as to manner, time or place, are evaluative or use generic terms[4] to act as implicit derogations, for example in the Core Rules, indicates the deliberate sanctioning of discretion by rules. Indeed, the use of rules in this way prompts the thought that the definition of discretion adopted in the leading studies of discretion in bureaucracies could be amended. Hawkins and Galligan define discretion as interstitial: it is 'the space ... between legal rules in which legal actors may exercise choice'.[5] The use of rule type to distribute discretion suggests that discretion may be not only the space *between* rules but *within* rules in which legal actors may exercise choice.

In contrast, increased specification has been used in an attempt to exert greater control over the interpretation and application of the rule, both by regulators and by the regulated. Despite the problems to which precise and complex rules can lead, such rules, which have sanctions attached for their breach, are prevalent in

[3] J. Raz, 'The Rule of Law and its Virtue' (1977) 93 *LQR* 195; F. Hayek, *Law, Legislation and Liberty* (London, 1982); for parallels in accountancy, D. McBarnet and C. Whelan, 'The Elusive Spirit of the Law: Formalism and the Limits of Legal Control' (1991) 54 *MLR* 848.

[4] For the different ways in which a rule may be vague, see the discussion in Ch. 1, text accompanying n. 58.

[5] K. Hawkins, 'The Use of Legal Discretion: Perspectives from Law and Social Science', in K. Hawkins (ed.), *Uses of Discretion* (Oxford, 1992), 11; D. J. Galligan, *Discretionary Powers* (Oxford, 1986), 20–4.

the rule books. One of the reasons for that detail has been to provide certainty. Another has been the concern that in its absence firms (and regulators) will do only the minimum necessary to ensure compliance with the rule. The issue here is not creative compliance but *inadequate* compliance: that the regulated will simply not act according to the standards of behaviour that the regulator requires unless that behaviour is specified. The question which is being asked is essentially, to what extent can the rule makers trust the regulated to behave as they want them to. Detailed rules are a sign of distrust.

It is clear that detailed rules do not ensure control, however, as both enforcement studies and the analysis of rules in chapter 1 suggest. Such rules facilitate creative compliance, are likely to lead to under-inclusiveness, and can simply displace discretion to another, less rule governed area. There thus appears to be a trade-off between the vague, imprecise rules demanded to counter creative compliance, and the more precise rules which the rule maker feels are demanded by the problem of inadequate compliance. It is important to deepen the analysis, however, to understand more fundamentally why regulation through detail cannot work. Here the analysis of rules, interpretation, and interpretive communities suggested assists.[6] Increasing precision is an attempt to render explicit the conduct expected in as wide a range of circumstances as possible. It is an attempt to substitute rules for the tacit understandings and informed reading which rules need, but which may not exist. As such, it can only fail: increased precision may reduce but can never eliminate the inherent indeterminacy of rules and does not in the end create the understanding which it is trying to replace.

The propensity for detailed rules to fail in this manner has been recognized, at least to an extent. In particular, the moves towards the creation of interpretive communities can be seen as attempts to find ways to escape the need for precise and complex rules. Three different aspects of this development can be identified. The first is the use of rule type, the second a change, in the level of rhetoric at least, of regulatory approach, and the third an increased emphasis on the regulatee's own attitude, education, training, and competence. Each is aimed at changing the internal attitude of

[6] Ch. 1, 30 *et seq.*

the regulated to the regulation; displacing the need for control by building up understandings within the regulatory system as to what the regulatee is meant to do, how it is meant to act.

The formation of the Principles, it is suggested, was an attempt to create a community of interpretation of rules through rules themselves. One of the essential elements of rules, as noted in chapter 1, is the reciprocal relationship on which rules rely between rule maker and rule interpreter; rules cannot apply themselves, and so for the rule to be applied in a way which will further the overall aims of the rule maker, then the person applying it has to share the rule maker's interpretation of it. However, more than one interpretation may be possible and the question arises as to which, and whose, is to be authoritative. One way of ensuring this reciprocity, and of ensuring the authority of the rule maker's interpretation, is for the rule maker to have the authority to make the final determination of the rule's application in a particular case, for rule maker to be the ultimate adjudicator. Bodies external to the regulatory system, whose own members are the regulator (including its enforcement officials) and the regulated, are thus excluded from interpretation; this resolves both the problem of reciprocity, and the problem of competing sources of authoritative determinations of the rule's application. The system is 'closed' in this way: the regulator's word is final. It is just this closure which is effected by the change in status of the Principles to that of disciplinary status only, that is, breach gives rise to sanctions imposed by the regulator, not by the court.[7]

The second aspect of the development of an interpretive community has been the attempt to change the regulatory approach to one which is more purposive. This has again in part been attempted through rules, and again through the Principles, this time through changing the structure of the rules. The move to rules which were simpler and less specific, which contained generic and evaluative terms, was an attempt to infuse greater purposiveness into the rules both in an attempt to make their application more certain (the regulatee, understanding the overall aim of the rule, would be able to act appropriately in circumstances which did not

[7] Although, as noted, the court's jurisdiction is not excluded completely; injunctions and restitution orders can be granted only by the court under s. 61 and the regulatory bodies are subject to judicial review.

appear to fit the rule, i.e., where the rule was referentially vague or indeterminate) and to require the regulatee to focus on the purpose of the rule by making mechanical compliance more difficult. Hence vaguer rules would assist with the problem of 'honest perplexity' as to the rule's application, and also thwart creatively compliant behaviour.

The development of interpretive communities can have significant implications for the uses of rules. The significance of such a development has lain beyond the particular issue of rule use, however; it has been that the characteristics of such communities are also those associated with a particular type of regulatory system, one of self-regulation. So an integral part of the development of interpretive communities has been the increased insistence on the self-regulatory nature of the system. The phrase 'self-regulation' has had in fact two, mutually existing, interpretations: the idea of 'regulation of the self' and the idea that the regulatory system should be collectivist, practitioner based, non-governmental, and non-bureaucratic.

The insistence by senior regulators that 'self-regulation' means 'regulation of the self' is a move to encourage internal regulation of the firm by the firm through its own procedures. It has been emphasized that the rules are not a detailed list of arcane requirements but statements of best business practice, and it is as such that they need to be read. Thus part of the aim behind the Principles was to lift the issue of compliance from compliance officers up into the boardroom, and to help senior executives to see the moral wood for the technical trees.

'Regulation of the self' is accompanied by an emphasis on the non-bureaucratic, partnership nature of a self-regulatory system, embodied in the advocation of a particular relationship between regulator and regulatee, that of a 'regulatory contract'. The regulator agrees not to interfere in the detailed operation of the regulated, but in return expects compliance which goes beyond mere obedience to the letter of the law.[8] It was this mutuality of understanding

[8] See e.g., D. Walker, 'Some Issues in the Regulation of Financial Services', lecture at the Irish Centre for Commercial Studies, University College, Dublin, 14 Nov. 1991; id., 'Financial Services Regulation, Mid-1988, and Some Elements in Prospect', speech to the Financial Times/Deloittes Conference, 5 July 1988; id., 'The Development of Principles and Conduct of Business Rules for Financial Services in the UK', speech to the Brussels Centre d'Etudes Financières, 29 May 1990.

and reciprocity between regulator and regulated which many had assumed would be part of a self-regulatory system, and the attempts to stimulate such reciprocity thus stemmed in part from a desire to emphasize the system's self-regulatory nature. The current chairman of SIB, Andrew Large, has reiterated the need for the reciprocal relationship between regulator and regulated which the notion of a 'regulatory contract' embraces and coupled it with an increased emphasis on ethics and education, echoing the idea that responsibility for regulation falls as much on the firm as on the regulator.

Large has also explicitly linked the nature of the regulator/regulated relationship with rule type and with the reading rules could expect: precise rules would be removed only if and to the extent that SIB felt able to rely on rising standards of competence and business ethics of the regulated.

> Rules will never be able to be dispensed with. But they should in a number of areas be able to become less prescriptive. I would hope that SIB will gradually feel able to rely more on rising standards of professionalism (in both the competence and ethical senses), particularly as confidence grows in the credibility of recognised bodies as enforcers. In this, the partnership nature of regulator and regulated comes to the fore: the more that the industry takes on board the challenge of today's consumers in insisting on quality of service, quality of product, and high ethical standards, the less prescriptive the regulator needs to be.[9]

The rules needed to regulate a particular activity, Large stressed, would be affected by the quality and training of those involved; they would also be affected by their ethical standards: 'strong ethics', Large argued, 'are the best antidote to a threat of over-regulation'.[10] Indeed, the need radically to improve the training and competence of those participating in investment business and the development of accredited training courses are emphasized as essential components of the regulatory regime. Less precise and prescriptive rules are offered as the 'reward' for developing a better regulatory attitude. The analysis of interpretive communities explains this interaction: rules are based on tacit understandings; they require an informed reading. The greater the shared understanding of the rule and practices it is addressing, the more the rule maker can rely on tacit understandings as to the aim of the rule and the context in which it operates, the less the need for

[9] Large Report, para. 6. [10] Ibid., para. 6.5.

precision, and the greater the degree to which simple, vague rules can be used.

Finally, the idea that a self-regulatory system should be reciprocal, practitioner based, non-governmental, and non-bureaucratic has involved certain assumptions not only as to the particular nature of the regulator/regulatee relationship (the regulatory contract), but as to the types of rules which should be adopted, and by which regulator. The emphasis on the self-regulatory characterization of the system has thus been significant in the use made of rules to define regulatory roles. So we have seen that the hostility expressed towards the initial rule books was directed as much to the role those rule books indicated SIB was playing in the regulatory system as it was to the detailed regulation which they imposed.[11] The introduction of the New Settlement and the structure of the Principles and Core Rules was deliberately designed to indicate a 'standing back' on SIB's part, allowing the practioner based self-regulatory bodies to form their own rule books; however the status and application of those rules was equally designed to ensure SIB still exerted control over the central elements of their rule books, albeit not over the detail. Rule type was thus used to define, and was defined by, the role that the rule issuer played in the regulatory system.

Limits of Rules; Trade-Offs in the Uses of Rules

One of the reasons why the creation of communities of interpretation is necessary, it has been suggested,[12] is because of the limits of rules themselves. Rules may require 'high standards of integrity and fair dealing',[13] exhort firms to act with 'due skill, care and diligence'[14] or provide that firms should recommend only products or transactions which will be 'suitable' for a customer,[15] but rules cannot in practice dictate quality, or at least not successfully. They need to be supplemented, and building shared understandings as to the meaning and application of the rules is one way in which this can be achieved: the replacement of inadequate compliance and creative compliance with instinctive compliance.

It would be naïve in the extreme to expect that training and improved levels of competence, while necessary, could be in any

[11] See Ch. 3. [12] See Ch. 1. [13] Principle 1. [14] Principle 2.
[15] Core Rule 16.

way sufficient to ensure an improved rate and quality of compliance. Enforcement has to be an essential part of the process. However, it is equally suggested that enforcement alone is not enough; it has to be accompanied by an understanding of the aims of the rules and willingness to comply with them. There may be an immediate tension, however, between creating that understanding, and so relying on the judgement of the regulatee, and facilitating enforcement. In particular, in trying to raise the standard of conduct of the regulated, there is a tension between what may be termed 'quantitative' and 'qualitative' rules and conduct: between rules which require conduct which can be easily monitored (and so rules which can be easily enforced) and between rules which require a high level of conduct involving the exercise of judgement. The latter may better express the aim of the rule maker and limit the potential for creative compliance, but conduct under them is difficult to monitor on a widespread scale. Conduct under the former, more precise rules is easy to monitor, but may result in a lower standard of conduct than the evaluative rule. This is because the rule focuses essentially on 'proxies' of quality. Instead of requiring 'high standards of integrity and fair dealing', for example, to aid monitoring the rule may focus on measurable outputs or aspects of behaviour which serve as indicators of quality: the number of policies surrendered, for example, or times for responding to complaints. Of themselves, these do not represent overall quality, they are simply measurable proxies for it, and may indeed serve to undermine it: promoting or facilitating the mechanical and unthinking compliance that it may have been the aim of the purposive rule to override. This tension between achieving a high quality of conduct and enabling enforcement perhaps presents the tension between formalism and substantiveness in a different guise, one not of bureaucratic rationality but of regulatory effectiveness.[16]

Two examples may serve to illustrate the tension: the suitability rule and the best execution rule. Both aim to improve standards of business conduct, the suitability rule by requiring advisers only to recommend products which are suitable for the investor,[17] the best execution rule requiring dealers to obtain the best price available.[18] However, monitoring whether advice really was suitable or

[16] On formal and substantive rationality, see M. Weber, *Economy and Society*, eds., G. Roch and C. Wittich (New York, 1968).

[17] Core Rule 16.

[18] Core Rule 22.

the price the best available is a time consuming and perhaps impossible task given the number and variety of transactions involved. So proxies of quality have been adopted: in the case of best execution it is that the prices quoted at the time of the transaction will be taken as the best price, even though most trades are done at better prices; in the case of the suitability rule it is that the adviser must complete a fact find and a 'reason why' letter, even though this may end up being simply a record keeping exercise. In both, the need to have some form of measurable conduct to enable enforcement means that the overall standard of conduct which may result may be lower than that which may optimally be demanded.

Given the limitations of rules, and the trade-offs involved in ameliorating these limitations, it is important to consider the interaction of rules with regulatory technique; to ask the question, what are rules being used to do? Is there an alternative strategy which could be adopted which might not involve rules, or which may involve only particular types of rules? Initially, as we have seen, this question was not asked: rule obsession marked the early phases of the regulation. There have subsequently been moves away from a reliance uniquely on rules, particularly detailed rules, in two different sets of regulatory relationships: between regulator and regulatee, and between regulators themselves.

In imposing regulation on regulatees, changes in the use of rules have been accompanied by a change in the regulatory technique adopted. Instead of using detailed rules to impose regulation, vaguer rules have been used in conjunction with a change in technique, viz. the co-optation of other participants in the market into the regulatory process to aid monitoring and implementation. This is in effect a move away from the situation in which the regulator has the sole responsibility for ensuring the 'success' of the regulation. So in the regulation of soft commissions the attempt to use detailed rules to specify when a soft commission arrangement could or could not be entered into was discarded and replaced by the imposition of a duty on the fund manager to ensure that the soft commission arrangement would not operate to the disadvantage of the investor.[19] By placing the duty of monitoring the transaction on the fund manager, and so relying on his or her judgement, the regulator was relieved of the need to write a detailed rule which attempted to specify in advance the

[19] See Ch. 5.

range of situations, out of the thousands possible, in which such an arrangement would or would not be harmful. In a situation of a wide range of possible circumstances, of change and fluctuation in products and business practices, under- or over-inclusion would be highly likely, and such a precise structure could further serve to aid creative compliance, exploiting the under-inclusiveness of the rule. Instead of specification, therefore, there was an imposition of the duty of judgement onto the fund manager. Unfortunately, as we have seen, the duty is inchoately expressed, and for this reason at least the technique may not in practice work as initially hoped, at least by some of the regulators.

The second example differs slightly, as the change in regulatory technique adopted impacts not simply on rule type, but on the role played by rules. It concerns the regulation of the inter-regulatory relationship, an issue which has occupied a significant amount of regulatory, and political, time and attention. Initially SIB attempted to exert control over the SROs, and in particular their rule books, indirectly through rules, by requiring their rules to be equivalent to SIB's. The New Settlement also aimed to control the SROs through rules, again indirectly, this time by making SIB's rules applicable to the members of SROs. In the Large reforms, the role of rules in regulating inter-regulatory relations has been replaced by a move away from rules to management-orientated techniques of statements of objectives and management plans. What has occurred is a redefinition of the problem of the inter-regulator relationship as essentially a management problem; management techniques rather than rules are now being used in an attempt to define that relationship.

Making Rules

Thus portrayed, the rule making decision appears to have been a conscious and tactical one, and to a degree it has. However, rule making has in practice displayed varying degrees of sophistication and awareness of the nature and potential uses of rules. Moreover, rule making has not occurred in a vacuum. Whilst particular uses have been made of rules, it is clear that the rule making decision has been, and is likely to be, affected by considerations which range far beyond the very particular one of how best to use rules. Such an observation is not surprising. Both theoretical and empirically based studies of policy making, decision making, and regulatory agencies in a range of literatures stress the multiplicity of factors which may or do affect policy and decision making, examples of many if not all of which have been relevant to financial services rule makers.

Such factors include the role of interest groups in policy formation,[20] and in particular the impact of the lack of consumer involvement on agency decision making, especially in such an area as this which is characterized by considerable technical complexity,[21] the political environment in which the agency operates, which may affect the level of support the agency has within the key political institutions and the political sensitivity of the issues with which it deals,[22] and the degree of autonomy which it enjoys, both operational and financial, from the political process.[23] The organizational

[20] This study has noted the role of different interests in the pre-legislative and legislative stages and throughout the regulatory process, although, as noted below, these interests have not always been determinative. The role ascribed to interest groups in the literature varies. In theories of regulation, both the capture theory and private interest theories emphasize the role of interest groups in ensuring that regulation is conducted in their own interests: G. J. Stigler, 'The Theory of Economic Regulation' (1971) 2 *Bell J Econ. and Mgt. Sci.* 1; R. A. Posner, 'Taxation by Regulation' (1971) 2 *Bell J Econ. and Mgt. Sci.* 22; id., 'Theories of Economic Regulation' (1975) 5 *Bell J Econ. and Mgt. Sci.* 335; S. Peltzmann, 'Towards a More General Theory of Reguation' (1976) 19 *J Law and Econ.* 211; see also J. Q. Wilson, *The Politics of Regulation* (New York, 1980); B. A. Ackerman and W. T. Hassler, *Clean Coal, Dirty Air* (Yale, 1981). On the capture theory see M. H. Bernstein, *Regulating Business by Independent Commission* (New York, 1955); G. Kolko, *The Triumph of Conservatism* (New York, 1965), R. Cranston, 'Regulation and Deregulation: General Issues' (1982) 5 *UNSW LJ* 1. On the formation and impact of interest groups see M. Olson, *The Logic of Collective Action* (Harvard, 1965) and id., *Rise and Decline of Nations* (Yale, 1982).

[21] P. C. Yeager, *The Limits of Law: The Public Regulation of Private Pollution* (Cambridge, 1991); M. J. Trebilcock, J. R. Prichard, L. Waverman, 'The Consumer Interest and the Regulatory Process', in A. J. Duggan and L. W. Darrall (eds.), *Consumer Protection Law and Theory* (Toronto, 1980); M. J. Trebilcock, 'Winners and Losers in the Regulatory System: Why Must the Consumer Always Lose?' (1975) 13 *Osgoode Hall LR* 619.

[22] This is most famously set out in Bernstein's 'life cycle' theory of regulation: M. H. Bernstein, *Regulating Business by Independent Commission* (New York, 1955); see also J. M. Landis, *The Administrative Process* (Yale, 1938).

[23] Bernstein, *Regulating Business*; id., 'The Regulatory Process: A Framework for Analysis' (1961) 26 *L&CP* 329. UK studies of the impact of governmental involvement in the regulatory process include R. Baldwin, *Regulating the Airlines* (Oxford, 1985); id., 'Civil Aviation Regulation', in R. Baldwin and C. McCrudden, *Regulation and Public Law* (London, 1987); C. McCrudden, 'Codes in a Cold Climate: Administrative Rule Making by the Commission for Racial Equality' (1988) 51 *MLR* 409.

structure is also noted to affect the policy making process, with the interests represented in the organization, the distribution of authority within it, the levels at which decisions are taken, the degree of autonomy which decision makers have within the organization, and the backgrounds and competence of staff all being emphasized in different studies as relevant.[24] Organizational structure can encourage policy makers to take a top-down approach to decision making, inhibit feedback on the operation of those policies, and foster unrealistic assumptions concerning the division between policy and implementation.[25] The structure of the decision process also affects the decision: empirical studies highlight the impact that participative processes can have on agency operation, in particular, rules can become increasingly complex as accommodations of particular positions are made; and indeed as we have seen the rule maker may deliberately adopt a rule structure which facilitates such accommodation. Alternatively the need for political compromise could mean that agreement is reached only as to the broadest statements of policies, resulting in vague, widely drawn rules,[26] and again as we have seen such rules may, implicitly or explicitly, provide discretion to others involved in the regulatory process, be they regulators, enforcers, adjudicators or the regulated. Finally, the interests and values of agency officials themselves are also attributed a role of varying significance within different analyses. In economic theory the content and nature of these interests are

[24] Galligan, *Discretionary Powers* at 134; Cranston, 'Regulation and Deregulation'; Baldwin, *Rules and Government*, 169–74. Economic theories of the role of institutions in policy formation (which go under the broad label of new institutionalism or positive political theory) place particular emphasis on institutional structure: see in particular M. D. McCubbins, R. G. Noll, and B. R. Weingast, 'Administrative Procedures as Instruments of Political Control' (1987) 3 *J Law, Econ. and Org.* 243 and 'Structure, Process, Politics and Policy: Administrative Arrangements and the Political Control of Agencies' (1989) 75 *Virginia LR* 431; R. L. Calvert, M. C. McCubbins, and B. R. Weingast, 'A Theory of Political Control and Agency Discretion' (1989) 33 *Am. J Pol. Sci.* 588; J. R. Macey, 'Organisational Design and Political Control of Administrative Agencies' (1992) 8 *J Law, Econ. and Org.* 52; M. J. Horn and K. A. Shepsle, 'Commentary: Structure, Process, Politics and Policy' (1989) *Va. LR* 499; J. R. Macey, 'Separated Powers and Positive Political Theory: The Tug of War over Administrative Agencies' (1992) 80 *Geo. LR* 671.

[25] See Baldwin, *Rules and Government*, 167–9; C. Ham and M. Hill, *Policy Process in the Modern Capitalist State* (London, 1984); S. Barratt and C. Fudge (eds.), *Policy and Action* (London, 1981); D. S. Van Mater and C. E. Van Horn, 'The Policy Implementation Process' (1975) *Administration and Society* 455.

[26] Diver, 'Regulatory Precision'.

assumed and assigned to officials. Officials, as rational actors, are assumed to act to maximize their self-interest which is defined as, for example, increasing their power and that of the agency (greater budgets, larger area of competence) and furthering their own careers.[27] This is echoed in the 'revolving door' phenomenon familiar in much American literature: that officials will curry favour with regulatees as they will be seeking jobs from them when they leave the agency.[28] Non-economic approaches also highlight the importance of the perceptions, moral attitude, and norms of agency officials in the decision process, including perceptions as to the position of the agency, its values, and goals,[29] but in contrast to economic approaches do not assume these to take a particular form.[30]

Emphasizing then the multiplicity of factors to which a rule maker is subject, both as a policy maker and decision maker within an organization, is not a novel or surprising exercise. However, this of itself does not indicate how those factors impact on the rule making process, although it does suggest that single-cause analyses oversimplify the process. Indeed, rule making by financial services regulators shows rule making to be a complex and subtle process not readily reducible to simple causal formula: 'it's all because of *x*'. Examining that rule making process suggests, however, that simply identifying the different factors which affect the rule making decision does not take us very far in understanding that decision; we need to go further and understand and explain how they impacted and why they did so at the particular time and in the particular way they did. In so doing we should not see factors as discrete 'inputs' into the regulatory process, each entering

[27] A. Downs, *Inside Bureaucracy* (Boston, 1967), W. A. Niskansen, *Bureaucracy and Representative Government* (Chicago, 1971), G. Tullock, *The Politics of Bureaucracy* (New York, 1965), J. Buchanan and G. Tullock, *The Calculus of Consent* (Michigan, 1962), D. C. Mueller, *Public Choice* (Cambridge, 1979, rev. ed. 1989). More recent economic analysis has attempted to extend the range of recognized interests: see, e.g., M. E. Levine and J. L. Forrence, 'Regulatory Capture, Public Interest and the Public Agenda: Towards a Synthesis' (1990) 6 *J Law, Econ. and Org.* 167; K. S. Cook and M. Levi (eds.), *The Limits of Rationality* (Chicago, 1990).

[28] For a discussion see Cranston, 'Regulation and Deregulation'.

[29] P. Schuck, 'Organization Theory and the Teaching of Administrative Law' (1983) *Jnl. of Legal Education* 13. Moreover, as Katzmann's study indicates, differences between officials within the organization as to their own values, role, and backgrounds can also affect the way in which the agency operates: R. A. Katzmann, *Regulatory Bureaucracy* (Harvard, 1980).

[30] For contrasting approaches to the role and definition of interests, see references cited at n. 34.

in its separate container. Rather it is the fact and nature of their interaction which is significant, and which, it is suggested, enables us to understand more clearly the nature of the rule making process. Moreover, in understanding that process it is important to distinguish the fact that the rule maker is subject to a range of influences from the strategic and non-strategic use of rules: simply because a decision is influenced by a range of different factors and constrained in a variety of ways does not necessarily mean that within those constraints a decision cannot be strategically made (although whether that strategy ultimately proves to have been the right one is yet another matter).

In making these suggestions, we move from the broader focus of policy making into the more particular focus of decision making to address the question of how, given a context of competing demands from politicians and interested groups, of particular organizational structures, and taking into account the norms, perceptions, and values of those making the decision, all of which it is suggested play a role in the rule making process, rule makers make decisions on rules. Decision making theories divide broadly into two camps: rationalists and non-rationalists, although the line between the two is not always clearly drawn.[31] The rational model of economic theory sees decisions as purposive choices made by rational actors working with a clear set of individual or organizational goals. Decision makers are assumed to survey the likely outcomes of various courses of action that are possible, and to anticipate all likely consequences. Decision making is thus seen as intentional, consequential, and optimizing.

[31] In many respects the old adage holds true: 'economics is all about how people make choices; sociology is all about how they don't have any choices to make' (J. Duesenberry, 'Comment on "An Economic Analysis of Fertility"', in *Demographic and Economic Change in Developed Countries* (Princeton, 1960), 233, cited in M. Granovetter, 'Economic Action and Social Structure', in M. Granovetter and R. Swedberg (eds.), *The Sociology of Economic Life* (Colorado, 1992), 56. The different theories may nevertheless better be represented as positions on a spectrum between the 'choices' / 'no choices' poles. In the legal or socio-legal literature on discretion and decision making, two of the theories dominate the traditional discussion: rationalism and incrementalism, see Hawkins, 'Using Legal Discretion', 20–4; Galligan, *Discretionary Powers*, 117–28, Ham and Hill, *Policy Process in the Modern Capitalist State*, Ch. 5, and G. Smith and D. May, 'The Artificial Debate between Rationalist and Incrementalist Models of Decision Making' (1980) 8 *Policy and Politics* 147; for a model which combines elements of the rational and incremental approaches see A. Etzioni, 'Mixed Scanning: A "Third" Approach to Decision Making' (1967) *Pub. Admin. Rev.* 27; 'new institutionalism', discussed below and see references cited at n. 34, has not thus far formed a central part of that debate.

Alternative models challenge the picture of organizational and bureaucratic behaviour which rationalists paint. The incrementalist model of decision making advanced by Lindblom suggested that organizations proceed on an incremental basis, making marginal adjustments to particular solutions.[32] The emphasis is on finding solutions to particular problems. The method used is not a rational overview of all available alternatives, but an accommodation of conflicting interests and considerations within an established pattern of decision making. Only a restricted number of policy alternatives and consequences are envisaged or reviewed. Analysis may be fragmented between different participants, limited to a few familiar alternatives, and only some consequences explored. Goals and values may be intertwined with the empirical aspects of the problem, means and ends chosen simultaneously.

The comprehensively rational model of economics has been modified by Simon's notion of 'bounded rationality', which recognized the limits on the decision makers' knowledge and ability. Decision makers, Simon argued, do not and cannot undertake the full survey of outcomes and consequences that the rational model assumes, and do not work on the basis of full information. Rather decision makers have limited information, foresight, and resources and make their decisions within these limits. Moreover, decision makers 'satisfice', rather than optimize, taking the first satisfactory solution encountered.[33]

This model has been developed in certain strands of new institutionalism.[34] March and Olsen argue that human action is an

[32] See C. Lindblom, 'The Science of Muddling Through' (1959) 19 *Pub. Admin. Rev.* 79.

[33] H. Simon, *Administrative Behaviour* (New York, 1975). For a discussion of the impact of Simon's theory on decision making theories, see C. R. Miller, 'The Rhetoric of Decision Science, or Herbert A. Simon Says', in H. W. Simons (ed.), *The Rhetorical Turn: Invention and Persuasion in the Conduct of Inquiry* (Chicago, 1990).

[34] There are broadly three main strands to new institutionalism: economic, political/historical, and sociological, although the boundaries between them are not clear cut. In economics see O. E. Williamson, *Markets and Hierarchies* (New York, 1975); id., *The Economic Institutions of Capitalism: Firms, Markets, Relational Contracting* (New York, 1985); D. C. North, *Institutions, Institutional Change, and Economic Performance* (Cambridge, 1990); K. S. Cook and M. Levi (eds.), *The Limits of Rationality* (Chicago, 1990); in broadly the political/historical field see J. G. March and J. P. Olsen, 'The New Institutionalism: Organizational Factors in Political Life' (1984) 75 *Am. Pol. Sci. Rev.* 734; *eid.*, *Rediscovering Institutions* (New York, 1989); T. Skocpol, 'Bringing the State Back In: Strategies of Analysis in Current Research', in P. Evans, D. Rueschemeyer, and T. Skocpol (eds.), *Bringing the State Back In* (London,

attempt to satisfice, but the expectations which actors aim to fulfil are context specific and deeply embedded in cultural, socio-economic, and political fields or structures.[35] Although individuals may act in a relatively purposive way, in doing so the rules they follow are defined by the context in which they are operating, and are followed even when doing so may not be in their self-interest. Action is the fulfilment of duties and obligations. Individuals behave not according to their self-interest but according to what they consider appropriate. What is appropriate for a particular person in a particular situation is defined by the political and social system and transmitted through socialization.[36] Explanations of repetitive action within organizations again are not due to rational strategies of minimizing transaction costs or other pursuits of self-interest, but to their 'taken-for-granted quality and their reproduction in structures that are to some extent self-sustaining'.[37] When there are no clear guidelines on how to act, individuals dip into a 'garbage can' of possible solutions which are possibly random and represent a haphazard response to a new situation.[38] The political order is seen not as the outcome of reason (rational actors) and competition and coercion (conflicts of interests, bargaining, power) but of inefficient history, accidental coincidences of events, endogenous processes, norms of appropriateness, of duties, obligations, roles, and rules.[39]

Sociological variants of new institutionalism go further than the

1985); P. Hall, *Governing the Economy* (London, 1986); G. J. Ikenberry, 'Conclusion: An Institutional Approach to American Foreign Economic Policy', in G. J. Ikenberry, D. A. Lade, and M. Mastanduno (eds.), *The State and Foreign Economic Policy* (New York, 1988); K. Thelen and S. Steinmo, 'Historical Institutionalism in Comparative Politics', in S. Steinmo, K. Thelen, and F. Longstreth, *Structuring Politics: Historical Institutionalism in Comparative Analysis* (Cambridge, 1992); in the sociological/organizational school, see e.g.: J. W. Meyer and B. Rowan, 'Institutionalized Organisations: Formal Structure as Myth and Ceremony' (1977) *Am. J Sociol.* 340; R. Scott, 'The Adolescence of Institutional Theory' (1987) 32 *Admin. Sci. Qly.* 493; P. DiMaggio and W. Powell, 'Introduction' in P. DiMaggio and W. Powell (eds.), *The New Institutionalism in Organisational Analysis* (Chicago, 1991); M. Granovetter and R. Swedberg (eds.), *The Sociology of Economic Life* (Colorado, 1992). For a useful review and comparison of the different approaches see T. Koeble, 'The New Institutionalism in Political Science and Sociology' (1995) *Comparative Politics* 231; see also R. E. Goodin, 'Institutions and their Design', in id. (ed.), *The Theory of Institutional Design* (Cambridge, 1996).

[35] March and Olsen, *Rediscovering Institutions*, 9–19.

[36] Ibid., 23–4; *eid.*, 'The New Institutionalism', 741.

[37] Powell and DiMaggio, 'Introduction', 9.

[38] March and Olsen, *Rediscovering Institutions*, 12–13.

[39] March and Olsen, 'The New Institutionalism', 743–4.

political or historical strands in denying any role for rational action in decision making, even in a bounded form. The new institutionalists in sociology play down the significance of the individual as an agent or as a significant variable in a decision. They see individual decisions as the product of a far larger frame of reference of cultural, political or social relationships over which they have no control.[40] It is the larger, extrainstitutional, and systemic factors of culture and history which both shape *and determine* choices. Institutions are themselves dependent on their cultural, political or social context. They stress the importance of the embeddedness of individuals in this wider context. Cognitive and cultural embeddedness explains why individuals cannot conceive of alternative arrangements or ways of doing things. Indeed Granovetter argues that individuals are so embedded that it is almost absurd to speak of utility-maximizing and rational behaviour in a strictly economic sense. What is rational depends on the context in which it is viewed.[41]

The emphasis of particularly the sociological approach to new institutionalism echoes that of Hawkins's model of 'natural' decision making.[42] In analysing the behaviour of legal decision makers (for example bureaucrats, parole board members) in making individualized decisions Hawkins stresses that a holistic approach to analysing such decisions should be adopted. Decisions should be seen not as discrete entities but rather as relatively complex, subtle, and part of or the culmination of a process in which external constraints such as organizational and occupational rules, norms, procedures, and resources also operate.[43] He uses the notion of a 'decision frame' to understand how and why decisions are actually made.[44] A decision frame is the 'structure of knowledge, experience,

[40] Powell and DiMaggio, 'Introduction'; M. Granovetter, 'Economic Action and Social Structure: The Problem of Embeddedness', in Granovetter and Swedberg, *The Sociology of Economic Life.*

[41] Ibid.

[42] K. Hawkins, 'Discretion in Making Legal Decisions' (1986) 43 *Wash. & Lee LR* 1161; id., 'Using Legal Discretion', 24–35. By legal decision making Hawkins means decisions such as granting parole or enforcing rules which have binary outcome (parole, no parole), and which may be made by formal adjudication, negotiation or mediation: 'Discretion in Making Legal Decisions', 1168–71.

[43] Hawkins, 'Discretion in Making Legal Decisions', 1187; id., 'Using Legal Discretion', 27–35.

[44] Galligan also talks of the importance of understanding the 'framework' through which problems are seen and decisions approached as providing a starting-point for the analysis of decision making: *Discretionary Powers*, 124–6; see also D. J. Gifford, 'Decisions, Decisional Referents, and Administrative Justice' (1972) 37 *Law and Contemp. Problems* 3.

values and meanings that the decision-maker shares with others and brings to a choice . . . a master code which shapes, typifies, informs and even confirms the character of choices'. It may comprise moral values, institutional ideology or organizational values. It may change as the priorities accorded the values brought to any decision task change. Different decision frames may produce different outcomes, different decisions on the same information.[45]

Although the differences between the different models of decision making may be more of degree rather than kind, at least in some respects, the natural model of decision making and non-economic strands of new institutionalism emphasize, *inter alia*, the causal complexity and context dependency of decision making, the role of history, and the significance of the decision makers' 'world view' to a far greater extent than certainly the comprehensively rational model of decision making. It is the latter, however, which is often assumed to be the decision process which accompanies rule making, and rules are indeed often seen as a better mode of decision making than discretion simply because they involve such a comprehensive and rational survey of options and consideration of implications.[46] Examining the rule making process of financial services regulators, however, suggests that it is the characterization of decision making captured in the natural model of decision making and the non-economic strands of new institutionalism, rather than that of comprehensive rationality, which accord better with the reality of regulatory rule making.

The analysis of rule making offered here both differs from and adds to that of new institutionalism, and, to the extent that they are similar, the model of natural decision making.[47] First, it has

[45] Hawkins, 'Using Legal Discretion', 24–6; id., 'Discretion in Making Legal Decisions', 1190–5; P. K. Manning, '"Big Bang" Decisions: Notes on a Naturalistic Approach', in K. Hawkins (ed.), *The Uses of Discretion*.

[46] For a classic statement of the advantages of rules which assumes such a model of decision making, see D. L. Shapiro, 'The Choice of Rulemaking or Adjudication in the Development of Administrative Policy' (1965) 78 *Harvard LR* 921.

[47] With respect to new institutionalism, there is perhaps a danger in suggesting that there is a clearly defined theory of new institutionalism. Rather, by its own admission, new institutionalism is rather less coherent, being described by some of its advocates as an 'approach and not a theory' (Ikenberry, 'An Institutional Approach', 241, who adds '[i]t presents a set of problems and variables, but it does not pretend to provide the basis for a formal and parsimonious test of propositions that researchers can test in a simple fashion'), an 'empirically based prejudice' (March and Olsen, 'The New Institutionalism', 747) which reasons inductively

been stressed above that it is important to separate out the question of the degree of strategy involved in the decision from the issue of the isolation of the decision maker from external and internal pressures. In this, the role which this study has noted for strategic action on the part of rule makers runs counter to the sociological emphasis on the deep contextual embeddedness of individuals which denies a role for rational or strategic action, albeit of a restricted nature.[48] The rule making decision has involved a varying degree of strategy, albeit one shaped and constrained by the context in which it was made.[49] Moreover, it is suggested that in understanding the rule making decision, the particular nature of that decision has to be recognized: the decision is affected not only by its context but by its inherent properties, which in the case of rule making are those of rules. A strategic use of rules thus requires awareness of the nature and limitations of rules. Further, rules also play a significant symbolic role in which not simply the content but the structure and status of the rule play an important part. Thus the nature of rules, and the assumptions which attach to the use of different types of rules, provide a particular dimension to the rule making decision which differentiates it both from the generalized policy decision and the individualized discretionary decision.

The following discussion focuses on the role and interaction of several key elements in the process of rule making by financial services regulators explored in the previous chapters: the organizational

from events rather than deductively from theory (Thelen and Steinmo, 'Historical Institutionalism', 12). It also self-confessedly has difficulties explaining change in institutions: for discussions and attempts to address this issue see Thelen and Steinmo, 'Historical Institutionalism', 15–26; Powell and DiMaggio, 'Introduction', 30–1.

[48] This is not to say that strategy is always present, nor that it is always successful and its outcomes predicted. For discussion of the different roles attributed to strategy in the different strands of new institutionalism see Granovetter, 'Economic Action and Social Structure', who attempts to find a middle way between the 'over-socialised' model of action of sociology and the 'under-socialised' model of economics; see also Powell and DiMaggio, 'Introduction'; Thelen and Steinmo, 'Historical Institutionalism in Comparative Politics'; Koeble, 'The New Institutionalism in Political Science and Sociology'. The sociological emphasis is stressed in the natural model of decision making: Hawkins, 'Using Legal Discretion'.

[49] It is the fact that strategy is so shaped by contextual factors, such as history, institutional structures, norms, and perceptions, however, which distinguishes this analysis from the economic model of rational decision making. Moreover, strategy may not always be present; nor are decisions ever free from unintended consequences and unforeseen effects.

and legal structure, the norms and perceptions of those involved in and observing the process, the rhetoric of self-regulation which imbues that process, interest groups, the nature of the market, and the internal dynamic of regulation itself. Certain of these elements may be constant, structuring or permeating all rule making decisions; the pressures they exert may always push in one direction, or may change over time. Others may be ephemeral; their coincidence accidental, altering the course of the decision, creating space in which the decision can be made, or acting as catalysts, reacting with a constant factor with the result that factor exerts a different impact than it may otherwise have done.

The most obvious constant, structuring factor is the legal framework, the distribution of power between different institutions or bodies. Most significantly, in conferring rule making powers the legal framework determines what types of rules can be used, by stipulating that they must be made by statutory instrument, for example, or their legal status and the sanction that should attach to them, and so may either restrict or facilitate the uses which can be made of rules. Further, the legal framework creates 'entry points' and indeed 'veto points' in the rule making process,[50] enabling, prohibiting or limiting the extent to which other bodies may be involved. In distributing powers of recognition, supervision, and regulation throughout the regulatory system it also structures the relations between regulatory bodies.

Simply noting the map of legal powers does not however of itself indicate how those powers will be used, or what the implications of the institutional structure would be. It is the interaction of this structure with other aspects of the regulatory context which is of importance, including its history, the nature of the market being regulated and its participants, the political context and the perceptions of those institutions involved in the regulatory process both as to the existence and nature of the problems or issues which need to be addressed and the responses which should be made to them. These in turn involve both institutional self-interest, but also a strong sense of appropriateness, of what appears to that body to be the 'right' thing to do.

[50] Other veto or entry points (or 'windows') may be more fluid. For a discussion see E. Immergut, 'The Rules of the Game: The Logic of Health Policy Making in France, Switzerland and Sweden', in Thelen and Steinmo, *Structuring Politics*; J. W. Kingdom, *Agendas, Alternatives and Public Policies* (Boston, 1984), 173–204.

One example of the impact of this interaction on the particular use made by a body of its institutional position is the role of the DTI in the formation of the initial rule books. In not conferring powers on SIB directly but instead requiring it to be approved by the DTI before powers would be transferred to it, the Act deliberately gave the DTI a brief 'window' in the formation of the regulation and a crucial opportunity to influence the form of the initial rule books. The way in which this power was used, the implications of allowing the DTI an entry point into the process, was itself a product of the historical reasons for that distribution of authority, the DTI's own concerns as to its position, and the degree of uncertainty and flux which existed in the industry. Concerns that the system as a whole would degenerate into a regulatory cartel, and the fact that it was precluded by the terms of the Act from having any continuing role in shaping the rules of the regulators in turn affected how the DTI used this window, prompting demands from the DTI for SIB to increase the detail and specification in its initial rules. Combined with SIB's own attitude, its own emphasis on the need for detail to ensure consistency, certainty, and control over the regulated's behaviour and SROs' rules, these factors in combination led to the detailed nature and complexity of the initial rule books.

The OFT's involvement in the regulatory process provides a further example of the influence of its history on the pattern of the institutional structure and of the interaction of that structure with other factors. The anti-competitive nature of the Stock Exchange's rules and the adverse effect which they were perceived to have had on London's competitiveness highlighted the need for a rigorous review of the regulation to prevent anti-competitive practices; however the experience of the case brought to the Restrictive Practices Court by the OFT against the Stock Exchange in 1979–83 illustrated that litigation in the RPC was not necessarily the most effective way to perform this review, hence the removal of the regulatory system from the regime of general competition law. The role of the OFT as a substitute review body was at least in part in response to the effective sidelining of the OFT in the Goodison-Parkinson agreement.[51] The significance of the OFT's role has, however, arisen not simply because the Act endowed the

[51] See Ch. 2, n. 31.

OFT with the task of carrying out a competition review, but because of the particular interaction of the institutions involved: the OFT's assertiveness over the FSA regulators, the difference in perceptions between it and the FSA regulators as to what regulation to adopt to achieve investor protection objectives, even though those objectives are shared, and the varying degree of receptiveness of the Government to OFT reports and its consequent giving of the necessary legal directions.

The development of retail regulation in particular has been characterized by a dialogue, indeed almost dialectic between the OFT and the FSA regulators, with the OFT repeatedly finding that the rules made were anti-competitive to a significant degree. The FSA regulators and the OFT have differed in their perceptions of the nature of the markets being regulated, the consequences to which the regulation has led, and the skill and sophistication of the investor. As we have seen, the OFT saw the retail market as divided into two distinct parts: the market for advice, and the market for sales. Independent financial advisers (IFAs) operated in the former; IFAs and tied agents in the latter. The fact that they operated in distinct market areas, the OFT argued, meant that different rules could apply to each without either suffering a competitive disadvantage. SIB argued there was one market, and so the potential that differential regulatory treatment could result in one suffering a competitive disadvantage. Further, the OFT had a higher assessment than SIB and Lautro of the investors' ability and willingness to seek out and process information about an investment product and to conduct their own comparisons, leading directly to conflicts over disclosure policy.

Regulators' own perceptions, of the issues to be addressed, the ways in which they should be addressed, and of their own role, play an important and inevitable role in their decision process. Regulators mediate the demands different interest groups make on them, politicians, media, regulated, consumer bodies, and other regulators. In so doing, March and Olsen's suggestion that actors act in accordance with their own norms of appropriateness appears well borne out by the experience of regulatory rule making thus far.[52] The statutorily stated and politically expected objectives of regulation are wide-ranging, potentially conflicting, and raise as

[52] March and Olsen, 'The New Institutionalism', 741.

many questions as they purport to answer. They include investor protection, the prevention and detection of fraud and market manipulation, raising the standards of business in the market-place, the provision of confidence in the markets, the importance of competition, the facilitation of market efficiency, and the promotion of London as a financial centre. Given the range of objectives and the heterogeneity of the industry it is clear that they cannot all be met simultaneously or through the same means and the regulators have to perform the inevitable balancing act. Nor is it immediately clear what the objectives require in any particular circumstance. What is 'protection' and to whom should it be given? Does investor protection require paternalistic measures, or is it served by a competitive market-place in which the investor has freedom to choose between different products or courses of action? How does 'market efficiency' relate to competition? Should the rules aim to treat different sectors of the market equivalently, or impose requirements which might give an advantage to one sector of the market over another? The regulators' interpretation of those objectives, their assessment of what course would best fulfil them is an essential element in the rule making process.

These perceptions and the norms which inform the rule making decisions are themselves defined in part by the institutional structure, and by its characterization as a system of self-regulation. The significance of the institutional structure is not simply that it is federal, with consequent tensions between the role of the centre and the outlying bodies, although this is relevant. It is the ambiguity inherent in the structure as to the respective roles of the regulators and the nature of rules which they should produce, and the coupling of this structure with the rhetoric which surrounds it, the description of the system as one of 'self-regulation within a statutory framework', which have exerted such an impact on regulatory rule making.

In order to understand the nature and reasons for the particular influence this has had, it is necessary to appreciate its history. The institutional structure is the product of history and the particular market context in which the regulation operates. Its formation is a study in design and coincidence: Gower's proposals provided solutions to problems which were unanticipated when he wrote, and the emergence of which meant that those proposals were implemented, only slightly modified, when they may otherwise not have been. In Gower's own words, reflecting on the impact of the Stock Exchange agreement and Big Bang, the increased incidence of fraud, and the change in the Bank of England's attitude to regulation in prompting the passing of the FSA despite the initial hostile reactions to his proposals, '[e]vents . . . achieved what arguments and persuasion would not have done'.[53]

The system of 'mandated' self-regulation which was implemented[54] itself reflects the complex meshing of governmental and non-governmental regulatory arrangements which characterized the pre-FSA era. The FSA was essentially, to use Moran's words, 'a codification, institutionalisation and juridification' of these corporatist arrangements, whereby rules became more elaborate and statute-based and organizations acquired greater (legislative) authority.[55] The ultimate form of the division of powers between SIB and the recognized bodies was in turn due to the competing views as to the merits or otherwise of statutory and non-statutory systems, themselves in turn affected by the coincidences of events immediately prior to the Act, in particular the increase in the publicized incidence of fraud. The (partly deliberate) lack of clarity as to the nature of the relationship between SIB and the SROs in the White Paper, the confusion in the debates leading up to the Act, and the incremental additions and amendments to that structure in the legislative process resulted in a structure in which the respective roles of SIB and the recognized bodies were ill-defined, with certain centralizing aspects sitting alongside preserved areas of autonomy for those bodies.

The particular nature of the structure, its unusual combination of statutory and non-statutory elements, of public and private, has had a significant impact on the uses made of rules, and was the principal motivation for the New Settlement, as we have seen. It has also had a deeper, more complex impact. It has affected the perceived legitimacy of the regulatory system, the extent to which it is accepted, its rules, decisions, processes seen as valid reasons for action by those it regulates, and the light in which its actions are viewed by its media and political observers.[56] These different

[53] L. C. B. Gower, 'Big Bang and City Regulation' (1988) 51 *MLR* 1, 10.

[54] See Ch. 1, 79.

[55] M. Moran, *Politics of the Financial Services Revolution* (London, 1991), 13.

[56] The notion of legitimacy being adopted here is that of Weber: Weber, *Economy and Society*, 218. For a fuller discussion of legitimacy see in particular D. Beetham, *The Legitimation of Power* (London, 1991); J. Habermas, *Legitimation Crisis* (London,

groups form different legitimacy communities, each demanding a different criteria of acceptability.[57] Here the hybrid nature of the system means that it has suffered. It has fallen between broadly two potential sources of legitimacy, and had difficulty tapping either. Moreover, it has been tarred with the illegitimate aspects of both. A pure self-regulatory system may derive legitimacy (acceptability) from its regulatees: it is 'one of them'. However, from those outside the system it is subject to the charge of lack of accountability and self-interested regulation, particularly if it is a monopoly regulator or regulating a significant area of social or economic activity. A statutory system can borrow, as it were, from the legitimacy of the State, but may nevertheless be treated by those it is regulating as an unacceptable and unwarranted intrusion into their affairs. Statutory regulatory systems in particular can have low levels of acceptability amongst those being regulated.[58]

Many aspects of the changes in the regulatory and rule system, and indeed of the current debate surrounding that system, have at their root the search for legitimacy. The thrust behind the initial rule books, that which did not get lost in the haste and confusion of those early days, was to show that SIB was, to adapt a phrase, 'tough on investor protection, tough on the causes of investor protection'. The New Settlement was largely aimed at gaining the acceptance of the regulatees, particularly the City, who it was feared had been alienated by the form the initial regulation had taken. The norms of appropriateness which have had such an impact have themselves been shaped by the same concern. The public, via the media, meanwhile voice concern that the system is one of self-interested regulation, and the endless reversals of policy in the retail sector following OFT recommendations, the widespread breaches of regulation, highlighted all too clearly in the misselling of home income plans and personal pensions, and the Maxwell affair, have done much to vindicate their charges. As we have seen, the regulators are currently distancing themselves from the description 'self-regulators' and adopting that of 'independent regulators' in

1976); J. Freedman, *Crisis and Legitimacy* (Cambridge, 1978); and with particular respect to bureaucracies, G. E. Frug, 'The Ideology of Bureaucracy in American Law' (1984) 97 *Harvard LR* 1277.

[57] For the development of the idea of 'legitimacy communities' see R. Barker, *Political Legitimacy and the State* (Oxford, 1990).

[58] Hawkins, *Environment and Enforcement*, 10–14, discusses the hostility of business to regulation and the 'moral ambivalence' which surrounds it.

an attempt to gain recognition and acceptance as effective regulators, not instruments of industry interests.

The rhetoric of self-regulation and light in which self-regulation is viewed has had a further and very particular impact on the uses which have been made of rules. This is in large part because of a strong assumed association of rule type and regulatory approach made by those both within and observing the regulatory system. The association of rule type with regulatory approach means that as the political climate varies in the demands it makes for the intensity of the regulation, so pressures for different types of rules are exerted. These vary with different groups: politicians, the regulated, the media; over time, with different constituencies making different demands in different periods; and between markets. Different types of rules are assumed to follow almost inexorably from particular types of regulatory systems. These assumptions were clear in the debates surrounding the formation of the Act: that self-regulation was seen to mean 'flexible' rules sensitively applied; statutory regulation was associated with detailed, 'rigid' rules.

Different types of rules have thus been perceived as involving particular regulatory approaches, tough or flexible, self-regulatory or statutory, and as having different levels of efficacy. Detailed rules are associated with greater control, and so have been equated in the rhetoric surrounding the regulation with tough regulation, with upholding investor protection; they have also been associated with a system of statutory, bureaucratic regulation which it is feared would stifle innovation and competitiveness. Vague rules are associated with self-regulation, which is flexible and adaptable, but also with self-interested and 'light' regulation which does not further investor protection. These assumptions are illustrated in the expectations surrounding the use of the Principles: that the consequence of the more general rule would be to alter the perceptions of the regulation, increase its acceptability, and increase compliance.

The association of rule type with a particular type of regulatory system, self- or statutory, has meant that rule type has played a significant part in defining the roles of regulators within the regulatory structure. Thus SIB's initial concern to set the standard for and control the contents of the SROs' rule books through detailed rules, whilst perfectly legal, was for many a violation of the spirit of self-regulation and contrary to the intentions of the Act, or more particularly the intentions of some of those behind it. The move by SIB to broader, vaguer rules (the Principles) and rules of an 'intermediate level of generality' (the Core Rules) was, as noted above, an attempt to reinforce the 'self-regulatory' element of the system and to signal a 'step back' from regulating to supervising on the part of SIB.

Assumptions as to the association of rule type and the characterization of the regulatory system are paralleled by assumptions as to rule type and the 'rigour' of regulation. Detailed rules are associated with strong (but rigid) regulation, vaguer rules with a lax (but sensitive) regime. The initial demand of the Government was for tough regulation, and so detailed rules; this then changed to requiring a more flexible regulatory approach, and so a different type of rule. These assumptions were shared by SIB. In forming its initial rules SIB also argued that detailed rules were necessary to ensure high standards of behaviour, given the competitive environment and actors who varied considerably in their competence and honesty.[59] Although its view changed with its chairman, in introducing the Principles the regulators were concerned to convince those who were worried about regulatory laxity that the Principles would be meaningful, and enforceable. As one official stated, 'one of the aims was to sell the idea that rules did not have to be as specific as the old rule book to be effective'. Paradoxically, the Principles are now used by SIB to defend itself against charges of over-regulation.[60] Different approaches are seen as appropriate in different market areas. Detailed rules are perceived as necessary in market areas where private, individual investors are involved, where the objective of investor protection is seen to be of greater concern. In contrast, in the wholesale market where mainly professional investors participate, investor protection concerns are outweighed by concerns for market efficiency, prompted by fears that 'over-regulation' will drive business from London. More substantive, purposive regulation which gives greater flexibility is thus demanded.

Perceptions and assumptions thus play significant roles, although they themselves are shaped by a multitude of factors including the structure and nature of the institutional framework; they also change. The market context in which the regulation is operating

[59] SIB, *The SIB Rulebook: An Overview*, Oct. 1987, para. 10.

[60] See, e.g., the response of Mr Andrew Large to the Treasury and Civil Service Select Committee, Financial Services Regulation, Minutes of Evidence 1992/3, HC Paper no. 733-i, para. 39.

plays a role in this process; it also affects the uses of rules in quite a particular way. Again, the relationship is reciprocal, even reflexive, one affecting and affected by the other. The demands of interest groups clearly play a significant role in the rule making decision and the clamour of self-interest on the part of these groups can be deafening, although as indicated they do not necessarily play a straightforwardly deterministic role in policy and rule formation. These demands, and their expression, are in turn shaped, and indeed created, by the regulatory system and its institutional structure. Regulation can confer competitive advantage or disadvantage, and so is sought or fought on this basis. In creating a regulatory *status quo* the regulation itself creates particular interests for different groups, who in turn argue against any change in the regulation which would adversely affect their (regulation-created) position. The institutional structure affects how these interests are expressed. The division of authority between different bodies within the structure means that interested groups, particularly regulatees, have, as one regulator put it, 'three bites at the cherry': they can go to their SRO, to SIB, and ultimately the Treasury, arguing their case at each point and attempting to play one off against the other.

The institutional structure itself is in part a product of the market context. The institutional pattern of the SROs broadly reflects a functional division between different market activities: broking and dealing, managing, marketing and advising, with an effective division between the wholesale and retail sectors which the formation of PIA more clearly enforces. That the structure should reflect the market context is unsurprising: the Act did not impose particular regulatory 'groupings' on different areas of the market but through permitting SROs to form themselves allowed the market to choose its own regulatory structure. As the market itself changes structure, this calls into question the organization of regulatory responsibilities, as the current debate on regulation of conglomerates (which combine banking and securities activities) indicates. It also means that the differences between different market participants can themselves receive institutional expression: so in the best execution and soft commission rules the differences between brokers and fund managers were manifested in a difference between their regulators, SFA and IMRO.

The market context also affects the uses which have been made of rules, not only because of the impact of interest groups or the approach to regulation (and so to rules) which is seen by a range of participants and observers in the process to be appropriate or desirable, but because that market context raises particular concerns which have to be addressed. The regulatory process responds to changes in the market environment, the attention of the rule making process may shift following such changes and its priorities altered. The market context also affects the rule making decision in other, less obvious ways. It exerts a particular influence on rule structure and the uses which are made of rules due to the degree of flux and uncertainty which it may be experiencing, the complexity of the behaviour and arrangements being regulated, and the particular susceptibility to regulation of the market in financial products which are essentially legal constructs.

As the analysis of rules indicates, in forming its rules the regulator has to make assessments of the causal relations between particular legal and financial arrangements, particular ways of conducting business, and particular harms or goals. The more complex these arrangements, the greater the degree of innovation and change in those practices, the more difficult it is to discern which aspect of them sits in that causal relationship, even if the 'harm' or 'goal' can be readily defined. The market context may also affect the degree to which the regulator can expect an informed and sympathetic reading of rules or an opportunistic strategy of creative compliance. The significance of interpretation for the uses of rules has been noted above. The market context shapes the extent to which different interpretive strategies may exist and how they may be used within a particular regulatory area, and so in part explains why regulators may pay particular attention to rule type in addressing them. The opportunistic use of rules is prevalent in financial and business regulation, and supports a large contingent of professional advisers. The incentives are great, significant amounts of money can be made or saved. Moreover, creative compliance is possible because what is being regulated are artificial, legal and financial, constructs. It is possible for the regulated to arrange their affairs so as to comply with the letter but not the spirit of rules. Creative compliance is thus an issue in financial regulation where it may not be in other areas. Regulators attend to the question of how rule type may address the question of creative compliance simply because creative compliance is a prevalent problem. This in turn suggests that rule type may be a significant concern for regulators in some areas rather than others simply because the areas being regulated have different characteristics.

Finally, both the rule making process and in particular the uses made of rules are affected by the regulatory system's own dynamics. Regulation creates its own policy momentum, with new policies becoming necessary to correct unintended consequences, to mediate policy clashes, and to uphold and protect existing policies. Decisions made at one point in time shape and affect those made at another.[61] Different demands are made. The same problems receive different solutions. In the retail sector, for example, the problem of formulating rules of disclosure has been addressed in part through adjusting the process in order to include wider sources of information. From the almost exclusive reliance on actuaries as advisers the process has opened up through attempts to involve a greater number of consumer groups, to commissioned reports from expert, but non-industry, advisers and an increasing reliance on market research to test the effectiveness of the disclosures required. Different uses have been made of rules. As noted above, the question of how to address the inevitable tension between certainty and flexibility has received different answers, and ways of defining the respective roles of regulators have similarly evolved: initially defined through close supervision of their rule books, then through the use of rules to define their roles, the relationship of SIB to the SROs and other recognized bodies, as we have seen, is now being principally structured through the use of management-type techniques.

The dynamic of the regulatory system may affect the uses made of rules in a more fundamental manner. The evolution of the financial services regulatory system suggests that the stage the system is at in its evolutionary process affects its rule making, in particular in two respects: the ability to engage in compliance-orientated rule making, and the creation of interpretive communities. Rule makers, Baldwin sensibly argues, in forming rules should take into account the demands of different enforcement strategies. The approach that enforcement officials take is shaped by the particular characteristics of the regulatee: whether it is well or ill intentioned, well or ill informed. Rules, whilst not determining the approach taken,

[61] For a discussion of the effect of previous decisions and policies on subsequent ones in macro-politics, see R. Rose, 'Inheritance before Choice in Public Policy' (1990) 2 *J Theo. Pols.* 263.

can facilitate those approaches: prosecution-orientated approaches may require precise rules, compliance strategies, particularly of advice and education, require simple, targeted rules and guidance. In order to ensure that rules are compliance-orientated, rule makers should liaise with enforcement officials in forming and revising rules; however as Baldwin notes the ability of rule makers to engage in such a process may be hindered by their internal organizational structure and processes.[62] It is suggested that ability is also affected by the stage the system has reached in its evolution. In short, when the system is being set up, before it is brought into operation and indeed in the early days of its operation, the information on its enforcement is simply not available. The rules cannot benefit from experience in enforcement as there is no history of enforcement; rule makers can only anticipate likely enforcement strategies, bearing in mind the likely characteristics of the regulatees. There is a necessary delay, in other words, before that information can be brought on-line, and so before a truly informed compliance strategy of rule making could be adopted. This delay in turn militates against such an approach ever being reflected in the rules; this information only appears after the rules are formed, so to be taken into account requires rule revisions. Rule changes demand regulatory time and attention, resources which may have been diverted elsewhere; they are also costly for the regulatee. So unless there is a pressing urgency for a change in a particular rule or set of rules the revision may not occur.

Evolution of the system also affects the uses that can be made of rules as it is through greater experience of the operation and demands of the rules, by both regulators and regulatees, that an informed understanding of the rules may develop. This may in turn enable rules to become less specific. It may be possible, as regulation becomes more familiar, for interpretive communities to evolve, particularly if the rules are supplemented by training and education both formally and as part of the enforcement process. Unless the regulation is building on an existing interpretive community, it cannot simply with the production of rules create one instantaneously. The experience of implementation and enforcement of the rule can serve to build understandings as to the rule's interpretation; however this is likely to be a slow, and relatively *ad*

[62] Baldwin, *Rules and Government*, Ch. 6.

hoc process. Formal training and education as to the rule's application and ways of complying with it needs to be systematically and extensively conducted; regulation should not rely on a compliance approach to enforcement as the sole means for its provision. This will take time, however; so just as rules may play a role in creating such communities, uses of rules which depend on the creation of interpretive communities may thus have to evolve with that community.

Conclusion: Towards a Theory of Rule Making

Understanding rule making thus requires an understanding of policy making, of decision making within organizations or bureaucracies, and of the nature of rules, their limitations and potential. In understanding rule making it is important, however, to separate the question of the strategic use of rules from the contextual constraints to which a rule maker may be subject. The strategy which can be adopted, and the extent to which one can, will be shaped by and vary with the context. The adoption of particular strategies of rule use (as opposed to the strategic development of the policy which forms the substantive content of the rule), is, however, always dependent on two things: the rule maker's own awareness of the limitations and uses of rules, and the legal powers with which he or she is endowed. A regulatory body may be directly constrained in the use it can make of rules if its legal powers restrict the types of rules which it can make, for example by requiring it to make rules of a particular status. It may also be indirectly constrained: for example, if its rules are enforceable in court at the suit of an individual (not the regulator), then the creation of an interpretive community is rendered more difficult, with the implications this then has for rule use.[63] If the body is thus either directly or indirectly constrained in the types of rules it can form or the uses it can otherwise make of rules, then any rule maker, no matter how sophisticated, can only make a limited use of rules.

Even if a rule maker is aware of the potential uses of rules and

[63] The exclusion of the courts from the interpretation and application of regulatory rules does, however, have its own drawbacks, notably the lack of accountability which this may entail.

has sufficient legal powers, and so can adopt a strategy of rule use, the rule making decision is shaped by the context or environment in which it is made. This analysis thus suggests an approach to regulatory rule making which is contextual, stressing the history of the system, its legal framework, the area which it is regulating, its sensitivity to political and interest group demands, which emphasizes the role of the agency itself in the process and the norms and perceptions of its officials, and which is dynamic, recognizing the changing configuration of factors, the evolution of the regulatory system, and the tensions and policies which the regulatory process can itself create.

Although any analysis of rule making may thus be context dependent, there are nonetheless aspects of rule making in financial services which are potentially generalizable to other areas, and which may form the basis for developing a positive theory of rule making. First, the importance of the design of the regulatory system; second, the significance of the market context; third, the circumstances in which interpretive communities can be built; and fourth, the relevance of the regulatory system's own evolution.

Firstly, the design of the regulatory system can have the most direct impact on rule making. The significance of the legal ability to make rules of a range of different types has been noted above; the legal structure may also determine the extent to which other strategies for using rules, notably the use and development of interpretive communities and the adoption of a conversational model of regulation, may be possible. The design of the system may affect rule use less directly, however; the association of the system's design with particular regulatory approaches and with particular types of rules may play a dominant role in shaping the rule strategy adopted; indeed the assumptions may be so strong that they may override any ability to adopt a strategy at all. The association, in other words, of statutory regulation with detailed rules and of self-regulation with vaguer (and non-legally sanctioned) rules, although by no means either politically or analytically necessary, is so strong that it may simply dominate the rule making decision, either because it is so forcefully put that the rule maker cannot for a range of reasons resist, or because the association is so embedded in the rule maker's own perceptions of what type of rule should be adopted. The design and characterization of the regulatory system may thus matter, not because it determines what uses of rules are lawful, but because it determines what uses of rules are deemed to be appropriate and acceptable.

Secondly, the market context can affect the uses which can be, and may need to be, made of rules in two ways. It may affect the likelihood of the under- or over-inclusiveness of rules, and it may affect the interpretation which the rule maker can expect of the rules made. Rules, as noted above, are generalizations: they group together particular instances or attributes of an object or event and generalize from them to build up a category or definition which then forms the operative basis of the rule. In deciding which attributes to include in the generalization, the rule maker has to search for those which are causally relevant to the aim of the rule: the goal which is sought to be achieved or the harm avoided. The more complex the object or occurrence, the greater the degree of change to which they are subject, and the greater the difficulty in determining the relationship of probable causality, the more likely that the rule will be over- or under-inclusive. In these circumstances, the rule maker will encounter considerable difficulty in making rules, and the use of precise rules of legal status will only exacerbate such over- or under-inclusion. As indicated in chapter 1, a strategic use of rules would then require the mitigation of such problems of inclusiveness, and indeed indeterminacy, through, for example, the combination of different rule types within a system of rules, the development of interpretive communities, and / or the adoption of a conversational model of regulation.

The market context may also affect the interpretive strategy which the rule maker can expect from those subject to the rules, and in particular the extent to which a strategy of creative compliance exists. In areas such as tax, accountancy, and financial services such a strategy is prevalent; in other areas it may not be.[64] Creative compliance is not an interpretive strategy which will exist in equal measure across all regulatory regimes; strategies of rule use which

[64] It is notable, e.g., that in his analysis of health and safety regulation the type of regulatee which is most likely to adopt this strategy, the well-informed but ill intentioned, was absent from Baldwin's classification: R. Baldwin, 'Why Rules Don't Work' (1991) 51 *MLR* 321. Baldwin notes some of the difficulties which may be encountered in creatively complying with particular provisions: *Rules and Government*, 186 n. 103.

are designed to counter it may thus be more relevant, and the need for them more pressing, in some areas rather than others.[65]

Both the design of the regulatory system and the market context are relevant for the third point, the potential for the use and / or development of interpretive communities. The significance of such communities for rule use has been noted above and explored more fully in chapter 1. A number of preconditions are necessary for the development of such communities, however. Most notably, the reciprocity or mutuality of interpretation between regulated and regulator as to the meaning and requirements of a set of relatively technical rules, based in turn on shared tacit understandings, is unlikely to arise spontaneously and needs to be actively developed, ideally through both formal training and education, reinforced in the enforcement process. The need for the closure of the system, on the other hand, arises only if the regulator cannot otherwise ensure that its interpretation is that which is authoritative. Closure entails its own problems, notably of accountability; it may nonetheless be the only, or most direct way, of ensuring such authoritativeness.

Finally, as noted, the stage the system is at in its evolution may affect its use of rules, particularly the ability of the rule maker to utilize information about the enforceability of the rules, and so to adopt rules which assist in that process; and to use interpretive communities. Both are particularly difficult in the early stages of the system's development. Moreover, to the extent that rule use relies on the experience of the rule's operation, for example to test the inclusiveness of the rule and the degree of its indeterminacy, then again the earlier the system is in its development, the more this inhibits the effective use of rules.[66]

[65] The significant variable is probably the regulation rather than the firm: it remains possible for the same firm to adopt different strategies in response to different regulatory regimes. A finance house may creatively comply with financial regulation (and indeed employment regulation) but not with the health and safety regulation to which it is also subject. This prompts the obvious question, what determines whether creative compliance is a strategy that will be adopted by the regulatee?

[66] Indeed, it is notable that some of the greatest advocates of rules share the assumption that rule making will be a continual process, and that rules will not precede regulation, but rather evolve over the course of its operation: K. C. Davis, *Discretionary Justice* (Illinois, 1971), Ch. 2; H. J. Friendly, *The Federal Administrative Agencies: The Need for a Better Definition of Standards* (Harvard, 1962).

Thus in developing a theory of regulatory rule making this study suggests both normative and positive elements of such a theory. Positively, it is suggested that rule making should be seen as a form of both policy making and organizational of bureaucratic decision making; and that the nature of rules themselves is a significant aspect of the decision, differentiating it from generalized policy making on the one hand and individualized discretionary decision making on the other. Normatively, building on an analysis of the nature of rules, it has been suggested that some of their inherent limitations may be ameliorated through the use of rule type, the development of interpretive communities, and the adoption of a conversational model of regulation. Thus through an integration of a theoretical analysis of the nature of rules and their interpretative and an empirical analysis of the use of rules and their formation, a model of rule making can be developed which seeks to explain how in fact rules are used and to suggest ways in which they could be used.

Bibliography

Aaranson, P. H., Gellhorn, E., Robinson, G. O., 'A Theory of Legislative Delegation' (1982) 68 *Cornell LR* 1.

Ackerman, B. A., and Hassler, W. T., *Clean Coal, Dirty Air* (Yale, 1981).

Adler, M. J., and Asquith, S., 'Discretion and Power', in Adler, M. J., and Asquith, S., *Discretion and Welfare* (London, 1981).

Akerlof, G., 'The Market for "Lemons": Qualitative Uncertainty and the Market Mechanism' (1970) 84 *Qly. Journal of Economics* 488.

Alexander, L., and Kress, K., 'Against Legal Principles', in Marmor, A., (ed.), *Law and Interpretation* (Oxford, 1996).

Allen, C. K., *Law and Orders* (London, 1965).

Altman, A., 'Legal Realism, Critical Legal Studies, and Dworkin' (1986) 15 *Phil. & Pub. Aff.* 205.

Asimov, M. A., 'Delegated Legislation in the US and UK' (1983) 3 *OJLS* 253.

———, 'Nonlegislative Rulemaking and Regulatory Reform' (1985) 35 *Duke LJ* 381.

Atiyah, P. S., and Summers, R. S., *Form and Substance in Anglo-American Law* (Oxford, 1987).

Ayers, I., and Braithwaite, J., *Responsive Regulation* (Oxford, 1992).

Baker, G. P., and Hacker, P. M. S., *Wittgenstein: Understanding and Meaning* (Oxford, 1980).

——— and ———, *Scepticism, Rules and Language* (Oxford, 1984).

——— and ———, *Wittgenstein: Rules, Grammar and Necessity* (Oxford, 1985).

Baldwin, R., *Regulating the Airlines* (Oxford, 1985).

———, 'Health and Safety at Work: Consensus and Self Regulation', in Baldwin, R. and McCrudden, C., *Regulation and Public Law* (London, 1987).

———, 'Accounting for Discretion' (1990) 10 *OJLS* 422.

———, 'Why Rules Don't Work' (1991) 53 *MLR* 321.

———, *Rules and Government* (Oxford, 1995).

———, and Hawkins, K., 'Discretionary Justice: Davis Reconsidered' (1984) *Public Law* 570.

———, and Houghton, J., 'Circular Arguments: The Status and Legitimacy of Administrative Rules' (1986) *Public Law* 239.

———, and McCrudden, C., *Regulation and Public Law* (London, 1987).

Bardach, E., and Kagan, R. A., *Going by the Book: The Problem of Regulatory Unreasonableness* (Philadelphia, 1982).

Barendt, E., Barron, A., Herberg, J., and Jowell, J., 'Public Law' (1993) 46 *Current Legal Problems* 103.

Barker, A., *Quangos in Britain* (London, 1982).

Barker, R., *Political Legitimacy and the State* (Oxford, 1990).

Barratt, S., and Fudge, C., (eds.), *Policy and Action: Essays on the Implementation of Public Policy* (London, 1981).

Beales, H., Craswell, R., and Salop, S., 'The efficient regulation of consumer information' (1981) 24 *Journal of Law and Economics* 491.

Beatson, J., 'Legislative Control of Administrative Rule Making: Lessons from the Experience' (1979) 12 *Cornell Int'l. LJ* 199.

Beetham, D., *The Legitimation of Power* (London, 1991).

Bell, J., 'Discretionary Decision Making: A Jurisprudential View', in Hawkins, K., (ed.), *The Uses of Discretion* (Oxford, 1992).

Bennion, F., *Principles of Statutory Interpretation* (London, 1984).

Bernstein, M. H., *Regulating Business by Independent Commission* (New York, 1955).

———, 'The Regulatory Process: A Framework for Analysis' (1961) 26 *L & CP* 239.

Bix, B., *Law, Language and Legal Determinacy* (Oxford, 1993).

———, 'Questions in Legal Interpretation', in Marmor, A., (ed.), *Law and Interpretation* (Oxford, 1996).

Black, J. M., '"Which Arrow?" Rule Type and Regulatory Policy' (1995) *Public Law* 96.

———, 'Consitutionalising Self-Regulation' (1996) 59 *MLR* 24.

Blair, M., 'Regulation of the Conduct of Investment Business: SIB's Proposal' (1989) *BJIBFL* 398.

———, 'Europe 1992 and the Harmonisation of Standards for the Regulation of Financial Institutions' (1990) *Canadian Business LJ* 97.

———, *Financial Services: The New Core Rules* (London, 1991).

Bowers, F., *Linguistic Aspects of Legislative Expression* (University of British Columbia, Canada, 1989).

Boyer, B. B., 'Alternatives to Administrative Trial-Type Hearings for Resolving Complex Scientific, Economic and Social Issues' (1972) *Mich. LR* 111.

Bradley, C., 'Competitive Deregulation of Financial Services Activity in Europe after 1992' (1991) 11 *OLJS* 545.

Braybrooke, D., and Lindblom, C., *A Strategy of Decision: Policy Evaluation as a Social Process* (New York, 1963).

Breyer, S., *Regulation and its Reform* (Harvard, 1982).

Brink, D., 'Legal Theory, Legal Interpretation, and Judicial Review' (1988) 17 *Phi. & Pub. Aff.* 105.

———, 'Semantics and Legal Interpretation (Further Thoughts)' (1989) 2 *Canadian Journal of Law and Jurisprudence* 181.

Buchanan, J., and Tullock, G., *The Calculus of Consent* (Michigan, 1962).

Business Performance Group, *Disclosure in the Retail Financial Products Market* (London School of Economics, 1991).

Butterworth's *Financial Services Law and Practice* (London, 1987, updated).

Calvert, R., McCubbins, M., and Weingast, B., 'A Theory of Political Control of Agency Discretion' (1989) *Am. J Pol. Sci.* 588.

Chambliss, W. J., and Seidman, R. B., *Law, Order and Power* (Mass., 2nd ed., 1981).

City Research Project, *Key Issues for the Square Mile: Interim Report* (Corporation of London and London Business School, July 1992).

Clarke, M., *Regulating the City* (Oxford, 1986).

Coggan, P., *The Money Machine: How the City Works* (London, 1989).

Coleman, J. L., and Leiter, B., 'Determinacy, Objectivity and Authority', in Marmor, A., (ed.), *Law and Interpretation* (Oxford, 1996).

Comaroff, J. L., and Roberts, S., *Rules and Processes: The Cultural Logic of Dispute in an African Context* (Chicago, 1981).

Cook, K. S., and Levi, M., (eds.), *The Limits of Rationality* (Chicago, 1990).

Cotterell, R., *The Sociology of Law, An Introduction* (London, 2nd ed., 1992).

Craig, P. P., *Administrative Law* (London, 3rd ed., 1993).

Cranston, R., *Regulating Business: Law and Consumer Agencies* (London, 1979).

——————, 'Regulation and Deregulation: General Issues' (1982) 5 *UNSW LJ* 1.

——————, *Consumers and the Law* (London, 2nd ed., 1984).

Cushman, R., *The Independent Regulatory Commissions* (Oxford, 1941).

Daintith, T. C., 'A Legal Analysis of Economic Policy' (1982) 9 *J Law & Soc.* 191.

——————, 'Law as a Policy Instrument: Comparative Perspectives', in id. (ed.), *Law as an Instrument of Economic Policy: Comparative and Critical Approaches* (Berlin, 1988).

——————, 'A Regulatory Space Agency?' (1989) 9 *OJLS* 534.

——————, 'The Techniques of Government', in Jowell, J., and Oliver, D., (eds.), *The Changing Constitution* (Oxford, 3rd ed., 1994).

Danzig, R., 'A Comment on the Jurisprudence of the UCC' (1975) 27 *Stanford LR* 621.

Davis, K. C., *Administrative Law Treatise* (Illinois, 1958).

——————, *Discretionary Justice* (Illinois, 1971).

Di Maggio, P., and Powell, W., 'Introduction', in Di Maggio, P. D., and Powell, W., (eds.), *The New Institutionalism in Organisational Analysis* (Chicago, 1991).

Diver, C. S., 'Policy Making Paradigms in Administrative Law' (1981) 95 *Harvard LR* 393.

——————, 'The Optimal Precision of Administrative Rules' (1983) 93 *Yale LJ* 65.

Diver, C. S., 'Regulatory Precision' in Hawkins, K. and Thomas, J. M., (eds.), *Making Regulatory Policy* (Pittsburgh, 1989).

Downs, A., *Inside Bureaucracy* (Boston, 1967).

Dworkin, R., *Taking Rights Seriously* (London, 1977).

Edwards, G., and Sharansky, I., *The Policy Predicament: Making and Implementing Public Policy* (New York, 1978).

Ehrlich, I., and Posner, R., 'An Economic Analysis of Legal Rulemaking' (1974) 3 *J Legal Studies* 257.

Elliott, E. D., 'Reinventing Rulemaking' (1992) 41 *Duke LJ* 1490.

Etzioni, A., 'Mixed Scanning: A "Third" Approach to Decision Making' (1967) *Pub. Admin. Rev.* 27.

Finn, P. D., *Fiduciary Obligations* (Sydney, 1977).

Fiovail, M. P., 'Legislator Uncertainty, Legislative Control and the Delegation of Legislative Power' (1986) 2 (1) *J Law & Economic Organisation* 33.

Fish, S., *Is there a Text in This Class?* (Cambridge, Mass., 1980).

——————, 'Fish v. Fiss' (1984) 36 *Stanford LR* 1325.

——————, 'Don't Know Much About the Middle Ages: Posner on Law and Literature' (1988) 97 *Yale LJ* 777.

——————, *Doing What Comes Naturally* (Oxford, 1989).

Fiss, O. M., 'Objectivity and Interpretation' (1982) 34 *Stanford LR* 739.

Franks, J., and Mayer, C., *Risk, Regulation and Investor Protection: The Case of Investment Management* (Oxford, 1989).

——————, and Schaefer, S., *The Costs and Effectiveness of the UK Financial Regulatory System* (City Research Project, London Business School, March 1993).

Freedman, J., *Crisis and Legitimacy* (Cambridge, 1978).

Friedman, L. M., 'Legal Rules and the Process of Social Change' (1967) 19 *Stanford LR* 786.

Friendly, H. J., *The Federal Administrative Agencies: The Need for a Better Definition of Standards* (Harvard, 1962).

Frug, G. E., 'The Ideology of Bureaucracy in American Law' (1984) 97 *Harvard LR* 1277.

Fuller, L. L., 'Positivism and Fidelity to Law—A Reply to Professor Hart' (1958) 71 *Harvard LR* 630.

——————, *The Morality of Law* (New Haven, rev. ed., 1969).

——————, 'The Forms and Limits of Adjudication' (1978) 92 *Harvard LJ* 353.

Galanter, M., 'Legality and its Discontents: A Preliminary Assessment of Current Theories of Legalization and Delegalization' (1980) *Jahrburch fur Rechtssozolgie und Rechtstheorie* 11.

Galligan, D. J., *Discretionary Powers: A Legal Study of Official Discretion* (Oxford, 1986).

Ganz, G., 'Legitimate Expectation', in Harlow, C., (ed.), *Public Law and Politics* (London, 1986).

———, *Quasi-Legislation: Recent Developments in Delegated Legislation* (London, 1987).

George, E., 'Changes in the structure of Financial Markets: A View from London' (1985) *BEQB* 76.

Gifford, D. J., 'Communication of Legal Standards, Policy Development and Effective Conduct Regulation' (1971) 56 *Cornell LR* 409.

———, 'Decisions, Decisional Referents, and Administrative Justice' (1972) 37 *Law and Contemp. Problems* 3.

———, 'Discretionary Decisionmaking in the Regulatory Agencies; A Conceptual Framework' (1983) 57 *South Calif. LR* 101.

Goode, R. M., *Conflicts of Interest in the Changing Financial World* (London, 1986).

Goodhart, C., and Schoenmaker, D., *Institutional Separation between Supervisory and Monetary Agencies* (Special Paper No. 25, LSE Financial Markets Group, 1993).

Goodin, R. E., 'Welfare, Rights and Discretion' (1986) 6 *OJLS* 232.

———, 'Institutions and their Design' in ———, (ed.), *The Theory of Institutional Design* (Cambridge, 1996).

Goodison, N., 'The Regulation of Financial Services in the UK' (1985) *SEQ* 24.

Gottlieb, G., *The Logic of Choice* (London, 1968).

Gower, L. C. B., *Review of Investor Protection: A Discussion Document* (London, 1982).

———, *Review of Investor Protection: Report, Part I*, Cmnd. 9125 (London, 1984).

———, *Review of Investor Protection: Report, Part II* (London, 1985).

———, 'Big Bang and City Regulation' (1988) *MLR* 1.

Gowland, D., *The Regulation of Financial Markets in the 1990s* (London, 1990).

Graff, G., '"Keep off the Grass," "Drop Dead," and Other Indeterminacies; A Response to Stanford Levinson' (1982) 60 *Texas LR* 405.

Graham, C., 'Self-Regulation', in Genn, H., and Richardson, G., *Administrative Law and Government Action* (Oxford, 1995).

Granovetter, M., 'Economic Action and Social Structure: The Problem of Embeddedness', in Granovetter, M., and Swedberg, R., (eds.), *The Sociology of Economic Life* (Colorado, 1992).

———, and Swedberg, R., (eds.), *The Sociology of Economic Life* (Colorado, 1992).

Habermas, J., *Legitimation Crisis* (London, 1976).

Hague, D. C., McKenzie, W. J. M., and Barker, A., *Public Policy and Private Interests: The Institutions of Compromise* (London, 1975).

Hall, P., *Governing the Economy* (London, 1986).

Ham, C., and Hill, M., *Policy Process in the Modern Capitalist State* (London, 1984).

Hancher, L., and Moran, M., 'Organising Regulatory Space', in Hancher, L., and Moran, M., (eds.), *Capitalism, Culture and Regulation* (Oxford, 1989).

Handler, J. F., *The Conditions of Discretion: Autonomy, Community, Bureaucracy* (New York, 1986).

Hart, H., and Sachs, A., *The Legal Process* (Tentative ed., 1958).

Hart, H. L. A., 'Positivism and the Separation of Law and Morals' (1958) 71 *Harvard LR* 593.

——, *The Concept of Law* (Oxford, 1961).

——, 'Definition and Theory in Jurisprudence', in *Essays in Jurisprudence and Philosophy* (Oxford, 1983).

Harter, P., 'Negotiating Regulation' (1982) 71 *Georgetown LJ* 1.

Hawkins, K., *Environment and Enforcement* (Oxford, 1984).

——, 'Discretion in Making Legal Decision' (1986) 43 *Washington and Lee LR* 1161.

——, 'Compliance Strategy, Prosecution Policy and Aunt Sally' (1990) 20 *BJ Crim.* 444.

——, 'The Use of Legal Discretion: Perspectives from Law and Social Science', in Hawkins, K., (ed.), *The Uses of Discretion* (Oxford 1992).

——, (ed.), *The Uses of Discretion* (Oxford, 1992).

——, and Thomas, J. M., (eds.), *Enforcing Regulation* (Boston, 1984).

——, and ——, 'Rule Making and Discretion: Implications for Designing Regulatory Policy', in Hawkins, K., and Thomas, J. M., (eds.), *Making Regulatory Policy* (Pittsburgh, 1989).

——, and ——, (eds.), *Making Regulatory Policy* (Pittsburgh, 1989).

Hayek, F., *The Constitution of Liberty* (Chicago, 1960).

——, *The Road to Serfdom* (London, 1964).

Hirsch, W. Z., 'Reducing Law's Uncertainty and Complexity' (1974) 21 *UCLA LR* 1233.

Holland, J., 'Self Regulation and the Financial Aspects of Corporate Governance' (1996) *JBL* 127.

Hood, C., *Administrative Analysis: An Introduction to Rules, Enforcement and Organisation* (London, 1986).

Horn, M. J., and Shepsle, K. A., 'Commentary: Structure, Process, Politics and Policy' (1989) *Va. LR* 499.

Horwitz, R. B., *The Irony of Regulatory Reform The Deregulation of the American Telecommunications Industry* (Oxford, 1989).

Hutter, B., *The Reasonable Arm of the Law* (Oxford, 1988).

Ikenberry, G. J., 'Conclusion: An Institutional Approach to American Foreign Economic Policy', in Ikenberry, G. J., Lade, D. A., and Mastanduno, M., (eds.), *The State and Foreign Economic Policy* (New York, 1988).

Immergut, E. M., 'The Rules of the Game: The Logic of Health Policy Making in France, Switzerland and Sweden', in Thelen, K., and Steinmo, S., *Structuring Politics: Historical Institutionalism in Comparative Analysis* (Cambridge, 1990).

Jaffe, J. L., 'The Illusion of the Ideal Administration' (1977) 86 *Harvard LJ* 1183.

Johnston, J. S., 'Uncertainty, Chaos, and the Torts Process: An Economic Analysis of Legal Form' (1991) 76 *Cornell LR* 341.

Jones, L., 'The Changing Securities Market, A Stock Exchange View' (1984) *Company Lawyer* 97–100.

Jones, T. H., 'Administrative Law, Regulation and Legitimacy (1989) 16 *J Law and Soc.* 410.

——————, 'Regulatory Policy and Rule-Making' (1991) *Anglo-American LR* 131.

Jowell, J. L., 'The Legal Control of Administrative Discretion' (1973) *Public Law* 179.

——————, *Law and Bureaucracy, Administrative Discretion and the Limits of Legal Action* (New York, 1975).

Kagan, R. A., *Regulatory Justice, Implementing a Wage Price Freeze* (New York, 1978).

Katzmann, R. A., *Regulatory Bureaucracy: The Federal Trade Commission and Anti-Trust Policy* (Cambridge, 1980).

Kay, J., and Vickers, J., 'Regulatory Reform: An Appraisal', in Majone, G., (ed.), *Deregulation or Re-Regulation: Regulatory Reform in Europe and the US* (New York, 1990).

Kempson, R. M., *Semantic Theory* (Cambridge, 1977).

Kennedy, D., 'Legal Formality' (1973) 2 *J Leg. Stud.* 351.

——————, 'Form and Substance in Private Law Adjudication' (1976) 89 *Harvard LR* 1685.

Kingdom, J. W., *Agendas, Alternatives and Public Policies* (Boston, 1984).

Koch, C. H., and Martin, B., 'FTC Rulemaking Through Negotiation' (1983) 61 *North Carolina LR* 275.

Koeble, T., 'The New Institutionalism in Political Science and Sociology' (1995) *Comparative Politics* 231.

Kolko, G., *The Triumph of Conservatism* (New York, 1965).

Kress, K, 'Legal Indeterminacy' (1989) 77 *Calif. LR* 283.

Kripke, S., *Wittgenstein on Rules and Private Language* (Cambridge, Mass., 1982).

Kurzon, D., *It Is Hereby Performed: Explanations of Legal Speech Acts* (Philadelphia, 1986).

Landes, R., and Posner, R. A., 'The Private Enforcement of Law' (1975) *JLS* 1.

Landis, J. M., *The Administrative Process* (New Haven, 1938).

Law Commission, *Fiduciary Duties and Regulatory Rules, A Consultation Paper,* CP No. 124 (London, 1992).

——, *Fiduciary Duties and Regulatory Rules,* Report No. 236 (London, 1995).

Leigh Pemberton, R., 'Changing Boundaries in Financial Services' (1984) *BEQB* 40.

——, 'The Future of the Securities Market' (1984) *BEQB* 189.

——, 'The UK Approach to Financial Regulation' (1986) *BEQB* 48.

——, 'The Markets, the City and the Economy' (1988) *BEQB* 59.

——, 'Takeovers and Standards in the City' (1989) *BEQB* 545.

Lempert, R., 'Discretion in a Behavioural Perspective', in Hawkins, K., (ed.), *The Uses of Discretion* (Oxford, 1992).

Levi, M., *Regulating Fraud: White Collar Crime and the Criminal Process* (London, 1987).

Levine, M. E., and Forrence, J. L., 'Regulatory Capture, Public Interest and the Public Agenda: Towards a Synthesis' (1990) 6 *J Law, Econ. & Org.* 167.

Lindblom, C., 'The Science of Muddling Through' (1959) 19 *Pub. Admin. Rev.* 79.

——, *The Intelligence of Democracy: Decision Making Through Mutual Adjustment* (New York, 1965).

Linklaters and Paines, *Unit Trusts: Law and Practice* (London, 1989).

Llewellyn, D. T., *The Regulation and Supervision of Financial Institutions* (London, 1986).

——, 'The Changing Structure of Regulation in the British Financial System', in Button, K., and Swann, D., (eds.), *The Age of Regulatory Reform* (Oxford, 1989).

Llewellyn, K., *Common Law Tradition* (Boston, 1960).

——, *Jurisprudence* (Chicago, 1962).

Lomax, D., *London Markets After the Financial Services Act 1986* (London, 1987).

Lomnicka, E. Z., and Powell, J. L., *Encyclopedia of Financial Services Law* (London, 1987, updated).

Long, S., 'Social Control and Civil Law: The Case of Income Tax Enforcement', in Ross, H. L., (ed.), *Law and Deviance* (California, 1981).

Lowi, T. J., *The End of Liberalism* (New York, 2nd ed., 1979).

MacCormick, N., *Legal Reasoning and Legal Theory* (Oxford, 1978).

Macey, J. R., 'Organisational Design and Political Control of Administrative Agencies' (1992) 8 *J Law, Econ. and Org.* 52.

———, 'Separated Powers and Positive Political Theory: The Tug of War over Administrative Agencies' (1992) 80 *Geo. LR* 671.

Maley, Y., 'The Language of the Law' in Gibbons, J., (ed.), *Language and the Law* (London, 1994).

Manning, P. K., 'Big Bang Decisions: Notes on a Naturalistic Approach', in Hawkins, K., (ed.), *The Uses of Discretion* (Oxford, 1992).

March, J. G., and Olsen, J. P., 'The New Institutionalism: Organisational Factors in Political Life' (1984) 75 *Am. Pol. Sci. Rev.* 734.

———, and ———, *Rediscovering Institutions* (New York, 1989).

Marmor, A., 'Three Concepts of Objectivity', in Marmor, A., (ed.), *Law and Interpretation* (Oxford, 1996).

———, (ed.), *Law and Interpretation: Essays in Legal Philosophy* (Oxford, 1996).

Mayer, C., *The Changing Structure of Financial Markets* (*Amex. Bank Review*, Special Paper, 1987).

McBarnet, D., 'It's Not What You Do, But The Way That You Do It: Tax Evasion, Tax Avoidance and the Boundaries of Deviance', in Downes, D., (ed.), *Unravelling Criminal Justice* (London, 1991).

———, and Whelan, C., 'The Elusive Spirit of the Law: Formalism and the Struggle for Legal Control' (1991) 54 *MLR* 848.

———, ———, 'Beyond Control: Law, Management and Corporate Governance', in McCaherty, J., Picciotto, S., and Scott, C., (eds.), *Corporate Control and Accountability* (Oxford, 1993).

McCrudden, C., 'Codes in a Cold Climate: Administrative Rule Making by the Commission for Racial Equality' (1988) 51 *MLR* 409.

———, 'The Northern Ireland Fair Employment White Paper: A Critical Assessment' (1988) 17 *ILJ* 162.

McCubbins, M. D., Noll, R., and Weingast, B. R., 'Administrative Procedures and Instruments of Political Control' (1987) 3 *J Law, Econ. & Org.* 243.

———, 'Structure, Process, Politics and Policy: Administrative Arrangements and the Political Control of Agencies' (1989) 75 *Virginia LR* 431.

McDowell, J., 'Non-Cognitivism and Rule-Following', in Holtzman, S., and Leich, C., (eds.), *Wittgenstein: To Follow a Rule* (London, 1981).

McGarity, T. O., 'Regulatory Analysis and Regulatory Reform' (1987) 65 *Texas LR* 1243.

———, 'The Internal Structure of EPA Rulemaking' (1991) 54 *Law and Contemp. Prob.* 57.

———, 'Some Thoughts on "Deossifying" the Rulemaking Process' (1992) *41 Duke LJ* 1385.

McGinn, C., *Wittgenstein on Meaning* (Oxford, 1984).

McRae, H., *Developments in the Retail Savings Markets* (Business Performance Group, LSE, 1992).

McRae, H., and Cairncross, F., *Capital City* (London, 1992).
Meyer, J. W., and Rowan, B., 'Institutionalised Organisations: Formal Structure as Myth and Ceremony' (1977) *Am. J Sociol.* 340.
Miers, D., and Page, A. C., *Legislation* (London, 1982).
Miller, C. R., 'The Rhetoric of Decision Science or Herbert A. Simon Says', in Simons, H. W., (ed.), *The Rhetorical Turn: Invention and Persuasion in the Conduct of Inquiry* (Chicago, 1990).
Mitchell, J., *Saving and Investments, Consumer Issues; An Occasional Paper to the OFT* (OFT, June 1992).
Moore, M., 'A Natural Law Theory of Interpretation' (1985) 58 *S Calif. LR* 277.
——, 'The Interpretive Turn in Modern Theory: A Turn for the Worse?' (1989) 41 *Stanford LR* 871.
Moran, M., *The Politics of Banking* (London, 2nd ed., 1986).
——, 'Politics and Law in Financial Regulation', in Graham, C., and Prosser, T., *Waiving the Rules: The Constitution under Thatcherism* (Oxford, 1988).
——, 'Investor Protection and the Culture of Capitalism', in Hancher, L., and Moran, M., *Capitalism, Culture and Regulation* (Oxford, 1989).
——, *The Politics of the Financial Services Revolution: The UK, US and Japan* (London, 1991).
Morgan, G., and Knight, D., *The Financial Services Act: The Origins, Consequences and Future of a Regulatory Regime* (Financial Services Research Centre, University of Manchester Institute of Science and Technology, September 1990).
Mortimer, K., 'The Securities and Investments Board', in Seldon, A., (ed.), *Financial Regulation—or Over-Regulation?* (London, 1988).
Mueller, D. C., *Public Choice* (Cambridge, 1979, rev. ed. 1989).
Niskansen, W. A., *Bureaucracy and Representative Government* (Chicago, 1971).
Nonet, P., and Selznick, P., *Law and Society in Transition: Towards Responsive Law* (New York, 1978).
North, D. C., *Institutions, Institutional Change and Economic Performance* (Cambridge, 1990).
Ogus, A., *Regulation: Legal Form and Economic Theory* (Oxford, 1994).
——, 'Re-thinking Self Regulation' (1995) 15 *OJLS* 97.
Olson, M., *The Logic of Collective Action* (Harvard, 1965).
——, *Rise and Decline of Nations* (Yale, 1982).
Page, A. C., 'Self-Regulation and Codes of Practice' (1980) *JBL* 24.
——, 'Self-Regulation: The Constitutional Dimension' (1986) 49 *MLR* 141.
——, and Ferguson, R. B., *Investor Protection* (London, 1992).
Pearce, F., and Tombs, S., 'Ideology, Hegemony and Empiricism' (1990) 20 *BJ Crim.* 423.

Peltzman, S., 'Towards a More General Theory of Regulation' (1976) 19 *J Law and Econ.* 211.

Pierce, R. J., 'Two Problems in Administrative Law: Political Polarity on the District of Columbia Circuit and Judicial Deterrence of Agency Rulemaking' (1988) *Duke LJ* 300.

Poser, R., *International Securities Regulation: London's 'Big Bang' and the European Securities Markets* (Boston, 1991).

Posner, R. A., 'Taxation by Regulation' (1971) 2 *Bell J Econ. and Man. Sci.* 22.

——, 'Theories of Economic Regulation' (1974) 5 *Bell J Econ. and Man. Sci.* 335.

——, 'Law and Literature: A Relation Reargued' (1986) 72 *Virginia LR* 1351.

——, *An Economic Analysis of Law* (Boston, 1986).

Price Waterhouse World Regulatory Practice, *Banking and Securities Regulation in Europe: A Survey of Senior Management Views* (Price Waterhouse, February 1990).

Prichard, J. R., and Waverman, L., 'The Consumer Interest and the Regulatory Process', in Duggan, A. J., and Darrall, L. W., (eds.), *Consumer Protection Law and Theory* (Toronto, 1980).

Pound, R., *Jurisprudence* (St Paul, 1959).

Ramsay, I., *Rationales for Intervention in the Consumer Marketplace* (OFT, 1984).

——, 'The Office of Fair Trading: Policing the Consumer Marketplace', in Baldwin, R., and McCrudden, C., *Regulation and Public Law* (London, 1987).

——, *Consumer Protection: Text and Materials* (London, 1989).

Raz, J., 'Legal Principles and the Limits of the Law' (1972) 81 *Yale LJ* 823.

——, 'The Rule of Law and its Virtue' (1977) 93 *LQR* 195.

Reid, M., *All Change in the City: The Revolution in Britain's Financial Sector* (London, 1988).

Report of a Committee to Review the Functioning of Financial Institutions, chaired by Harold Wilson, Cmnd. 7934 (London, 1980).

Report of the Committee on Company Law, chaired by Lord Jenkins, Cmnd. 1749 (London, 1962).

Report of the Committee on Fraud Trials, chaired by Lord Roskill (London, 1980).

Report of the Hansard Society Commission on the Legislative Process, 'Making the Law', chaired by Lord Rippon (London, 1992).

Richardson, G. M., with Ogus, A. I., and Burrows, P., *Policing Pollution; A Study of Regulation and Enforcement* (Oxford, 1983).

Robinson, G. O., 'The Making of Administrative Policy: Another Look at Rule Making and Adjudication in Administrative Procedure Reform' (1970) 118 *U Pa. LR* 485.

Rose, R., 'Inheritance before Choice in Public Policy' (1990) 2 *J Theoretical Politics* 263.
Sabatier, P., and Mazmanian, D., 'The Conditions of Effective Implementation: A Guide to Accomplishing Policy Objectives' (1979) *UCLR* 481.
Sainsbury, R. M., 'Is There a Higher Order Vagueness?' (1991) 41 *Philosophical Qly.* 167.
Schauer, F., 'Formalism' (1988) 97 *Yale LJ* 509.
——, *Playing by the Rules: A Philosophical Examination of Rule-Based Decision Making in Law and in Life* (Oxford, 1991).
Schklar, J., *Legalism* (Harvard, 1964).
Schneider, C. E., 'Discretion and Rules: A Lawyer's View', in Hawkins, K., (ed.), *The Uses of Discretion* (Oxford, 1992).
Schuck, P. H., 'Organisation Theory and the Teaching of Administrative Law' (1983) *Journal of Legal Education* 13.
——, 'When the Exception Becomes the Rule: Regulatory Equity and the Formulation of Agency Policy through an Exceptions Process' (1984) *Duke LJ* 163.
Scott, R., 'The Adolescence of Institutional Theory' (1987) 32 *Admin. Sci. Qly.* 493.
Seldon, A., (ed.), *Financial Regulation—or Over-Regulation?* (London, 1988).
Shapiro, D. L., 'The Choice of Rule Making or Adjudication in the Development of Administrative Policy' (1965) 78 *Harvard LR* 921.
Shapiro, S. P., *Wayward Capitalists: Target of the Securities and Exchange Commission* (New Haven, 1984).
Simon, H. A., *Administrative Behaviour* (New York, 1945).
Singer, J., 'The Player and the Cards: Nihilism and Legal Theory' (1984) 94 *Yale LJ* 1.
Skocpol, T., 'Bringing the State Back In: Strategies of Analysis in Current Research', in Evans, P., Rueschemeyer, D., and Skocpol, T., (eds.), *Bringing the State Back In* (London, 1985).
Smith, G., and May, D., 'The Artificial Debate between Rationalist and Incrementalist Models of Decision Making' (1980) 8 *Policy and Politics* 147.
Steinmo, S., Thelen, K., and Longstreth, F., (eds.), *Structuring Politics: Historical Institutionalism in Comparative Analysis* (Cambridge, 1992).
Stevens, R. B., and Yamey, B. S., *The Restrictive Practices Court* (Oxford, 1965).
Stewart, R. B., 'The Reformation of American Administrative Law' (1975) 88 *Harvard LR* 1669.
Stigler, G., 'The Theory of Economic Regulation' (1971) 2 *Bell J Econ. and Man. Sci.* 1.
Stiglitz, J., and Weiss, A., 'Credit Rationing in Markets with Imperfect Information' (1981) 71 *American Economic Review* 393.

Stock Exchange, *Conflicts of Interest and their Regulation, Discussion Document* (1984) *SEQ* 18.

Strauss, P., 'The Rulemaking Continuum' (1992) 41 *Duke LJ* 1463.

Streeck, W., and Schmitter, P. C., 'Community, market, state—and associations? The prospective contribution of interest governance to social order', in Streeck, W., and Schmitter, P. C., (eds.), *Private Interest Government, Beyond Market and State* (Sage, 1985).

Summers, R. S., 'The Technique Element in Law' (1971) 59 *Calif. LR* 733.

——————, and Howard, C., *Law, its Nature Function and Limits* (New York, 1972).

Surrey, S., 'Complexity and the Internal Revenue Code: The Problem of Management of Tax Detail' (1964) 34 *Law and Contemp. Probs.* 673.

Tapper, C., 'A Note on Principles' (1971) 34 *MLR* 628.

Teubner, G., 'Juridification: Concepts, Aspects, Limits, Solutions', in Teubner, G., (ed.), *Juridification of the Social Sphere* (Berlin, 1987).

Thelen, K., and Steinmo, S., 'Historical Institutionalism in Comparative Politics', in Steinmo, S., Thelen, K., and Longstreth, F., (eds.), *Structuring Politics: Historical Institutionalism in Comparative Analysis* (Cambridge, 1992).

Trebilcock, M. J., 'Winners and Losers in the Regulatory System: Must the Consumer Always Lose?' (1975) 13 *Osgoode Hall LR* 619.

Tullock, G., *The Politics of Bureaucracy* (New York, 1965).

Tushnet, M., *Red, White and Blue* (Harvard, 1988).

Twining, W., *Karl Llewellyn and the Realist Movement* (London, 1973).

——————, and Miers, D., *How To Do Things With Rules* (London, 3rd ed., 1991).

Vaughan, J., *The Regulation of Unit Trusts* (London, 1990).

Vogel, D., *National Styles of Regulation* (Ithaca, 1986).

Waismann, F., 'Verifiability', in Flew, A. G. N., (ed.), *Logic and Language First Series* (Oxford, 1951).

Walker, D., 'Financial Services: The Principles Initiative' (1989) *BJIBFL* 51.

——————, 'The New Settlement in Financial Services', *Law Society Gazette,* 26 July 1989.

Weber, M., *Economy and Society,* eds. Roch, G., and Wittich, C. (New York, 1968).

Whittaker, A. M., 'Financial Services, Developing the Regulatory Structure' (1989) *BJIBFL* 5.

——————, 'Legal Technique in City Regulation' (1990) 43 *Current Legal Problems* 35.

Williams, G., 'Language and the Law' (1945) 61 *LQR* 71, 179, 293, 384; and (1946) 62 *LQR* 387.

Williamson, O. E., *Markets and Hierarchies* (New York, 1975).

Williamson, O. E., *The Economic Institutions of Capitalism: Firms, Markets, Relational Contracting* (New York, 1985).
Wilson, J. Q., *The Politics of Regulation* (New York, 1980).
Woellnar, R. H., 'Law and Business Risk Raking' (1982) *Aust. Bus. LR* 391.
Wolf, C., 'A Theory of Non-Market Failure: Framework for Implementation' (1979) 22 *J Law and Econ.* 107.
Wright, C., Critical Notice (1989) 98 *Mind* 289.
Yablon, C., 'The Indeterminacy of the Law: Critical Legal Studies and the Problem of Legal Explanation' (1985) 6 *Cardozo LR* 917.
——————, 'Law and Metaphysics' (1987) 96 *Yale LJ* 613.
Yeager, P. C., *The Limits of the Law: The Public Regulation of Private Pollution* (Cambridge, 1992).
Zander, M., *The Lawmaking Process* (London, 4th ed., 1990).

Official and Regulatory Publications

CSI, *Annual Reports*, 1979–85.
——————, *Draft Code of Conduct on the Management of Conflicts of Interest* (CSI, 1984).
DTI, *Amendments to the Prevention of Frauds (Investments) Act 1958*, Cmnd. 6893 (London, 1977).
——————, *Financial Services in the UK: A New Framework for Investor Protection*, Cmnd. 9432 (London, 1985).
——————, *Insurance Intermediaries*, Cmnd. 6715 (London, 1977).
——————, *Possible Changes to the FSA* 1986 (London, 1989).
——————, *Releasing Enterprises*, Cmnd. 512 (London, 1988).
Fimbra, *Annual Reports*, 1989–92.
——————, *Fimbra Rules*, 1988 (amended).
——————, *Response to SIB Review of Retail Regulation*, August 1991.
——————, *Submission to Sir Kenneth Clucas of Fimbra's Views on the Advantages of Forming a New Retail Regulator*, November 1991.
Formation Committee, *The Personal Investor Authority, A Consultative Paper*, September 1992.
IMRO, *Annual Reports*, 1989–92.
——————, *IMRO Rules*, August 1991 (as amended).
——————, *IMRO Rules, Consultation Document*, November 1990.
——————, *IMRO Rules*, 1988.
——————, *Modification Note*, December 1989.
——————, *Submission to Sir Kenneth Clucas*, December 1991.
——————, *Submission to the House of Commons Social Security Committee*, February 1992.
Investment Ombudsman, *Annual Reports*, 1991–5.

Large, A., *Financial Services Regulation: Making the Two Tier System Work*, SIB, May 1993.

Lautro, *Annual Reports*, 1989–92.

————, *Disclosure*, CB No. 11, October 1991.

————, *Lautro Rules*, 1988 (amended).

————, *Product Disclosure, Illustrations, Indirect Benefits and Other Matters*, CB No. 13, March 1993.

MacDonald, O., *Report on Training and Competence in the Financial Services Industry*, SIB, May 1990.

Miller, T., *Curbing the Sale of Unsuitable Products, A Report to the SIB*, SIB, May 1993.

OFT, *Fair Trading and Life Insurance Savings Products, A Report by the Director General of Fair Trading*, March 1993.

————, *Financial Services Act* 1986, *Regulatory Costs and the Availability of Independent Advice, The rules of Fimbra and other regulatory bodies: A Report by the Director General for Fair Trading to the Secretary of State for Trade and Industry*, April 1990.

————, *Financial Services Act* 1986, *The Disclosure of Information about Life Insurance Products and Commissions Paid to Independent Advisers, The New Requirements of the Securities and Investments Board: A Report by the Director General of Fair Trading to the Secretary of State for Trade and Industry*, April 1990.

————, *Independent Financial Advisers and the Impact of Commission Disclosure by London Economics Ltd*, October 1992.

————, *Savings and Investments, Consumer Issues, An Occasional Paper to the OFT* by Mitchell, J., and Weisner, H., June 1992.

————, *Securities and Investment Board: A Report by the Director General of Fair Trading to the Secretary of State for Trade and Industry*, March 1987.

————, *Study of Insurance Intermediaries' Costs: Report of a Survey by Arthur Young*, August 1987.

————, *The Financial Intermediaries, Managers and Brokers Regulatory Organisation: A Report by the Director General of Fair Trading to the Secretary of State for Trade and Industry*, December 1987.

————, *The Investment Management Regulatory Organisation: A Report by the Director General of Fair Trading to the Secretary of State for Trade and Industry*, January 1988.

————, *The Life Assurance and Unit Trust Regulatory Organisation: A Report by the Director General of Fair Trading to the Secretary of State for Trade and Industry*, March 1988.

————, *The Marketing and Sale of Investment-Linked Insurance Products, The Rules of the Securities and Investments Board and the Life Assurance and Unit Trust Regulatory Organisation: A Report by the Director General of Fair Trading to the Chancellor of the Exchequer*, March 1993.

OFT, *The Marketing and Sale of Unsuitable Products, A Report to the SIB*, SIB, May 1993.

———, *The Securities Association: A Report by the Director General of Fair Trading to the Secretary of State for Trade and Industry*, February 1988.

PIA, *PIA Rule Book*, 1994 (as amended).

Retail Regulation Review: Report of a study by Sir Kenneth Clucas on a new SRO for the Retail Sector, SIB, March 1992.

Review of Retail Regulation: Consumer Research by Taylor Nelson Financial, SIB Disclosures Research Report, January 1992.

SIB, *Achieving and Judging Adequacy*, CP 39, April 1990.

———, *A Forward Look*, October 1989.

———, *Annual Reports*, 1987–93.

———, *A Wider Basis for SIB's Principles of Conduct: The Next Stage of the New Approach*, March 1989.

———, *Broker Funds*, April 1987.

———, *Broker Funds and Broker Unit Trusts*, CP 26, July 1989.

———, *Broker Funds and Broker Unit Trusts, A Policy Statement*, February 1990.

———, *Broker Funds, A Policy Statement*, May 1991.

———, *Broker Funds: Future Regulation*, CP 48, November 1990.

———, *Conduct of Business Rules: A New Approach*, November 1988.

———, *Consultative Document on the Control of the Oil Markets*, February 1988.

———, *Core Conduct of Business Rules*, January 1991.

———, *Core Conduct of Business Rules: Commencement for Members of IMRO*, CP 54, August 1991.

———, *Core Conduct of Business Rules: Commencement for Members of SFA*, CP 55, December 1991.

———, *Dedesignation of the Core Conduct of Business Rules, The Client Money Rules and the Financial Supervision Rules*, CP 83, August 1994.

———, *Draft Rules and Regulations*, 1986.

———, *EC Second Banking Co-ordination Directive*, CP 68, December 1992.

———, *Financial Services (Client Money) Regulations*, 1991.

———, *Financial Services (Client Money) (Supplementary) Regulations* 1991.

———, *Financial Services (Compensation for Investors) Rules* 1990.

———, *Financial Services (Conduct of Business) Rules* 1987.

———, *Financial Services (Conduct of Business) Rules* 1990.

———, *Financial Services (Conduct of Business) (Amendment) Rules* 1988 (No. 8) 17 March 1988.

———, *Financial Services (Conduct of Business) (Amendment No. 2) Rules* 1988 (No. 21) 28 April 1988.

———, *Financial Services (Conduct of Business) (Amendment No. 3) Rules* 1988 (No. 23) 3 May 1988.

———, *Financial Services (Conduct of Business) (Amendment No. 4) Rules* 1988 (No. 26) 27 May 1988.

———, *Financial Services (European Institutions) Instrument* 1993.

———, *Financial Services (Interim) Rules and Regulations* 1988 (No. 22) 28 April 1988.

———, *Financial Services (Misc. Amendments) Rules and Regulations* 1988 (No. 13) 21 April 1988.

———, *Financial Services (Misc. Amendments) (No. 2) Rules and Regulations* 1988 (No. 27) 16 June 1988.

———, *Financial Services (Oil Markets) Rules and Regulations* 1988 (No. 11) 31 March 1988.

———, *Financial Services (Regulated Schemes) Regulations* 1991.

———, *Financial Services (Transitional) Rules and Regulations* 1988 (No.14) 12 April 1988.

———, *Financial Supervision Rules* 1990.

———, *Financial Supervision (Amendment) Rules*, CP 57, December 1991.

———, *Further Amendments Proposed to the February 1987 Drafts of Rules, Regulations and Orders to be made by SIB additional to those published in April 1987*, August 1987.

———, *Know Your Customer*, CP 8, November 1988.

———, *Life Assurance and Unit Trust Disclosure*, CP 23, May 1989.

———, *Life Assurance and Unit Trust Disclosure*, CP 27 Parts 1 and 2, August 1989.

———, *Life Assurance and Unit Trust Disclosure: Outstanding Matters*, CP 30, November 1989.

———, *Life Assurance: Disclosure of Commissions and Other Matters*, CP 77, February 1994.

———, *Management and Budget Plans*, 1995–7.

———, *Permitted Persons*, December 1987.

———, *Proposals for Amended Client Money Regulations*, CP 53, April 1991.

———, *Regulation of the Conduct of Investment Business: A Proposal*, August 1989.

———, *Regulation of the Marketing of Investment Products and Services, A Policy Statement*, March 1991.

———, *Regulation of the Marketing of Investment Services and Products: Report of a Review Committee*, March 1990.

———, *Retail Regulation: Issues for Review*, April 1991.

———, *Retail Regulation Review, Disclosure and Standards of Advice, A Policy Statement*, May 1992.

———, *Retail Regulation Review: Disclosure, Polarisation and Standards of Advice*, CP 60, March 1992.

———, *Retail Regulation Review*, Discussion Paper 2, Polarisation, September 1991.

SIB, *Retail Regulation Review*, Discussion Paper 3, Disclosure, October 1991.
———, *Review of the Investors' Compensation Scheme*, CP 28, August 1989.
———, *Review of the Investors' Compensation Scheme* 2, CP 36, February 1990.
———, *Soft Commission Arrangements in the Securities Markets: A Discussion Paper*, February 1989.
———, *Soft Commission Arrangements in the Securities Market, Policy Statement*, July 1990.
———, *Soft Commission Arrangements in the Securities Market, Second Policy Statement*, February 1991.
———, *Soft Commission Arrangements in the Securities Market: Soft for Net*, CP 46, November 1990.
———, *Soft Commissions in the Securities Markets*, CP 29, October 1989.
———, *Soft Commissions: Recent Developments*, CP 56 and Policy Statement, December 1991.
———, *SRO Limits for Compensation Costs*, CP 41, May 1990.
———, *Statements of Principle*, March 1990.
———, *The Financial Services Act and the Press*, March 1988.
———, *The Proposed Core Rules*, CP 42, October 1990.
———, *The Proposed Core Rules: Derogations and other certain points*, CP 47, November 1990.
———, *The Proposed Principles for Investment Business*, CP 33, January 1990.
———, *The Securities and Investments Board's Application for the Designated Agency Status under the terms of the Financial Services Act and the Revised Rule Book*, February 1987.
———, *The SIB Rulebook: An Overview*, October 1987.
——— and MIBOC, *Life Assurance and Unit Trusts: Independent Intermediaries, Tied Agents and Company Representatives*, December 1985.
——— and ———, *Life Assurance Companies, Disclosure of Expenses and Charges*, December 1986.
——— and ———, *Life Assurance, Unit Trust and the Investor*, April 1986.
——— and ———, *Product Disclosure: Illustrations, Surrender Values and Past Performance*, July 1986.
SFA, *Annual Reports*, 1991–5.
———, *Consultative Document on the New Conduct of Business Rules*, Board Notice 2, Parts 1–3, April 1991.
———, *Professional Dealing Handbook*, December 1991.
———, *SFA Rule Book*, December 1991 (as amended).
Social Security Select Committee, *Report on the Operation of Pension Funds*, 1991/2 HC Paper No. 61–1.

Trade and Industry Select Committee, *The Securities and Investments Board*, Minutes of Evidence, 1990/1 HC Paper 131.

——————, *The Securities and Investments Board*, Minutes of Evidence, 1991/2 HC Paper 162-i.

Treasury and Civil Service Select Committee, *Financial Services Regulation*, Minutes of Evidence, 1992/3 HC Paper 733-i.

——————, Fourth Report, *Retail Financial Services Regulation: An Interim Report*, 1993/4 HC Paper 236.

——————, Sixth Report, *The Regulation of Financial Services in the UK*, Volume I, 1995/6 HC Paper 332-I.

TSA, *Annual Reports*, 1989–91.

——————, *Conduct of Business Rules, Notes and Appendices*, October 1990.

——————, *Revised Conduct of Business Rules, Consultative Document*, Board Notice 220, October 1990.

——————, *TSA Rule Book* 1988.

Index